The World's Greatest Cities

timeout.com

Editorial
Editor Jessica Cargill Thompson
Deputy Editor Simon Coppock
Copy Editor Holly Pick
Consultant Editor Marcus Webb
Research (Metropolists) Paul Fairclough
Research (Instant Passports) Ruth-Ellen Davis,
Anna Leach, Kohinoor Sahota, April Welsh
Proofreader Mandy Martinez

Managing Director Peter Fiennes
Editorial Director Ruth Jarvis
Business Manager Dan Allen
Editorial Manager Holly Pick
Assistant Management Accountant Ija Krasnikova

Design
Art Director Scott Moore
Art Editor Pinelope Kourmouzoglou
Senior Designer Henry Elphick
Graphic Designers Kei Ishimaru, Nicola Wilson
Advertising Designer Jodi Sher

Picture Desk
Picture Editor Jael Marschner
Deputy Picture Editor Lynn Chambers
Picture Researcher Gemma Walters
Picture Desk Assistant Marzena Zoladz
Picture Librarian Christina Theisen

Advertising
Commercial Director Mark Phillips
International Advertising Manager Kasimir Berger

Marketing
Marketing Manager Yvonne Poon
**Sales & Marketing Director, North America
 & Latin America** Lisa Levinson
Senior Publishing Brand Manager Luthfa Begum
Marketing Designer Anthony Huggins

Production
Group Production Director Mark Lamond
Production Manager Brendan McKeown
Production Controller Damian Bennett
Production Coordinator Kelly Fenlon

Time Out Group
Chairman Tony Elliott
Chief Executive Officer David King
Group General Manager/Director
 Nichola Coulthard
Time Out Communications Ltd MD David Pepper
Time Out International Ltd MD Cathy Runciman
**Time Out Magazine Ltd Publisher/
 Managing Director** Mark Elliott
Group IT Director Simon Chappell
Director of Marketing & Circulation
 Catherine Demajo

Time Out Guides Ltd
Universal House
251 Tottenham Court Road
London W1T 7AB
United Kingdom
Tel: +44 (0)20 7813 3000
Fax: +44 (0)20 7813 6001
Email: guides@timeout.com
www.timeout.com

Published by Time Out Guides Ltd, a wholly owned subsidiary of Time Out Group Ltd.
Time Out and the Time Out logo are trademarks of Time Out Group Ltd.

© Time Out Group Ltd 2009

10 9 8 7 6 5 4 3 2 1

This edition first published in Great Britain in 2009 by Ebury Publishing.
A Random House Group Company
20 Vauxhall Bridge Road, London SW1V 2SA

Random House Australia Pty Ltd 20 Alfred Street, Milsons Point, Sydney, New South Wales 2061, Australia
Random House New Zealand Ltd 18 Poland Road, Glenfield, Auckland 10, New Zealand
Random House South Africa (Pty) Ltd Isle of Houghton, Corner Boundary Road & Carse O'Gowrie,
Houghton 2198, South Africa

Random House UK Limited Reg. No. 954009

For further distribution details, see www.timeout.com.

ISBN: 978-1-84670-1412

A CIP catalogue record for this book is available from the British Library.

Printed and bound in Singapore by Tien Wah Press Ltd.

The Random House Group Limited supports The Forest Stewardship Council (FSC), the leading
international forest certification organisation. All our titles that are printed on Greenpeace approved
FSC certified paper carry the FSC logo. Our paper procurement policy can be found at
http://www.rbooks.co.uk/environment.

Time Out carbon-offsets its flights with Trees for Cities (www.treesforcities.org).

Whilst every effort has been made by the authors and the publisher to ensure that the information contained in
this guide is accurate and up-to-date as at the date of publication, the publisher cannot accept responsibility
for any errors it may contain. The publisher accepts no responsibility or liability for any inconvenience, loss,
injury or death sustained by anyone as a result of any advice or information contained in this guide.

Front cover photograh Shibuya Crossing, Tokyo, by Tom Bonaventure/Getty Images.
Back cover photograhs San Francisco, by Elan Fleisher; Duomo, Florence, by Gianluca Moggi; Palm
Island, Dubai, by ITP Images.

Page 5 photograph Chicago, by Martha Williams.

Cities selected and ranked by Jessica Cargill Thompson, Peterjon Cresswell, Guy Dimond, Tony Elliott,
Peter Fiennes, Will Fulford-Jones, Sarah Guy, Ruth Jarvis, Chris Moss, Cath Phillips, Cathy Runciman,
Ros Sales, Aleida Strowger, Marcus Webb and Time Out's international editors.

Thanks to Peterjon Cresswell, Jeroen Bergmans, Dave Rimmer, Ros Sales, citymayors.com, Heloisa Souza
and Kira Matulovich at HSBC, Nadia Latif at travelintelligence.com, Anna Livia at LSE Urban Age Programme,
the editors of all Time Out's city guides, and the staff at Time Out's 30-plus international magazines.

© Copyright Time Out Group Ltd
All rights reserved

Europe

Edmonton
Calgary
Vancouver
Toronto Montréal
Markham
Westport
New York
Washington DC
San Francisco
Los Angeles
Tijuana Hamilton
Monterrey Miami
Jalisco Leon Merida
Mexico City Grand Cayman

Panama
Bogota

Brasília Salvador

São Paulo Rio de Janeiro
Curitiba

Buenos Aires

Glasgow Edinburgh
Newcastle
York
Leeds
Manchester Sheffield
Leicester
Swansea Milton Keynes
London
Cardiff
St. Helier Lille
Rouen Paris Strasbourg Prague Kraków Warsaw
Lyon
Nice
Toulouse Cannes
Istanbul
Athens
Valletta

Glasgow   Edinburgh

Manchester
London   Warsaw
Rouen   Lille Prague   Kraków
Paris Strasbourg
Lyon
Cannes
Toulouse   Strasbourg

Valletta   Athens   Istanbul

Beirut

Cairo   Amman
Dammam
Manama   Doha
Riyadh
Jeddah   Abu   Muscat
Dhabi

Islamabad
Lahore
Karachi   Chandigarh
Delhi
Ahmedabad

Mumbai   Kolkata
Pune   Hyderabad

Bangalore   Chennai   Bangkok

Colombo   Kuala Lumpur
Penang
Petaling
Medan   Jaya
Johor
Singapore   Bahru   Kuching

Shenyang
Beijing   Dalian
Tianjin
Qingdao   Seoul   Tokyo
Kobe   Yokohama

Suzhou
Chengdu   Wuhan   Shanghai
Chongqing   Guangzhou   Hangzhou
Dongguan   Xiamen
Shenzhen   Taipei
Macau   Taichung
Hong   Tainan
Kong   Kaohsiung

Caloocan   Mutinlupa
Makati City   Bonificio Global City
Manila   Quezon City
Pasig   San Juan
Kota   Cebu
Kinabalu   Davao
Bandar Seri Begawan
Kuala Belait

Jakarta   Surabaya
Bandung   Semarang

Brisbane
Perth   Sydney
Melbourne   Auckland

Contents

Pictured, left to right: Milan, Barcelona, New York, Rome, Miami, Vienna, Naples, Paris. Previous pages: Copenhagen, Stockholm, Hong Kong, Shanghai, Milan, Venice, Prague, Vienna.

Introduction

THE URBAN MILLENNIUM

From *Great Expectations* to *An American in Paris*, cities are the places where people go to achieve their dreams. And it seems that we are drawn to them in increasing numbers. In 2007, the UN-HABITAT programme announced that urban living had become so popular that half the people on earth now live in cities – an increase from just one tenth in 1900, and calculated to rise to three quarters by 2050. Demographers describe the 21st century as the 'urban millennium'.

No one knows exactly when the first city was founded, although archaeological research dates the city of Jericho back to 9000 BC and the settlements of Mesopotamia (now Iraq) to around 4,500 BC. Living in large groups has allowed mankind to indulge in all the activities we regard as characteristically human: conversation, exchange of ideas, exchange of goods and services, industry, creativity, invention. In other words, civilisation. The Sumerians of Mesopotamia came up with the wheel and written language; ancient Athens gave us philosophy; ancient Rome civil engineering and the western alphabet.

Alongside these high cultural achievements, cities have always been associated with hedonism, decadence, good times and/or godlessness (depending on your point of view). In biblical times it was Babylon and Sodom and Gomorrah; more recently gin-addled 18th-century London, fin-de-siècle Paris and 1930s Berlin; today the outrageous building programmes of Dubai and Shanghai, and the nightlife of Bangkok and Tel Aviv continue this spirit of unabashed excess.

Living in large communities creates its own problems – pollution, crime, violence, public health, housing, transport, traffic and social and economic inequality are all part of a delicately balanced metropolitan ecosystem that must also allow industry, expansion, entertainment and personal freedom. As the world's urban population soars towards a predicted 5 billion by 2030 (according to the United Nations' Population Fund) it is estimated that 100 million of us will be housed in shanty towns by 2020. Mumbai, Delhi, Rio de Janeiro and Cairo already have a significant proportion of their population consigned to slums and illegal favelas or, in the case of Cairo, tombs.

In selecting the 75 cities to feature in this book, we have taken into account their size and character along with their strengths and weaknesses. In short, how well do they function as cities? Some that have been included, such as Johannesburg, Bogotá, Belfast and Belgrade, have been through painful rehabilitation. Mexico City and Athens became renowned for extreme air pollution, but have cleaned up their act. Some vibrant cities that have not – Lagos, Abuja, Nairobi, Dhaka – still suffer from such extreme crime, corruption or poverty that they cannot currently be considered to be among the most successful, although Lagos in particular is one to watch over the next decade, its extreme expansion – an additional 58 people every hour – could result in either disaster or domination. Once great cities such as Kabul and Baghdad are still too close to conflict to be considered at this time.

Conversely, there are many world capitals either too small (Nuuk, in Greenland) or lacking the raw urban energy (Wellington, Oslo, Bern) to make the final 75. Other political capitals failed to match the cultural richness of their country's second or third cities (Warsaw, Canberra, Rabat, Ottawa, Pretoria). Some cities represent a type or region, hence Manchester in the north of England has been chosen over similarly worthy cities such as Liverpool, Leeds, and Newcastle; Vancouver just edged out Seattle.

Once a final selection of 75 had been made, we set about comparing them in six qualities we consider essential for a successful city: architecture; arts and culture; buzz; food and drink; quality of life; world status. Resident writers were asked to comment on their home city's strengths and weaknesses, with marks out of 10 given in each category. A panel of extraordinarily well-travelled experts was assembled, drawn from Time Out's Guides, International and Travel divisions, who assessed the scores from a global perspective and made adjustments for local cynicism or over-enthusiasm. The results are tabulated on page 17.

Architecture

All aspects of a city's physical form are considered in this category, including urban planning, streetscape and skyline, as well as the architecture itself.

Some cities are planned, but most have grown up organically, with varying commitment to urban aesthetics at different points in their history. A few stand out as man-made masterpieces: the ancient city of Sana'a with its mud brick skyscrapers; modernist Brasília, a giant concrete sculpture garden; the exquisite palaces of St Petersburg, Venice and Vienna; the temples of Kyoto; the canals of Amsterdam; the Haussmann streetplan of Paris; the skylines of Manhattan and Hong Kong. Some cities simply have a stunning natural setting: the sweeping bays of Rio de Janeiro; the mountains of Almaty; the hills and rocky crag of Edinburgh; Stockholm's archipelago.

Arts & Culture

Cities are, of course, places of inspiration where the best art is not only found but made, be it high art, indigenous culture or subculture. Seville has given the world flamenco, Buenos Aires tango, Rio samba. Havana, Dakar, Kingston and Chicago pulsate with home-made music. Kabuki came from Kyoto, New York lays claim to hip-hop, London to punk. St Petersburg has the Mariinsky Theatre, Milan has La Scala, Madrid the Prado, Florence the Uffizi, Paris the Louvre. Los Angeles made Hollywood and Mumbai made Bollywood. Currently there is a buzz around the art scenes of Berlin, Lisbon, Beijing, Mexico City, Buenos Aires and Miami.

But the two cities judged to be worth a 10 out of 10, reliably producing world-class art, theatre, music, literature and comedy, while generating a vibrant underground scene in parallel to the establishment, were London and New York.

Buzz

What is 'buzz'? This is a quality peculiar to cities, one that cannot be quantified or analysed, but just *is*. It's the feeling you get as your train pulls into the station, or when you return home after a trip. Sometimes called 'edge', it's the butterflies in your stomach that announce that this is a place of possibility where anything might happen.

Some of this frisson may come from less salubrious aspects of the city, making 'buzz' inversely proportional to the oft-tabulated 'quality of life'. But equally, it may be generated by creativity (London, Barcelona) or wild nightlife (Bangkok, Tel Aviv), party spirit (Buenos Aires, Naples) or streetlife (Paris, Tokyo, New York, Shanghai, Mumbai, Istanbul, Marrakech).

Food & Drink

As cities become increasingly multicultural and their citizens better travelled, the range of cuisines they offer becomes ever more complex. Many cities have their own regional triumphs (Naples invented the pizza, Dublin gave the world Guinness, Marseille bouillabaisse, Prague is the capital of pils, Vienna excels for cake) and anyone can eat extremely well in Marrakech, Belgrade, Beirut, Delhi and Seville. However, the restaurant and bar culture in these cities has yet to embrace other cuisines to the same high standards.

It is, in fact, Tokyo that currently boasts the most Michelin-starred restaurants of any city in the world, nearly twice the number of Paris (generally regarded as the arbiter of all things haute cuisine), while cosmopolitan New York and London offer an enviable spread of great bars and restaurants, with a broad range of international flavours.

Quality of Life

'Quality of living' surveys such as that by Mercer Human Resources Consulting (see Metropolists, page 341) are readily available, based on criteria such as political stability, crime, economy, health and sanitation, pollution, education, public services, transport, food and housing. Swiss cities – Zurich, Geneva, Bern – invariably do well, along with Vienna, Copenhagen, Auckland, Wellington and Vancouver. Only a few of these cities, however, make it into this book; as even Mercer admits, 'many lack a certain *je ne sais quoi*'. Clearly it is possible to be just too nice.

As this is not a geography text book, we have looked beyond the quantifiable statistics and asked what is it like to live in the city on a day-to-day basis. How easy is it to get around? Is there decent public space and facilities? Do citizens walk the streets with confidence or caution? What's the pollution like? Is it a good place to bring up children? Is it dark or frozen for a significant portion of the year? Is there a high degree of inequality? A sense of community? Is there enough decent housing for everyone?

Of course, the experiences of a shanty town dweller will differ enormously to those of a millionaire, so the dominant perspective will inevitably be that of a middle stratum, not so rich that they no longer engage fully with the city, nor so poor that they find themselves marginalised.

World Status

'World status', on the other hand, is very much the outsiders' perspective. What sort of influence – political, financial, cultural, historic – does a city wield? But here, of course, the geography of world power is shifting. Former colonial rulers cling to any last threads of importance, while the reins of world power have been pulled to the east – the fast-expanding cities of the Asian subcontinent and China. Most significantly, Beijing has emerged from decades of imposed isolation to be the power everyone wants to please.

The 'greatest cities'

Once all the above factors have been taken into account, it is New York that comes out on top, closely followed by the other perennial big-hitters London, Paris, Istanbul, Tokyo and Berlin. What do they have in common? They are all of a reasonable size – big enough to have multiple personalities. Many, though not all, rich in history, with waves of immigration injecting new concepts that are assimilated into the host culture. There is enough social freedom to allow creative anarchy. There is also, of course, the wealth that sustains a reasonable standard of living for a reasonable proportion of the inhabitants.

Cities of the future

As urban populations soar, today's cities are in flux. China, India and sub-Saharan Africa have the fastest growing cities on the planet, with the developing world predicted to absorb 95 per cent of urban growth over the next two decades. The challenge for these cities is whether they can emerge as the complex organisms required for a high quality of urban life, or single cells, soulless places where people simply work, eat and sleep. Along with the rest of the world, these cities will need to adapt to the demands of diminishing energy reserves and global warming. And while some urban areas grow into implausibly large 'metacities' demanding new methods of management, the majority of urban life will be in cities of fewer than 500,000 inhabitants, often in isolated locations where infrastructure is poor.

Contributors

Over the following pages you will hear from 75 different writers, each a resident, or recent resident, of the city they speak for. A number are editors of Time Out's many international magazines and guides; others are writers, reporters, architects, academics or other professionals. You'll find their biographies on page 346. Thanks are due to www.citymayors.com, which provided some of the statistics.

These are individual voices, expressing their own experience of their city, not a corporate Time Out take nor the standard tourist-centric view. This is explicitly not a book of potential holiday destinations, but of real life working cities, warts and all. Urban life as it is lived in all its colourful, chaotic glory.

Jessica Cargill Thompson, Editor

RANK	CITY	ARCHITECTURE	ARTS & CULTURE	BUZZ	FOOD & DRINK	QUALITY OF LIFE	WORLD STATUS	TOTAL/60
1	New York, USA	9	10	10	9	6	9	53
2	London, UK	7	10	9	9	6	9	50
3	Paris, France	9	9	6	9	7	8	48
4	Berlin, Germany	7	9	9	6	7	8	46
5=	Barcelona, Spain	9	7	8	8	8	4	44
5=	Chicago, USA	9	8	7	7	7	6	44
5=	Tokyo, Japan	7	6	9	10	4	8	44
8	Istanbul, Turkey	7	7	9	7	6	7	43
9=	Rome, Italy	9	7	7	6	6	7	42
9=	Sydney, Australia	7	6	7	7	10	5	42
11	San Francisco, USA	7	7	7	7	8	5	41
12=	Beijing, China	8	8	5	6	4	9	40
12=	Hong Kong, China	8	5	7	6	6	8	40
12=	Madrid, Spain	7	7	7	6	7	6	40
12=	Vienna, Austria	8	7	7	4	9	5	40
16=	Buenos Aires, Argentina	5	8	10	5	6	5	39
16=	Shanghai, China	7	4	8	6	7	7	39
18=	Melbourne, Australia	5	7	7	7	9	3	38
18=	Stockholm, Sweden	7	6	5	6	9	5	38
20=	Amsterdam, Netherlands	8	8	6	3	8	4	37
20=	Copenhagen, Denmark	6	6	5	6	10	4	37
20=	Los Angeles, USA	6	7	6	6	5	7	37
20=	Mexico City, Mexico	6	8	7	6	4	6	37
20=	Washington DC, USA	6	6	5	5	6	9	37
25=	Havana, Cuba	8	8	9	2	4	5	36
25=	Mumbai, India	4	6	10	6	3	7	36
25=	St Petersburg, Russia	9	10	6	3	5	3	36
28=	Brussels, Belgium	6	5	3	8	6	7	35
28=	Kyoto, Japan	8	7	2	8	8	2	35
28=	Lisbon, Portugal	7	7	7	4	7	3	35
28=	Rio de Janeiro, Brazil	8	6	8	4	5	4	35
28=	São Paulo, Brazil	6	7	7	6	2	7	35
28=	Tel Aviv, Israel	6	6	9	4	5	5	35
34=	Edinburgh, UK	9	5	5	4	7	4	34
34=	Moscow, Russia	4	7	7	4	4	8	34
34=	Seville, Spain	7	5	9	5	7	1	34
34=	Singapore	5	4	3	8	8	6	34
34=	Venice, Italy	10	8	4	2	5	5	34
39=	Bangkok, Thailand	3	6	9	6	4	5	33
39=	Beirut, Lebanon	4	6	9	5	4	5	33
39=	Cairo, Egypt	3	8	9	1	5	7	33
39=	Hanoi, Vietnam	7	4	8	6	4	4	33
39=	Kolkata, India	8	5	8	4	5	3	33
39=	Toronto, Canada	5	7	5	4	8	4	33
45=	Florence, Italy	7	7	4	5	6	3	32
45=	Krakow, Poland	9	6	6	2	8	1	32
45=	Prague, Czech Republic	8	6	5	4	6	3	32
48=	Glasgow, UK	6	6	7	3	6	3	31
48=	Seoul, South Korea	3	7	5	4	7	5	31
48=	Vancouver, Canada	4	4	4	7	9	3	31
51=	Athens, Greece	6	6	6	3	5	4	30
51=	Budapest, Hungary	8	6	5	4	5	2	30
51=	Delhi, India	6	6	5	2	4	7	30
51=	Miami, USA	6	4	4	6	6	4	30
51=	Naples, Italy	5	4	7	8	5	1	30
56=	Dubai , UAE	6	2	3	7	5	6	29
56=	Dublin, Republic of Ireland	6	5	4	5	6	3	29
58=	Bogotá, Colombia	5	7	7	3	3	3	28
58=	Brasília, Brazil	10	3	3	4	5	3	28
58=	Jakarta, Indonesia	4	5	6	3	4	6	28
58=	Manchester, UK	5	6	5	2	7	3	28
58=	Marseille, France	6	4	7	4	5	2	28
58=	Milan, Italy	4	5	5	4	5	5	28
64	Belgrade, Serbia	3	5	9	2	5	3	27
65	Cape Town, South Africa	6	4	4	4	5	3	26
66	Kuala Lumpur, Malaysia	3	3	3	6	7	3	25
67=	Belfast, UK	4	4	5	1	6	4	24
67=	Dakar, Senegal	5	4	8	1	5	1	24
67=	Marrakech, Morocco	6	3	6	4	4	1	24
70	Almaty, Kazakhstan	6	4	3	2	5	3	23
71=	Bucharest, Romania	4	7	4	1	4	2	22
71=	Sana'a, Yemen	10	2	7	1	1	1	22
73=	Kingston, Jamaica	2	5	8	2	3	1	21
73=	Manila, Philippines	7	2	4	2	3	3	21
75	Johannesburg, South Africa	2	5	2	2	1	7	19

World Map

THE 75 GREATEST CITIES

Vancouver

Toronto

Chicago

New York

San Francisco

Washington DC

Los Angeles

Miami

Havana

Mexico City

Kingston

Bogotá

Brasília

Rio de Janeiro

São Paulo

Buenos Aires

Europe

Stockholm

Copenhagen

Glasgow

Edinburgh

Belfast

Manchester

Dublin

Amsterdam

London

Berlin

Brussels

Prague

Krakow

Paris

Vienna

Budapest

Milan

Venice

Belgrade

Florence

Marseille

Bucharest

Rome

Madrid

Barcelona

Naples

Istanbul

Lisbon

Seville

Athens

Saint
Petersburg•

•Moscow

Almaty•

Beijing•

Seoul•

Tokyo•
Kyoto•

Beirut•
Tel Aviv•

Marrakech•

Cairo•

Shanghai•

Hong Kong•
Hanoi•

Delhi•

Dubai•

Mumbai•

Kolkata•

Sana'a•

Manila•

Bangkok•

Dakar•

Kuala Lumpur•

Singapore•

Jakarta•

Johannesburg•

Cape Town•

Sydney•

Melbourne•

Almaty

KAZAKHSTAN

Where ancient mountains edge up against modernity

Architecture
6

Arts & Culture
4

Buzz
3

Food & Drink
2

Quality of Life
5

World Status
3

Total
23/60

Rank
70

While cities like Istanbul, Moscow and Tokyo can overawe visitors by their sheer size, Almaty is just a small and cosy Babylon. Not so long ago it was all green hills and apple gardens; Almatintsy will, with sincere delight and out of deep sense of nostalgia, tell stories of the good old days when they used to catch mountain trout in the city irrigation canals that run down from the snow-covered peaks, of apples that grew to the size of a grapefruit. Nowadays, highways run where the city apple gardens used to be, and residents pay to fish for trout at the nearby hatchery.

There is still a touch of former, more bucolic times left among the modern arrivals. On the same street you may run across a stall selling hot, home-made samosas, and a luxury restaurant where they serve Château Lafite Rothschild at $14,000 a bottle. You can still get lost in Turkish and Chinese clothing markets so big they're like a city within a city. A Soviet-era Moskvich, a Porsche and a Lamborghini might be spotted on the same parking lot.

To escape, everyone – rich and poor – heads for the Zailijsky Alatau mountains. Visible from the city streets, they are an integral part of Almaty. Within 20 minutes you can leave the traffic jams and smog behind to find yourself nearly 1,800 metres above sea level, surrounded by nature. When spring comes, hundreds of *babushkas* in blue tights and bright headscarves start a pilgrimage to their piedmont dachas, where they cultivate 600 square metre plots of land – a legacy of the Soviet era, when smallholdings were given to every family to grow fresh food.

Each street is a potted history of the city. There, on the left, are a couple of three-storey houses with bas-reliefs and turrets – witnesses to the Stalin era. To the right are a couple of faceless

'Almaty is the city where I always feel comfortable. When I come here, for example, from Moscow, turn on the radio and hear ethnic Kazakh songs, I relax immediately. I realise why this city is my native town. It might be the case that to feel this, you have to leave and come back'

Erik Tastambekov film producer

Previous page: Almaty airport. Above: top, New Square (Republic Square) fountains; bottom, Kok Tobe wishing fountain. Top right and far right: café and cable car on Kok Tobe mountain

multi-storey blocks, a remnant of the 1970s. A little further and you might find the towering glass and metal of a 21st-century business centre. Just by turning into a side street, with its rickety old private houses, you may suddenly feel like you're in a Brazilian favela.

Food comes from the Dungan and Uighur cuisines, with lots of shashlyk and pilaf. A discerning gourmand can bite into a mutton head or feast on horsemeat, both Kazakh specialities, and the city food markets are full of fresh fruit and vegetables that look, smell and taste like the real home-grown ones should.

In Almaty, the motley local colour and chaos of the East lives side by side with the more usual European orderliness. The main thing about the city, though, isn't the avalanche of impressions you experience every day: it is the warm welcome offered to everyone who comes here. Which is why Almatintsy believe that anyone who visits must surely feel immediately at home.
Sergey Medvetsky

Instant Passport

Population
1,500,000

Area
325sq km

Where is it?
At the bottom of the Zailijsky Alatau mountains of the Northern Tien Shan range in the south-east of Kazakhstan

Climate
Extreme continental, with temperatures dropping from about 27°C to -14°C. April and May are rainiest, and smog can make summers humid

Ethnic mix
103 ethnicities, including Kazakhs, Russians, Uighurs, Turks, Azeri, Koreans, Tatars, Kurds, Germans, Ukrainians, Chechens, Uzbeks, Kyrgyz, Greeks, Dungans and Poles

Major sights
Sakas (Sacae) tribal hills; 1st City Firefighting Station; Kok Bazaar or 'Green Market', one of the first local food markets; the house of merchant Golovizin; Holy Ascension Cathedral

Insiders' tips
Shymbulak Mountain Resort, clothing and flea market; Alma-Arasan gorge, where everyone goes for a shashlyk; Arasan city sauna

Independence from Soviet Union gained
1991

Lost its capital status
1998, when the new capital Astana was created. It remains, however, the commercial hub of the country and its largest city

Tallest building
Esentai Tower (39 storeys)

Religion
There are 270 religious associations and 40 confessions in the city

Famous dish
Whole baked lamb (the head of which is a special delicacy), as served in Zheruyik Restaurant

Historical milestones
Leon Trotsky was exiled here in the late 1920s; temporary home of Mosfilm, the Soviet national movie production company, which was evacuated from Moscow during World War II; birthplace of Olzhas Sulejmenov, poet and founder of the Nevada-Semipalatinsk Movement, first anti-nuclear NGO in the Soviet Union

Famous fruit
Almaty means 'father of the apple' in Kazakh, and the area is famous for its fruit. The local variety is the Aport, a monstrous-sized fruit that can weigh up to a kilogram

National hobbies
Karaoke, hunting

Amsterdam

NETHERLANDS

Sex, drugs and civilised living

Samuel L Jackson's enthusiastic (expletive-filled) response to John Travolta's explanation of Amsterdam's singular weed policy in the film *Pulp Fiction* is typical of the conversations that inspire so many getaways. Once such visitors arrive, they usually find themselves endlessly looping back – just like the randy sailors did in the 17th century when the city was the richest port in the world – to Amsterdam's near geographic centre, the Red Light District. The way the city radiates out from this ancient inner pit and its flesh-squeegeed windows, once led a visiting Albert Camus to compare the circumscribing canals to the circles of Hell.

It is true that Amsterdam still has a certain reputation. But the recent 'I amsterdam' city-branding campaign has done much to distract the global imagination away from the sex and drugs and towards the 'creative capital', once home to Rembrandt, now abuzz with designers and advertising companies. Meanwhile, the city is gentrifying (locals call it 'frumpifying') quickly as the authorities are committed to making what is already the world's safest Red Light District into an area more conducive to wine bars and sushi joints. Many coffeeshops, where the sales of marijuana and hash are condoned, are being closed under pressure from the EU and a Christian Democrat-led national government. Meanwhile most of the major museums are undergoing extensive redevelopment and there's a city-bisecting construction site where an underground Metro will come – naturally all of these projects are running years, and millions of euros, behind schedule.

Aside from these big city problems, Amsterdam still has a loose and relaxed vibe, and this pocket-sized town can be crossed on bicycle in a mere 20 minutes. Leaving behind the chaos of the centre, there are the rarefied wandering opportunities of the Canal

Architecture
8

Arts & Culture
8

Buzz
6

Food & Drink
3

Quality of Life
8

World Status
4

Total
37/60

Rank
20

Ring, which in turn gives way to the more down-to-earth neighbourhoods of the Jordaan and the Pijp.

Even vice-meister Vincent (Travolta) noted more civilised Amster-delights: 'You can even walk into a movie theatre in Amsterdam and buy a beer. And I don't mean no paper cup, I'm talking about a glass of beer.'

Yes, this is still one hell of a town, a place where going with the flow remains an essential part of the lifestyle.
Steve Korver

Instant Passport

Population
1,160,000 (core city 729,000)

Area
219sq km

Where is it?
North Holland, on a former bog where the Amstel (now dammed) flows into the Het Ij bay

Climate
Technically maritime, but on a day-to-day basis, highly changeable

Ethnic mix
Germanic and Gallo-centric Dutch, Turkish, Moroccan, Antillean, Surinamese, Indonesian

Major sights
Rijksmuseum, Van Gogh Museum, Anne Frank House, Bloemenmarkt (the flower market), Ajax football stadium, the canals

Insiders' tips
The Jordaan, the Pijp, the art galleries of Bijlmermeer, the new venues gathering around the Waterfront

Where's the buzz?
The *grachtengordel* (girdle of canals), the Red Light District, Vondelpark

Number of canals
165

Total length of canals
75.5km

Number of bikes pulled from the canals each year
10,000

Number of bodies pulled from the canals each year
50

Traditional snack
Raw herring

Marijuana decriminalised
1976, although smoking in public is still technically illegal

Number of coffeeshops selling varieties of hashish and marijuana
Approximately 300

Number of Dutch Jews deported via Kamp Westerbrook during the Holocaust
140,000

Altitude
4m below sea level

Average height of the population
The Dutch are among the tallest people in the world, growing to an average of 1.8m (6ft) for men, 1.7m (5ft 7in) for women

Previous page: Reguliersgracht, on the corner with the Keizersgracht. Opposite: lighting up at a coffeehouse. Above: the Stadsschowburg (municipal theatre)

Get the local experience

More than 50 of the world's top destinations available

'We have a magnificent musical life in Amsterdam. There's a vibrant jazz scene and we have the Concertgebouw and the Muziekgebouw, quartets, incredible musicians and conductors that rival any I've seen elsewhere. In this respect, we are as great as any of the greatest cities in the world'

Job Cohen **Mayor of Amsterdam**

The Waterfront

The eastern docklands area of Amsterdam is a showcase for out-there experiments in modern urban living. Perhaps the most culturally significant location is the Muziekgebouw concert hall (*pictured*), centre of the city's modern classical and – in the Bimhuis, that brown box stuck on its flank – jazz music scenes. The Waterfront is also home to the likes of alternative burial store De Ode, where you can buy a designer coffin, and German architect Hans Kollhoff's imposing Piraeus building, with its eye-twisting inner court. The Borneo-Sporenburg peninsulas were carefully designed by urban planners and landscape architects West 8 with differently sized plots, specifically with the aim of encouraging the many illustrious participating architects to come up with creative low-rise housing; opposite the Borneo-Sporenburg, the crazed Whale residential complex – a mighty, raised, silver building designed by Frits van Dongen – is complemented by the folksier, floating Styrofoam park by Robert Jasper Grootveld's design studio.

The Waterfront is where you can see Amsterdam future: by 2012, the seven islands of IJburg are to house 45,000 people and the finest Dutch landscape and residential architecture, fusing progressive aesthetics with environmental friendliness. But you'll also find a vestige of Amsterdam past: the south-east of Zeeburg island is one of few 'free' places where squatters are still allowed to make their funky homes from trailers and boats. Despite government clamp-downs having left things a little less lively than they once were, they still host the city's more eccentric parties.

Athens

GREECE

Heavy with its own history

To live in Athens is to succumb to the schizophrenia of an ancient city that is actually very, very new. Cast an eye around the centre and you'll see the ancient city, the modern city – and little else, save for a Byzantine church or small monument. Ironically, more remains today of the city of Pericles than of the city of Leo von Klenze, Eduart Schaubert, Ernst Ziller and Stamatios Kleanthes, the architects and planners tasked with designing modern Greece's capital in the 1830s. Just a handful of neoclassical edifices have survived the vicious modernisation of the '50s, '60s, and '70s as it ripped through the city's fabric like a particularly nasty virus. It's as if, having raised such a perfect structure as the Parthenon, the Greeks are unable to bear the sight of anything else in Athens for too long.

At ground level, the city presents a totally different picture than when viewed from the air. What appears to be a viscous concrete mass spilling into the sea, at close range dissolves into self-contained neighbourhoods, each with their own character. The extraordinary Attic light loses its harshness, shrouding the city with the weightlessness of a halo. The city's charm is its ability to surprise: a sudden flash of the Parthenon between the narrow streets or an astonishing sunset reflected in the glass façade of a modern office building snatch your breath away and, with it, the day's frustrations.

Athens is a city that excites passions, equally those of the philhellene seeking out the glory that was Greece and those of the weary shop clerk struggling to get home in time for dinner. To outsiders, Athens groans under the weight of cultural baggage, from the unmatched aesthetic of Classical Greece to more contemporary representations of the 'Greek psyche' embodied

Architecture	6
Arts & Culture	6
Buzz	6
Food & Drink	3
Quality of Life	5
World Status	4
Total	30/60
Rank	51

Left: gazARTE bar-restaurant in the Gazi technopolis.
Above: centre, 'T Palace' at the King George Palace

'Athens is a great equaliser because there are so few genuine Athenians left. Money talks in the city, but it's also very easy for the common person to mingle with the rich and celebrities. We're very formal, but also very casual'

Antonis Kolonaki waiter

Opposite: top left, Olympic Stadium complex; top right, the university; centre left, church of Kapnikarea; centre middle, swimming pool at St George Lycabettus hotel; bottom left, K44 bar; bottom right, one of the boats in Piraeus harbour

in legendary figures like Zorba, Melina Mercouri, Aristotle Onassis, and Maria Callas. Reality bites: what enchants on the screen or as myth can seem childish in the context of daily life. Greeks willingly subscribe to the cliché of their country as the point where East meets West, but their identification with the 'West' goes no further than consumer lust; the passions and perspective beneath the cloak of Armani and Donna Karan are quite firmly rooted in the East. Reason follows a wayward path, propelled by a mixture of fatalism, paranoia, optimism and insouciance characteristic of a society forged from millennia of triumph and defeat.

Diane Shugart

Instant Passport

Population
3,685,000

Area
684sq km

Where is it?
In the south-east corner of Greece, sprawling across Attica's central plain. It is bounded on three sides by mountains with the sea to the south

Climate
Hot summers and late winters with some rain that alternate with warm, sunny days. Athens sits in a bowl in the mountains which causes the notorious air pollution

Ethnic mix
80% Greek, plus migrants from Albania, Russia and the Black Sea

Major sights
Acropolis (with Bernard Tschumi's new museum), National Archaeological Museum, Temple of Zeus, Theatre of Dionysus, Olympic stadium

Insiders' tips
Summer club-hopping along the coast, get into Greek music at a *rebetika* club on a winter Sunday

Where's the buzz?
Kolonaki cafés on weekdays, Thisseio and Monastiraki on weekend afternoons, Psyrri at night

Number of stones used to build the Parthenon
Approximately 13,400

Cost of the 2004 Olympic Games
€1.97 billion

Number of days of sunshine a year
300

Most frequent sight
The *periptero*, or corner kiosk

Most enduring summer tradition
Taking in a film at an open-air cinema

Most famous souvlaki
Thanassis or Bairaktaris at Monastiraki

Most annoying habit
Twirling worry beads

Most intense sports rivalry
Olympiakos versus Panathinaikos (football)

Best view of the city
Areios Pagos Hill, the rock from where Paul preached to the Athenians

Number of citizens per car
1.9. Athens traffic jams are legendary, even after midnight at weekends

Bangkok

THAILAND

The laid-back city that smiles on contradictions

Architecture
3

Arts & Culture
6

Buzz
9

Food & Drink
6

Quality of Life
4

World Status
5

Total
33/60

Rank
39

Only one thing in Bangkok is certain: ambiguity. An indirect culture of 'face' creates layers that puzzle and dazzle. The Thai capital embodies royal cosmology, yet it sprawls out unplanned across Central Thailand's delta. Temples abut playgrounds of naughty renown. Exquisite crafts gleam amid piles of concrete and tile. In this montage of uniform and impromptu, Thais somehow move with a dancer's grace, eat banquets for pennies and turn everything into a festival through *sanuk* — the urge, as they translate, 'to fun'.

Bangkok's identity blurs. It was bestowed an auspicious name 64 Thai syllables long, shortened to Krung Thep (City of Angels), then Siam was decreed Thailand. Yet all those names remain in use. Krung Thep echoes the layout of the ancient city-state Ayutthaya. In 1972 it became a twin town with Siam's intervening capital, Thonburi, across the Chao Phraya River; Bangkok was left not with one sacred and geographic centre, but two.

The complications persist. Bangkok has grown multiple city centres, laid non-integrated transit lines, paved the canals that formerly made the Thai lifestyle amphibious – roving vendors echo that floating market character. Upon this diversity, official Thai-ness adds self-conscious propriety. It calls itself the 'Land of Smiles', but there's a smile for every motivation: deference, defence, delight, disguise.

In a hierarchy under the venerated King, everyone has their place, whatever their origin. Only a little younger than the United States, Bangkok is Asia's melting pot. Thais are mostly Buddhist, effectively Hindu, invariably animist — except when they're Muslim. The old walled city displaced a Chinese enclave; today Sino-Thai

Far left: Phu Khao Thong, or the
Golden Mount. Middle, from top:
Knowledge Park; Damnoen
Saduak floating market; Chatuchak
weekend market. Above: Th Silom

Above: spectacular views from
Sirocco restaurant on the 63rd
floor of the State Tower

form the majority. In the dense maze of lanes, ethnic villages persist: Lao, Mon, Malay, Indian, Portuguese. Foreigners still shape quarters: Japanese, Korean, Brit. Many Western expats never leave, relishing the tolerance and chance to reinvent themselves.

Bangkok repeatedly adapts foreign fads, from Greco-Roman columns to the iconic tuk-tuk, which began as a Japanese motor-rickshaw. With its headquarters at teen hub Siam Square, the pop culture makeover continues: ethnochic design, boutique hotels, hip bars, indy arts, brand-name malls, open-air restaurants atop skyscrapers. Still, even the hippest visitor yearns to taste the exotic, orientalist Bangkok of tabloid hype.

Pull up a plastic stool to any pavement bar, temporarily pitched at Nana or Khao San Road. Sip from a bucket of vodka Red Bull, then goggle the cliché parade: tuk-tuks, streetfood, ladyboys, fried insects, copy watches, spirit houses, blind buskers, saffron-robed monks, numbered masseuses, elephants wandering by. It's like being a character in a so-called 'Bangkok Novel'. Few cities spawn their own literary genre. But this City of Angels rivals LA for tales of private eyes, seething underbellies and re-imagined history.

Some bemoan modernisation, but Thais flit between surface fashions, secure in their social creed: harmonious relationships trump abstract logic. Faced with jams, scams or disruption of plans, they sigh *mai pen rai* – 'never mind'.

Decades of breakneck development and relentless hospitality have taken their toll, but not compromised Bangkok's essence. By embracing every onslaught so warmly, Bangkok remains charmingly, ambiguously Thai.
Philip Cornwel-Smith

Street stalls

Makeshift vendor stalls remain integral to Thai life. Colonising any spare space by pedal or paddle, motor or manpower, they congregate at already congested places, such as soi mouths, shopping strips and tourist haunts. More than half of them are food stalls selling specific dishes at different times of day: doughnuts at breakfast, noodles at lunch, rolled dried squid after dark. Tell-tale bells, whistles and cries herald what's coming: a tinkling bell for coconut ice-cream, clacks of chopsticks announce cauldrons of noodle soup, hoots on a horn for fruit.

Instant Passport

Population
6,500,000, but with dramatic seasonal variations

Area
1,010sq km

Where is it?
Built around an artificial royal island in the Chao Phraya River delta in central Thailand

Climate
Tropical monsoon, with the rains at their most severe in September and October. The city is the world's hottest, its temperature averaging 27.8°C with 77% humidity

Ethnic mix
Thai, Chinese, Lao, Malay, Mon, Indian

Major sights
Grand Palace, Wat Pho, National Museum, Jim Thompson House, Wat Arun, Thonburi canals, Jatujak Weekend Market, Erawan Shrine, Vimarnmek Mansion, Khao San Road, Royal Barge Museum, Lumpini Park, Golden Mount

Insiders' tips
Thailand Creative & Design Centre, Chao Mae Tubtim phallic shrine, Origin cultural programmes, Bang Kra Jao forest, Bangkok Sculpture Centre, any festival

Where's the buzz?
Chinatown, Siam Square, Nana, Thonglor/Ekamai, Silom/Patpong, Banglamphu

Number of motorcycle taxis
114,452

Number of street vendors
Over a million

World's longest place name
Krung Thep (City of Angels), the old name for Bangkok, is short for a 64-syllable name meaning 'Great city of angels, the supreme repository of divine jewels, the great land unconquerable, the grand and foremost realm, the royal and delightful capital city of the nine noble gems, the highest regal dwelling and grand palace, the divine shelter and living place of the reincarnated spirits', transliterated as 'Krung Thep Mahanakhon Amon Rattanakosin Mahinthara Yuthaya Mahadilok Phop Noppharat Ratchathani Burirom Udomratchaniwet Mahasathan Amon Piman Awatan Sathit Sakkathattiya Witsanukam Prasit'

Spoonfuls of sugar consumed per person per day
20

Most famous kathoey or ladyboy
Nong Tum, who was also a champion Thai boxer during the late 1990s

National sport
Muay Thai, or Thai boxing, known for its brutal 'full-contact' rules. Matches can be bloody affairs

WHAT OTHER BANK WILL RECOGNISE YOU ON YOUR LATITUDE?

Mr Johnson

AIRPORT limousines

MR. JOHNSON

London: 51°N

Mumbai: 19

Mr Johnson

CITY CARS

Bangkok: 13°N

Wherever you are in the world, it's nice to be recognised.

With HSBC Premier, you'll be met with the same high quality of service wherever you are. You'll have access to our global network of Premier Centres so that you can always be sure of a warm welcome. In every one of them, you will be assisted by someone who is qualified to resolve your problems as quickly as you would expect back home.

To find out about a service that helps you get more out of the world, visit www.hsbcpremier.com

Barcelona

SPAIN

Imaginative and in love with the eccentric

Unassailable proof that what doesn't kill you makes you stronger, Barcelona over the centuries has been buffeted by invading forces, fleeced by trade restrictions and strangled by autocratic central governments – and every time has bounced back prouder and more audacious. After the 'grey years', the interminable period between the end of the civil war and Franco's dying breath, there was a huge zest for change, to move on to a new era. It stoked the desire to transform the city itself, while the bid for the 1992 Olympics and then the Games themselves provided extra incentive, not to mention cash.

The finest architects and urban planners were persuaded to take part in this vision. The axis upon which the project spun was the idea to 'turn Barcelona around' to face the sea, creating whole swathes of beach from what was virtual wasteland. Ugly high-rises flung up during the Franco regime were pulled down, derelict blocks razed to provide open spaces and parkland, and world-class artists and sculptors – Roy Lichtenstein, James Turrell, Claes Oldenburg and Rebecca Horn among them – commissioned to brighten up street corners. Along with the creation of the new Barcelona in bricks and mortar went the promotion of Barcelona-as-concept, a seductive cocktail of architecture, imagination, tradition, style, nightlife and primary colours.

Helped, in large part, by the legacy of Gaudí and his Modernista contemporaries, which provided the city with a unique foundation both architecturally and in spirit, this was perhaps the most spectacular, and certainly the most deliberate, of Barcelona's reinventions. It succeeded in large part because this image of creativity and vivacity – what writer Rose Macaulay described as its 'tempestuous, surging, irrepressible life and brio' – simply fitted

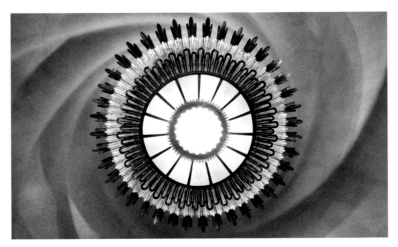

Architecture
9
Arts & Culture
7
Buzz
8
Food & Drink
8
Quality of Life
8
World Status
4
Total
44/60
Rank
5

Previous pages: left top to bottom, Torre Agbar, Plaça Reial, Casa Batlló; main picture, Calle Montcada. Top: left to right, Rebecca Horn's *Estel Ferit*, Mundial Bar, La Boqueria. Centre: left & far right, Park Güell; right, Font Màgica de Montjuïc. Bottom: left, Port Vell's Luz de Gas

'I love Barcelona for the sea and the mountains; for its sunny squares and markets; for its people – so warm and welcoming, yet hardworking and responsible; for its nightlife. Above all, I love it for all the rest, for all those indefinable qualities that make a city the perfect place to live'

Ferran Adrià **head chef at El Bulli**

Instant Passport

Population
3,900,000 (core city 1,454,000)

Area
803sq km

Where is it?
North-east Spain, between the Mediterranean and the Collserola hills

Climate
Temperate, but hot and humid in summer

Ethnic mix
European, Latin American, Pakistani, North African

Major sights
Sagrada Família, Museu Picasso, Casa Batlló, Catedral, Palau de la Música, MACBA, Fundació Joan Miró, MNAC, La Pedrera, Park Güell, Camp Nou

Insiders' tips
Museu Frederic Marès, CaixaFòrum exhibition space, old-fashioned tapas bars of Carrer Mercè, Hospital de Sant Pau, Els Encants fleamarket

Where's the buzz?
Late-night bars of the multicultural Raval, designer boutiques in the medieval streets of El Born

Percentage of Catalan speakers
74.6%

Number of parks and gardens
69

Number of registered architects
5,400

Number of members of FC Barcelona
156,366

Number of bar terraces
3,073

Number of fountains
220

Number of UNESCO World Heritage Sites
Nine (seven by Antoni Gaudí, two by Lluís Domènech i Montaner)

Year the building of the Sagrada Família began
1882

Year they expect to complete it
2026, the 100th anniversary of its architect Gaudí's death

Immortalised in
Private Life, *The City of Marvels*, *The Time of the Doves*, Carlos Ruiz Zafón's *The Shadow of the Wind*, *The Best of Worlds*, *Vicky Cristina Barcelona*, Whit Stillman's *Barcelona*

well with an idea of the city already held by many of its citizens. Thrown into the mix were the core values of nationalist pride and a delight in traditional ways, from dancing the sardana in front of the cathedral, to wheeling out papier-mâché giants and fire-breathing pantomime dragons at the first hint of a celebration. Barcelona's love of eccentricity had already brought about a wealth of quirky museums (such as those devoted to shoes, perfume, sewers, funeral carriages and mechanical toys), to which more were added. Its handsome but grimy façades were buffed up, its streets renamed and its churches restored. The glittering, buoyant result make the drab decades seem nothing but a collective bad dream.
Sally Davies

Architecture	
8	
Arts & Culture	
8	
Buzz	
5	
Food & Drink	
6	
Quality of Life	
4	
World Status	
9	
Total	
40/60	
Rank	
12	

Beijing

CHINA

A very cultural revolution

Over the past two millennia, this desert city has periodically been built and then raised and rebuilt at the whims of the latest conqueror. But it is the arrival of the Bling Dynasty, which invaded in the 1990s, that has been the making of Modern Beijing, for better and for worse. The city has again been built anew. Palaces in the form of towering buildings, Olympic Stadia and enormous theatres have replaced the Forbidden City and Temple of Heaven as key landmarks. The old city's low-rise courtyard homes and alley-way *hutong* dwellings have been brashly brushed aside beneath a veneer of reflective glass towers and ever-expanding ring roads.

The city's new economic might hasn't just changed its façade, it has changed its whole psyche. The dark years of the Cultural Revolution, which removed people's individuality in creating a classless nation, is a distant memory. Money is now king and climbing the social – or, rather, financial – ladder the new dream.

While the global economy falters, the world's most populous country continues to slowly steamroll its way across the globe. Its capital, which just a generation ago was cut off from the outside world, is now beginning to dominate the planet economically and increasingly politically. For it is in Beijing where the politicians decide the strength of the American dollar and will play it their way on subjects such as Tibet, human rights or banking systems, no matter what Björk, Sting or the Hollywood set have to say about it. From the loins of the massive gated community of Zhongnanhai – the physical and political heart of the city – is born the nation's wealth. Flash cars with white government number plates ignore the rules of the road on their way to gaudy nightclubs where bottles of expensive whisky are drunk, chunky Cuban cigars smoked and

Instant Passport

Population
8,614,000 (core city 7,362,000)

Area
748sq km

Where is it?
On the edge of the dusty plains of the Gobi desert, bordering Inner Mongolia

Climate
Dry: hot and dry in summer, cold and dry in winter

Ethnic mix
Almost entirely Han Chinese, with a sprinkling of Chinese minorities especially Uigurs from Xinjiang, as well as some Russians, Koreans and a smattering of Europeans

Major sights
Olympic Stadium, CCTV Tower, Temple of Heaven, Forbidden City, National Theatre, Tiananmen Square

Insiders' tips
Buy original Cultural Revolution posters from the western building at Panjiayuan dirt market, 798 Art District for contemporary art and design

Where's the buzz?
The Legation Quarter, where the former American Embassy is now home to international restaurants, bars and theatres; the revamped old bar area at Sanlitun, with design hotel the Opposite House as its centrepiece; China Bar on the 66th floor of the Park Hyatt, overlooking the entire city

Pollution
On an average day, five times higher than the level set by World Health Organisation safety standards

New cars on the street per day
1,300

Most popular street food
Xinjiang lamb kebabs

Best place for Chinese food
Provincial government offices

Year the Forbidden City was completed
1420

Number of surviving buildings in the Forbidden City
980

Number of ancient *hutong* streets
1989: 3,679; 2009: less than 500

Cost of the CCTV complex, half of which burnt down before opening
$730m. It was designed by architects OMA, led by Rem Koolhaas

Cost of a metro ticket
2RMB (roughly 30¢)

'I think these new buildings – the Bird's Nest, Water Cube, Egg, CCTV Tower and new airport – act as one to represent a new hope for a nation that has the desire and passion to change'
Ai Weiwei artist

Previous page: Tiananmen Square. Top: left, Peking Opera; middle, 'Bird's Nest' National Stadium; right, Ritz Carlton. Centre: left, Tiandi Theatre acrobats; middle, Dongdan PE Centre; right, Financial District. Bottom: left, China World mall; middle, Wanfujing street

modern-day concubines swarm. Graduates leaving Beijing's elite universities of Qinghua and Beida more often aspire to become a government official rather than an entrepreneur or the CEO of an international company, for the trappings of today's officialdom are akin to being a member of the old Emperor's court.

As the world's financial institutions continue to focus on a capital city whose economy seems to be one of the few still in the black, those with initiative, ingenuity (and the right connections) are managing to create a new social order – a nouveau upper-class that wants to distance themselves from their billion other brethren. And with ostentatious spending on private villas and designer handbags for mistresses becoming increasingly passé, a cultural class is helping create a new vibrant and contemporary city. As the '80s children, born into a modern city of double-figure economic growth and political calm, reach maturity, they are creating a new Chinese culture, mixing the best of the West with the romantic traditions of a bygone era, inspiring art, film, music and design that could see the city of fakers turn into a city of makers. Music venues with ironic names such as Mao Livehouse open for kids who aren't even aware rock 'n' roll was still banned when they were in nappies; and art galleries house kitsch paintings of a time not long gone by that is only known to their young contemporary creators through history books, but is still firmly fixed in the minds of their parents.
Tom Pattinson

Beirut

LEBANON

Enduring, anarchic and alluring

Architecture
4

Arts & Culture
6

Buzz
9

Food & Drink
5

Quality of Life
4

World Status
5

Total
33/60

Rank
39

Beirut is a woman, petite but not especially pretty. The average Beiruti will happily take time describing her features and highlights: he'll tell you how she was destroyed and then rebuilt half a dozen times, how her cooking is second to none and how, if you visit the iconic Pigeon's Rock (grasping your 20¢ coffee) in the very early hours of the morning, the sea melts into the city's night sky as the scattered fishing boats begin to light their oil lamps.

But ask any of the thousands of international expats that have made Beirut their home why they decided to stay, and they'll give the same answer: they know that they're in love with the place, they just aren't quite sure why.

Beirut is certainly a well-dressed lady. She's also steeped in culture: there are more sights, galleries and ruins here than you can shake a camera at, and she is equally at home in three languages – Arabic, French and English. She is always making music, drinking cocktails and dancing on the tables; she's wild and entertaining, and as attached to her nightlife as she is to her churches and mosques. But that isn't why you fall for her.

You love her because she's a living contradiction. She's rude, cheap, ugly – but for every person that'll threaten you for glancing at them, Beirut has ten that will open their homes to a complete stranger. For every beggar on the streets, you'll meet two Versace-clad elitists. For every $200 steak, you'll find a 50¢ meal fit for a king. For every destroyed building or break in the highway, you'll find a 2,000-year-old Roman bath or Byzantine church.

Beirut is anarchy, with as many independent governments as it has residents. She shuns mere maps and street names, preferring you to get lost in her alleys. Need to find that obscure art gallery?

Main picture: St George's Church. Above: top to bottom, old coins in Souk el Ahad; memorial to the assassinated Lebanese prime minister Rafik Hariri in Ain el Rimani; modern take on tabbouleh

'*Beirut has a fantastic mechanism of survival. You learn to believe in it*'

Bernard Khoury architect

Top: left, Downtown Beirut; right, Pigeon's Rock. Bottom, left to right: a basement nightclub in Saifi; ferris wheel on the Cornice; Saifi Village

Take a left at the butcher's, walk until you hear the caged birds, then make a sharp right at the store with the old couple sat out front.

Beirut will take you out and get you drunk, and treat you like a celebrity. She will make love to you all night and then leave you early in the morning, hungover, bruised and all alone – but still eager for more. And the more that she torments you, the more you'll love her for it.

Karl Baz

Instant Passport

Population
1,800,000

Area
648sq km

Where is it?
Western Lebanon, on a peninsula jutting out into the Mediterranean

Climate
Mediterranean, with hot, humid summers

Ethnic mix
Arab, with American and European minorities

Major sights
Al Omari Mosque, AUB Museum, the Corniche, Pigeon's Rock, Roman Baths, St George's Cathedral

Insiders' tips
Ghalayineh snacks, shoe-shiners on Hamra Street, poster salesmen in Downtown Beirut

Where's the buzz?
Gemmayzeh Street, Monot Street, Hamra Street, Downtown Beirut

Earliest evidence of civilisation
First mentioned in letters, dating to the 15th century BC, from the ancient Egyptian site of Tell el Amarna

Under French mandate
Until 1943

Consequences of internal conflict
At least 360,000 people (14% of the population) had at least one member of their family killed, wounded or kidnapped during the Lebanese civil war (1975-1990)

Length of Israel's military offensive in 2006
34 days, during which 1,000 Lebanese were killed

Education
Due to the lack of education during the civil war, 20% of Beirut's population aged over 20 are illiterate

Local flavours
Meze, houmous, kebab, baklava, fattoush (a salad mixed with pieces of toasted bread)

Man'oushes (bread with thyme) consumed per year
55 million

Major industries
Financial services, agriculture, tourism, food processing, jewellery, textiles, mineral and chemical products

Best way to spend a Sunday
At the races: Beirut's race track runs pure Arabians and is one of the few places in the Middle East to offer legal betting

Belfast

UK

Putting the Troubles behind it

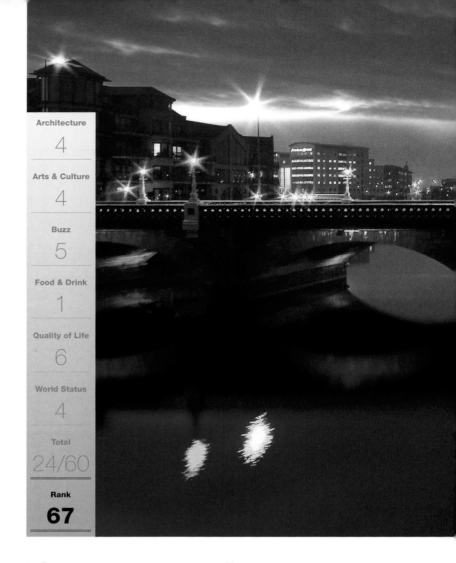

Architecture	4
Arts & Culture	4
Buzz	5
Food & Drink	1
Quality of Life	6
World Status	4
Total	24/60
Rank	**67**

One of the worst things you can do in Belfast is to take yourself too seriously. Get above your station and you'll be brought down to earth with a cutting 'catch yourself on'. In this city, few people get away with pretending to be something they're not. So when Northern Ireland's capital – once wholly overlooked on the tourism radar – began to emerge as a fashionable destination of choice, locals weren't quite sure what to do.

The bitter sectarian conflict, known euphemistically as 'The Troubles', as well as keeping visitors away for over thirty years, drummed a sense of cultural inferiority into Belfast's half a million inhabitants. London was trendier, Dublin more cosmopolitan, and teenagers left in droves to study or work away from home.

Having shrugged off its low self-esteem like an empowered guest on Oprah's couch, Belfast is turning its attention to the more positive chapters in its history. Dozens of cranes are busy transforming the remains of the city's sprawling shipyard into 'Titanic Quarter' – a satellite urban centre being constructed on the very spot where the iconic ship was built. It may seem strange to rally round the world's most infamous maritime disaster as a source of collective pride, but as a popular tourist T-shirt reads, 'she was alright when she left here'.

On the opposite side of the river Lagan, the Cathedral Quarter – once an area of post-industrial dereliction but now rehabilitated as the city's clubbing district – feels just like Barcelona, but with better banter up at the bar and less chance of getting your bag nicked. A brand new university campus, which was built partly to accommodate the growing numbers of local students who now choose to stay at home in Northern Ireland, will complete the transformation.

Top: Queens Bridge. Bottom: left, Ormeau Baths Gallery; right, traditional music at Madden's Bar

Ask locals what best symbolises Belfast's renaissance and many point to Victoria Square – the high-end, multi-storey mall whose attractive glass dome commands one of the best views of the city. But while the peace process has made way for Prada, there are subtler signs of transformation in other parts of the city. A new crop of arts venues, such as the Black Box theatre, with its penchant for burlesque revues, and the Golden Thread Gallery, a converted electricity switch room, keep creative types as busy as the shoppers. In the west, the Irish language is going through a fervent revival, with the patter of *Gaeilge* now reverberating round pubs, shops and cultural centres in Andersonstown and the Falls.

Sure, the anachronistic Sunday opening hours and mysterious lack of good espresso might irritate more aspirational inhabitants, but it's hard to begrudge a city that's dusted itself off as quickly as Belfast. Like anywhere undertaking a PR makeover, Belfast wants desperately to be liked and, despite being a bit rough around the edges, pulls it off with effortless charm.
Bryan Coll

Top: left to right, the Crown Bar, Stormont, Maritime Festival. Centre: left, Albert Clock; right, St George's Market. Below: left, Belfast Castle; right, Belfast Wheel and the City Hall

Instant Passport

Population
267,374

Area
115sq km

Where is it?
On the north-west coast of Northern Ireland, at the mouth of the River Lagan where it flows into Belfast Lough

Climate
Temperate with cool summers and very rainy, dark winters, particularly between October and January

Ethnic mix
98% white. The largest minority ethnic group within Belfast is the Chinese community (1,318 residents)

Religious mix
Protestant and other Christian 48.6%, Catholic 47.2%, non-religious or non-Christian 4.2%

Major sights
City Hall, Ulster Museum, West Belfast murals, Albert Memorial Clock, Belfast Cathedral, Crown Liquor Saloon, Custom House Square

Insiders' tips
Hot whiskey in the small but perfectly formed Bittles Bar, beside Victoria Square, before popping next door for a Paddy Pizza (made with local soda bread) at the Kitchen Bar; grab your seat early and leave any prudishness at the door for comedy nights at the Empire Music Hall on Tuesday; Saturday night clubbing with the city's cool kids (and drag queens) at Yello – don't bother turning up before 2am

Where's the buzz?
Cathedral Quarter, Upper Ormeau Road

Titanic launched
From Belfast on 31 May 1911

Most devastating World War II air raid
On 16 April 1941 Belfast suffered the worst air raid on any city outside London. The city was ill-prepared – it had just four public air raid shelters

IRA ceasefire
1994

Signing of the Belfast (Good Friday) Agreement
10 April 1998

Percentage of the population who are under 16
19.9% – one of the youngest populations in Europe

Famous people from Belfast
Bobby Sands, Brian Mawhinney, CS Lewis, Eamonn Holmes, George Best, Gerry Adams, James Galway, Kenneth Branagh, Van Morrison

Number of people who attended George Best's funeral in 2005
100,000

Harland and Wolff shipyards

The Harland and Wolff shipyards are destined to be forever remembered as the birthplace of the *Titanic*. When the 46,328-ton liner was completed for White Star Line in 1912, it was the biggest ship in the world – and Harland and Wolff the biggest shipyard.

The *Titanic* was only one of three sister-ships built by Harland and Wolff. It was preceded by the *Olympic* and – surprisingly, given the results of that encounter with the iceberg – it was followed by the *Britannia*, a ship almost as unlucky as its forebear. Ready just in time for World War I, the *Britannia* went into service as a hospital ship rather than a luxury cruiseliner, and was sunk by mines in 1916. Of the three vessels, only the *Olympic* pursued a healthy commercial career: it continued sailing until 1935.

Founded in 1861, the shipyards launched their last liner in the early 1960s. Harland and Wolff diversified, now engineering bridges, oil rigs and turbines, while parts of the dockyard are undergoing redevelopment as the 'Titanic Quarter', with a landmark £97m building the centrepiece.

Belgrade

SERBIA

Centuries-old survivor, looking to the future

<table>
<tr><td>Architecture</td><td>3</td></tr>
<tr><td>Arts & Culture</td><td>5</td></tr>
<tr><td>Buzz</td><td>9</td></tr>
<tr><td>Food & Drink</td><td>2</td></tr>
<tr><td>Quality of Life</td><td>5</td></tr>
<tr><td>World Status</td><td>3</td></tr>
<tr><td>Total</td><td>27/60</td></tr>
<tr><td>Rank</td><td>64</td></tr>
</table>

The Serbian capital lies atop and around twenty hills, and due to its strategic position holds a long and turbulent past. A Neolithic settlement started 8,000 years ago, it was later used by the Romans as a massive fortress, whose remnants are now the Kalemegdan park. Since then, it's been battered and bombed, leaving its streets a surreal mix of medieval and Ottoman, 18th-century monuments and World War II tanks and howitzers.

Let's not pretend. No one goes to Belgrade for the architecture or fresh air: what makes the city attractive is its relaxed approach to living, the great nightlife and a distinctive character that can only come with longevity. In spite of its history, Belgrade is a contemporary city in spirit, currently undergoing restoration of its former pride. Falling between East and West, it is a place where the Orient and Europe meet.

If New York is 'the city that never sleeps', Belgrade is a rough 'n' tumble, low-budget version. Cosy coffee shops, bars and clubs are places you go to throughout the week, not saved for weekends. Nightlife starts late – never before 10pm – and goes on well into the next morning. The Belgrade spirit, a sort of general openness to the world, mostly evolved in traditional restaurants (*kafanas*) with excellent traditional cuisine. Cigarettes, rakija (home-made traditional brandy) and coffee are all consumed with a clear conscience, because what's the point in life if you deny yourself small pleasures?

The food is a far cry from the low-fat, sugar-free menus of the rest of the world. The 19th-century *kafanas* of Skadarlija Street in the Bohemian Quarter serve traditional meat dishes, grilled lamb and beef goulash. There's no improvisation here: Serbian cuisine is straightforward, natural and tasty.

Above: middle, Trpezarija
Kralijevskog Dvora; bottom,
St Petka chapel

Above, top to bottom: a boat carnival on the Sava; Jugoslovensko Dramsko Pozoriste (Yugoslav Drama Theatre); crowds beneath the Pobednik ('Victor') statue on the walls of the Kalemegdan Citadel

Most cities faced with Belgrade's gruelling past, recent and historic, would crumble and fall into oblivion. But this capital is made of sterner stuff. It stands true, like an old lady who – in spite of her age – still looks amazing. Looking to the future, Belgrade will be *the* place in Europe. Not because it is full of beautiful women (while average monthly income is around €300, many women spend twice that amount on their appearance). Not because you can become a billionaire for only a euro (the hyperinflation of the 1990s has left behind old bank notes for 500 billion dinars, now sold as memorabilia). No, it's because Belgrade is a living, breathing jigsaw puzzle of Oriental kitsch, second-hand Europe, Soc-Realism and occasional contemporary pearls.
Slobodan Obradović

> *'To wake up in Belgrade this morning is quite an achievement for the day. To pursue the matter further would be regarded as vanity'*
>
> Dusko Radović **Serbian writer and poet**

Instant Passport

Population
2,000,000 (estimated)

Area
360sq km

Where is it?
On the Balkan peninsula in south-eastern Europe, at the confluence of the the Sava and Danube rivers

Climate
Moderate continental. A south-eastern and eastern wind called *košava* brings fair and dry weather in autumn and winter

Ethnic mix
Serbs (82.86%). The rest are Hungarians, Bosnians, Roma, Croats, Albanians, Slovaks, Vlachs, Romanians and Bulgarians

Major sights
Church of St Sava; the Kalemegdan Citadel; the ruins of NATO bombing; the grand House of Flowers, Tito's mausoleum

Insiders' tips
Little Ruzica church, which is cut into a steep hillside; late clubbing – don't even bother to head out until 10pm

Where's the buzz?
During the day, 'Circle of Two' (the inner part of the city centre); at night, on river barges on the New Belgrade side of both rivers

World's largest Christian Orthodox Church
Cathedral of St Sava

Celtic name
Singidun, meaning 'white city'

Oldest street
Kneza Mihaila, now one of the city's main shopping streets

NATO bombing campaign during the Kosovo War
24 March to 11 June 1999. Almost 1,000 aircraft were involved, resulting in approximately 500 civilian deaths. The objective was to force Yugoslav troops to withdraw from Kosovo, and led to the fall of Slobodan Milošević

Football triumphs
Red Star Belgrade has been both World and European club champion, winning the European Cup and Intercontinental Cup in 1991, as well as the Mitropa Cup in 1958 and 1968

Tennis triumphs
Novak Djoković was victorious in the Australian Open in 2008, the same year Ana Ivanović won the French Open. Jelena Janković was ranked world no.1 in 2008/9

Local flavours
Pljescavica, the grilled meat skewers served from street stalls

Most memorable graffiti
'If you're lost in Belgrade, don't despair. You're still in Belgrade'

Right: Helmut Jahn's Sony
Center. Above: top, Denkmal für
die ermordeten Juden Europas
(the Holocaust memorial in Mitte);
centre, the Konzerthaus

Architecture	7
Arts & Culture	9
Buzz	9
Food & Drink	6
Quality of Life	7
World Status	8
Total	46/60
Rank	4

Berlin

GERMANY

Finally finding its confidence

'Come to Berlin,' sings Barbara Morgenstern, one of the city's many noted electronic music artists, on her 2008 album *BM*, 'This place is in.' Like any Berliner abroad these days, on tour she'd encountered a newfound curiosity: 'Isn't Berlin the place to be?'

It is with no little bemusement that 21st-century Berlin, after stumbling through the past hundred years in a series of ugly and offbeat incarnations – teeming imperial capital, hotbed of Weimar Republic decadence, forbidding fascist metropolis, bombed-out city of rubble and ruins, bipolar Cold War anomaly – now finds itself cast as a mainstream capital of cool. Once more back at the political centre of things, it is now luxuriating in a quality wholly alien to its former self: confidence. One of Europe's most-visited cities, it greets an ever-increasing flow of tourists with an uncharacteristic friendliness that has surprised no one so much as itself since it pulled out all the stops for the 2006 FIFA World Cup finals. The city hosts one of the continent's most important film festivals; the Berlin Philharmonic, one of the world's best symphony orchestras, is only the centrepiece of a classical and opera scene big enough to satisfy three normal cities; the local art scene has begun to acquire international importance; and the post-techno pulse of the legendary Berlin nightlife still reverberates way past dawn.

Much of its attraction is to do with space. Not just the mostly late 19th-century layout of broad, tree-lined avenues, which has left Berlin as one of the only major European cities with streets wide enough for 21st-century traffic, but also the affordability of big, centrally located apartments that, apart from all the other advantages, means thousands of artists and writers, designers and musicians, have the time and space to pursue their interests.

Top: middle, the Reichstag; right, Shiro i Shiro. Centre: government buildings on the Spree. Below, left to right: East-Side Gallery, Fernsehturm, Gendarmenmarkt. Opposite: left, Galerie Max Hetzler; right, Kaiser-Wilhelm-Gedächtniskirche

'The city has definitely inspired the sounds of the clubs. It's never boring to go to a record shop or a club — something interesting will always happen. I feel like I live in the techno heart of Europe'

Sascha Funke DJ/producer

Although all the major unifying construction projects are now finished – the new government quarter, postmodern Potsdamer Platz, and a futuristic central station that ranks as the largest and most modern in Europe – and the Wall has been gone long enough for a generation that doesn't even remember it to have reached voting age, there are still some east/west differences and divisions. But the new Berlin continues its rise. Cultural collisions are celebrated these days, and the new centre of town has filled up with critical memorials to the victims of its former dark incarnations. This is never going to be a city where things are taken lightly, but contemporary Berlin is a refreshingly thoughtful and laid-back place – and still unique.

Dave Rimmer

Instant Passport

Population
3,387,000

Area
984sq km

Where is it?
On the River Spree in north-east Germany, 70km from the Polish border

Climate
Warm summers; cold, sub-zero winters

Ethnic mix
Mainly German. Of immigrant nationalities, the Turkish are by far the largest group. Other nationalities include Polish, Serbian and Russian

Major sights
Brandenburg Gate, Jüdisches Museum (the Jewish Museum), Reichstag, Denkmal für die ermordeten Juden Europas (the Holocaust memorial), Fernsehturm, Pergamonmuseum

Insiders' tips
Prenzlauer Berg, the lakes in the Grunewald, Bauhaus Archiv, Museum für Fotografie, Sunday fleamarkets

Where's the buzz?
Kastanienallee in Prenzlauer Berg, Bergmannstrasse in Kreuzberg, Mitte's Hackesche Höfe and Rosenthaler Strasse, Kurfürstendamm and Savignyplatz in Charlottenburg, Friedrichshain's Simon-Dach-Strasse

Continental Europe's biggest department store
KaDeWe (Kaufhaus des Westens, 'Department Store of the West'), on Tauentzienstrasse, opened in 1907. It has more than 60,000sq m of retail space and the food hall occupies the entire sixth floor

Length of the Berlin Wall
Approximately 155km when it stood from 1961 to 1989. Now only a few sections remain, including one on the north side of Topographie des Terrors and 1.3km of graffitied concrete rebranded the East-Side Gallery

Height of the Fernsehturm
365m. The television tower in Alexanderplatz is the second tallest tower in Europe, after Moscow's television tower (561m)

Beer and sausage consumption
Every year, the average German consumes 115 litres of beer and 30 kilos of sausage, half their annual meat consumption. The particular Berlin delicacy is the currywurst: a bratwurst seasoned with warm ketchup and curry powder

Dialect
Known as Berliner Schnauzer ('Berlin snout'), since it is coarse and peppered with French words

Immortalised in
Christopher Isherwood's *Goodbye to Berlin*, *Cabaret*, *M*, Len Deighton's *Funeral in Berlin*, *Emil and the Detectives*, Nabokov's *The Gift*, *Wings of Desire*, *Berlin Alexanderplatz*, *Christiane F*, *Good-Bye Lenin!*, David Bowie's *'Heroes'*, *The Lives of Others*

Berlin Hauptbahnhof

Odd to think that before the arrival of the Hauptbahnhof in 2006, Berlin never even had a central station. As if to make up for its tardiness in getting one, Von Gerkan Marg architects devised a grand design that has resulted in the biggest and most futuristic station in Europe; 14 overground platforms on two levels are covered by a barrel vault of delicately gridded glass and crossed in a north–south direction by a station hall 180 metres long and 40 metres wide. This hall gives access to the trains on each intersecting level and to the shopping centre, and the twin towers and arched central axis make an impressive dent on Berlin's skyline.

It's not just about scale though; the huge multi-level structure has all the facilities you'd expect of a thoroughly modern main station, including no fewer than 19 food and drink outlets (most of them, sadly, instantly familiar to train travellers from any number of other city stations across Europe). As such, it's not just an impressive hub for a whole European rail network, but stands as a functional and symbolic link between East and West Germany – after all, its operating train company, Deutsche Bahn AG, has only existed for a decade: East and West Germany's two rail organisations, Deutsche Bundesbahn and Deutsche Reichsbahn, had continued to operate separately for five years after the fall of the Berlin Wall.

For all the razzmatazz, there are still issues to resolve (notably, connections to the U-Bahn system are only now being put in place) and the station has not been universally popular with Berliners.

Architecture	5
Arts & Culture	7
Buzz	7
Food & Drink	3
Quality of Life	3
World Status	3
Total	28/60
Rank	58

Bogotá

COLOMBIA

An urban rehab success story

Like its introspective residents, Bogotá reveals its charms slowly. Although it boasts the cosmopolitan brio of any capital city – gourmet dining, yuppie pubs and around-the-clock convenience – its essence is in the past and the genteel *cachaco* who saunters along its opaque streets in buttoned-up dress and demeanour. Part of this reserve is a trick of nature. Bogotá only became a large city in the last 50 years and, owing to its isolation 2,600 metres up in the Andes, it doesn't dominate the rest of the country the way other Latin American megalopolises do.

Instead, the bulging city is a cultural crossroads that feels like a preternatural *pueblo*. Nowhere does the rich energy of Colombia's diversity pulsate more heavily than in La Candelaria, a warren of cobblestone streets, bohemian cafés and Spanish colonial churches. Here, as if straight out of a Gabriel García Márquez novel, Kogi Indians from the Caribbean coast can be spotted dodging traffic in their traditional white robes and waist-long hair.

Bogotá's innate modesty saved this outdoor museum from the wrecking ball. In 1949, after mass riots razed the city, Le Corbusier redrew the neighbourhood along rigid, modernist lines. The plan was scuttled and today the city's dominant building material, from hillside slum to wealthy enclave, is simple red brick. When the sun breaks through the year-round drizzle, the contrast with the verdant backdrop of Monserrate mountain is spellbinding.

Not everything recalls the past. Inspirational former mayor Enriqe Peñalosa (1998-2001) built on drastic reforms aimed at breaking down the inequalities between rich and poor (though the north is full of luxury appartments and shopping malls, elsewhere are vast areas of slums), introducing green initiatives, and driving out crime. Car use was restricted, housing and sewerage

Previous page: the city, with the
Plaza de Toros de Bogotá in the
foreground. Above: downtown
Bogotá. Left: human puppets at
a street festival

improved, public space prioritised, parks built or rebuilt, and the
mafia cleared out. The city is today held up as a role model of
urban reform. There are now nearly 350 kilometres of bicycle
paths and bendy red TransMilenio buses zip across the city, the
centrepieces of Bogotá's rebirth from the uncontrolled violence
that brought Colombia to its knees in the 1990s.

Although the city has largely shaken its reputation for drugs
and violence, the siege mentality persists in the form of ubiquitous
bulletproof cars and sniffer dogs at the entrances to shopping
malls. Luckily, playful residents of Locombia – the 'mad country' –
have adapted, and now the only mayhem most people will
encounter is the all-night partying in Parque 93 or the Zona
Rosa. It's just one more display of the city's surprising vitality
and sense of purpose in the face of adversity.
Joshua Goodman

Instant Passport

Population
7,000,000 (core city 6,422,000)

Area
518sq km

Climate
Mild and irregular, with dry and rainy seasons alternating throughout the year

Where is it?
2,640m above sea level, on a mountain-rimmed plateau in the Andes in central Colombia

Ethnic mix
Mestizo, white, mulatto, black, mixed black-Amerindian, Amerindian

Major sights
La Candelaria, Plaza de Bolívar, Museo del Oro, Cerro de Monserrate, Donación Botero, Quinta de Bolívar

Insiders' tips
Zona Rosa, La Macarena, restaurant and all-night party zone Andres Carné de Res

Where's the buzz?
Zona T, Parque 93, Usaquen, Botanical Garden

Independence from Spain
20 July 1810

Population growth
1985: 4,100,000; 1993: nearly 6,000,000

University population
Approximately 16% of the total number of inhabitants

Length of cycle paths in the city
344km

Murder rate
In the 1990s, 80 per 100,000 inhabitants; in 2005, 23 per 100,000 inhabitants – a reduction of 71%. Today Bogotá has a lower murder rate than São Paulo, Mexico City, Panama City, Detroit, Chicago, Rio de Janeiro, Caracas and Washington DC

Colombian cocaine cultivation
According to UN figures, 99,000 hectares in 2007 (27% increase from 2006), the equivalent of 600 metric tons of pure cocaine

Number of gold items from the pre-Hispanic cultures in Colombia held at the Museo del Oro
34,000 – it is one of the world's most important gold museums

Local flavours
Chocolate Santafereño (hot chocolate served with cheese and bread), ajiaco (stew of chicken and three different types of potato), canelazo (a hot drink made with cane sugar, cinnamon and aguardiente, the local firewater), coco rico (grilled chicken)

La Catedral Primada

The city's largest church stands on the east side of Plaza de Bolívar and is believed to mark the spot where the first mass was celebrated, shortly after Bogotá's foundation in 1538. Today's colossal structure is, in fact, the fourth to have been built here. The small, thatched original was replaced by a larger building between 1556 and 1565, but it collapsed due to poor foundations; another was reduced to ruins during the 1785 earthquake. The impressive neo-classical building that stands today was designed by the monk Domingo de Petrés and completed in 1823. Its vast, plain interior houses the tomb of Bogotá's founder, Gonzalo Jiménez de Quesada.

Brasília

Broad skies, sensational architecture

A sense of wide open space permeates day-to-day life in Brasília. The original urban plan envisaged an unobstructed view for all inhabitants, concentrating the few skyscrapers that there are in a small area. Everywhere, the immense blue sky invades the city. 'It's our sea!' some say. The evening sunset, a dusty blue fading to orange, is treated as a collective experience, watched and shared by the whole city.

Nestled in the central highlands of Brazil, the new capital was brought from Rio de Janeiro in 1960 to occupy 5,405 square miles of tropical savanna in the middle of nowhere, surrounded by natural springs. It was conceived by urban engineer Lúcio Costa, with principal buildings designed by Rio architect Oscar Niemeyer, and interventions from landscape designer Roberto Burle Marx. Costa's philosophy was that the city should be a concrete representation of a futurist and open-minded society; the unexpected outcome was that, as well as being a political hub, Brasília became a centre of mysticism. The mystic community believes Brasília to be the promised land prophesied in the dream of Dom Bosco, a 14th-century Italian priest celebrated in several churches and sanctuaries around the city. There are also an unusual number of alternative religions in the city such as Afro-descended Candomblé, ecumenical communities such as Vale do Amanhecer and Cidade Ecléctica, and Brazil's international holistic university.

In plan, the city is laid out like an aeroplane: the Monumental Axis of world-class government buildings corresponding to the 'fuselage', intersecting with the Residential Axis which forms the 'wings'. The original housing was conceived as a series of six-storey residential blocks or *quadra*, each of which would be a self-contained community, with local amenities close at hand,

Architecture	
10	
Arts & Culture	
3	
Buzz	
3	
Food & Drink	
4	
Quality of Life	
5	
World Status	
3	
Total	
28/60	
Rank	
58	

plenty of parking, and space for children to play outside. Grand, six-lane avenues would run the length of the Esplanade. Where the two axes cross is the bus terminal, flanked by hotels and the business district; in the 'cockpit' are the Praça dos Três Poderes and the main government buildings.

Inspired by the ideas of Le Corbusier, this strict geometric logic cuts Brasília up into the sorts of symmetrical spaces that, in spite of their stunning architecture, can feel dreary and monotonous. Unfortunately, such a highly organised urban plan did not take into account the natural expansion of the city, and the resulting sprawl means there are more cars than it was designed to cope with. Having grown far beyond its original 500,000 population, the city creates a rush-hour traffic jam that will soon become a real headache.

Brasília's setting – embraced by Lake Paranoá – gives it an ecological status widely discussed in environmental debates across the country. With its many natural springs and the wide biodiversity of its tropical savanna, it is part of the World Biosphere Net, officially recognised by the UNESCO MAB programme, which studies the relationship between man and the biosphere.

As the country's hub of politics and international congress, headquarters for national banks, media and telecoms companies,

Previous page: view along the Monumental Axis towards Congresso Nacional. Above: Catedral de Brasília. Opposite: flagpole near Praça dos Três Poderes

Instant Passport

Population
3,480,000 (core city 2,016,000)

Area
583sq km

Where is it?
On the Planalto Central plateau in the Federal District of central Brazil,
between the Preto River (to the east) and the Descoberto River (west)

Climate
Pleasant year-round, with few extremes in temperature. Rainy summers,
very dry winters

Ethnic mix
A concentrated further mix of the combination of African, European,
Latin and indigenous traces that characterises Brazil

Major sights
360° panoramas from the TV Tower; the Monument complex of Praça
dos Três Poderes, Catedral de Brasília, Museu da República, Biblioteca
Nacional and Teatro Nacional; Congresso Nacional; Palácio do Planalto;
Juscelino Kubitschek Memorial

Insiders' tips
Sunset by the lake at Ermida Dom Bosco; free Tuesday concerts at
the National Theatre and the Clube do Choro

Where's the buzz?
Lakes of the Parque da Cidade during the day, nightly entertainment
at the Gilberto Salomão, shopping at the craftworks fairground of the
TV Tower at weekends

Constructed
Over 41 months, from 1956 to 1961. Then-president Juscelino
Kubitschek used the motto '50 years in five' to express his ambition
to bring Brazil forward 50 years during his five-year term of office

Distance from nearest paved road in 1956
600km. It was 125km to the nearest railway, 190km to the airport

Inaugurated as Brazil's capital
21 April 1960, before it was actually complete

Buildings designed by Oscar Niemeyer
Congresso Nacional, Palácio do Planalto, University of Brazil, Palácio
dos Arcos, Catedral de Brasília, Teatro Nacional, Palácio da Alvorada

Length of shoreline of Lake Paranoá
80km. The lake was created for the city by damming the Paranoá River

Designated a UNESCO World Heritage site
1987

Number of satellite cities
16

In quotes
'Elegant monotony' (Simone de Beauvoir)

Brasília is also a multicultural place. At the city's conception, the
federal government called out for people from all over the country
to participate in the 'construction of the future'. Many different
accents meet here, and many different cultures. The international
community, represented by embassies and consulates, add to
the distinctive cosmopolitan touch Brasília has acquired.

Looking at itself and the world around it through the years,
Brasília has been able to maintain a cultural calendar that fulfils the
expectations of a global city. The great States Fair and Nations Fair
in June showcase national and international cuisine. The city holds
international film festivals, poetry gatherings and the International
Music Summer Course in January. Just some of the many worlds
Brasília can fly to in its aeroplane.

Jaqueline Fontenelle

Brussels

BELGIUM

A nod to the traditional, a wink at the unusual

Architecture	6
Arts & Culture	5
Buzz	3
Food & Drink	8
Quality of Life	6
World Status	7
Total	35/60
Rank	28

Our Brussels imaginings are often loaded with the one-dimensional bureaucratic face of the European Union, a place that seems to tell the rest of us how to live. The reality is that nothing could be further from the truth. Brussels is a city that routinely refuses to be staid and its residents live in a glorious state of laissez-faire; be whatever you want to be, do whatever you want to do and, as long as it doesn't affect me, nothing really matters.

In that sense, Brussels doesn't set out to make you love it like other, more glamorous cities. Take it or leave it, the city invites you to get under its skin, to breathe with it, to take part in its offbeat, sometimes bizarre, lifestyle. This is a roguish city with a generous party spirit and a nod to individuality – so it's no coincidence that its symbol is a statue of a little boy with a half smile on his face, peeing to his heart's content.

Brussels is a city with few set pieces, though its big draw, the Grand'Place, is one of the world's most perfect squares, dazzling in its Gothic and Italian Baroque authenticity. It's the living room of Brussels, echoing with the footsteps of Marx, Engels and Victor Hugo, and where free radical thinkers still sit and muse on life while nursing a Duvel beer. From here, all life radiates out in a busy, haphazard spiral. It's hard to find such a mix of outstanding restaurants, outlandish bars and quirky clubs that routinely turn the night into day.

It's all an urban enigma. Brussels is a bilingual city surrounded by Flanders but with a French-speaking majority. There is a certain linguistic tension in the air that sparks creative thought, philosophical posturing and political manoeuvres in the dark.

Left: Atomium. Above: top, the Hôtel de Ville from the Musée des Instruments de Musique; middle, the Manneken-Pis in one of his 725 outfits

'Brussels combines the sophistication of Paris, the cultural melting pot of London and the small scale of Amsterdam. It has the architectural splendour of the Grand'Place, the tiny Manneken-Pis and the largest number of diplomats in the world. I love Brussels because it is both confusing and exhilarating'

Paul Dujardin Director-General of BOZAR Centre for Fine Arts

This is a city always on the move, forever reassessing itself but, at the same time, comfortable in its skin. It is the birthplace of art nouveau, Jacques Brel and techno, home to Tintin, Magritte and the Breughels. Comic strip art reflects the national psyche while interior design and high Flemish fashion push it to the top of the style pile. It claims to have more green space than any other European city: parks, woods, the Forêt de Soignes, private gardens, cemeteries and sports fields cover a total of over 8,000ha, half the region's area.

Most importantly, Brussels will just be itself and will let you be yourself. Slip in next to the locals and soak it all up. The city may not take much notice of you but it'll know you're there, you'll feel it absorbing you. And when it hits home, it is cheekily irreverent and totally irresistible.

Gary Hills

Above: top, classic chess bar Le Greenwich; middle, fish restaurants on Ste-Catherine. Right: La Brouette, one of many fine buildings on Grand'Place

Instant Passport

Population
1,570,000

Area
712sq km

Where is it?
Flanders, north-west Belgium

Climate
A maritime temperate climate, with around 200 days of rain per year

Ethnic mix
More than a third of inhabitants are foreigners: 753,000 Belgian nationals, 295,000 other

Major sights
Grand'Place, Parc du Cinquantenaire, the Manneken-Pis, Royal Quarter, the Sablon district, the Atomium

Insiders' tips
Boutiques along rue Antoine Dansaert, daily flea market at Place du Jeu de Balle, fish restaurants in Ste Catherine

Where's the buzz?
St Géry, Rue du Marché au Charbon, Ixelles

Most famous dish
Moules frites (mussels and chips)

Number of Belgian beers
More than 800

Litres of beer consumed annually
150 litres per person

Lay-by lays
Two thirds of Belgians have had sex in their cars

World's biggest chocolate retailer
Brussels National Airport

Number of restaurants
2,000

Number of restaurants in the Michelin guide
300

First railway line on mainland Europe
Between Brussels and Mechelen, 1835

World's highest cable TV usage
97% of homes are cabled

World's biggest law courts
The Palais de Justice (26,000sq m)

World's deepest swimming pool
Nemo 33, Uccle (35m)

Bucharest

ROMANIA

Many eras making their mark

Architecture	4
Arts & Culture	7
Buzz	4
Food & Drink	1
Quality of Life	4
World Status	2
Total	22/60
Rank	**71**

Bucharest is a layered city, in fact several cities coexisting in a direct and sometimes rough relationship, each one unveiled in turn as you walk down the city's wide boulevards and the narrow streets hidden behind them.

There is a French-German Bucharest, defined by the 19th century buildings that make up the city's main landmarks: the Triumphal Arch, the Romanian Athenaeum, the house of the 'George Enescu Philharmonic', the Central University Library, and the Royal Palace (now the National Art Museum). There is an avant-garde Bucharest of 1920s villas and houses scattered in the central neighbourhoods, small architectural gems that remind the visitor of the most prosperous period of the city, between the First and the Second world wars. Many of these villas have been refurbished and transformed into restaurants and clubs that are crowded all year long. In the courtyards of the Gradina Icoanei area, you can still find hundred-year old trees (somehow surviving the uncontrolled construction fever of the past ten years) next to modern, glazed office buildings that are out of kilter with the prevailing architectural style.

There is a Byzantine Bucharest, situated within the old part of the city, called Curtea Veche. Step into the courtyard of Stavropoleos church (1742) in the Lipscani area and you'll find yourself among small isles of green gardens, surrounding Christian Orthodox churches with pillared patios and twisted columns. Their architectural style, Brâncovenesc, is named after Constantin Brâncoveanu, a generous prince who built large parts of the city when he ruled the region of Walachia, in the 17th century.

Finally, there is communist Bucharest, with its neighbourhoods of concrete apartment blocks lined up in monotonous rows along

Previous page: Biblioteca Centrala Universitara. Above: Villacross.
Opposite: top left, Romanian Athenaeum; top right, Green Hours.
Bottom: left, Studio Martin; right, Stavropoleos Monastery

wide boulevards – grey belts that surround the heart of the city. Its
most prominent landmark, the Casa Poporului or People's House
now houses the Romanian Parliament. Commissioned by dictator
Nicolae Ceauscu, it is the world's largest civilian administrative
building, dominating the central downtown area of Unirii Piazza.

Bucharest's charm and its character lies in the rough mix of old
and new, in the different heartbeats encountered every day, even in
a ten-minute walk, in the unexpected combinations of styles of
architecture. A city that lives several lives at the same time.

Anca Ionita

Instant Passport

Population
2,600,000

Area
228sq km

Where is it?
Between the river Danube and the Carpathian mountains on the banks of
the river Dâmbovita in southern Romania

Climate
Very hot summers (temperatures reaching 38°C) and mild winters with little
snow. The most beautiful time is spring, with temperatures around 15°C

Ethnic mix
Romanian; Hungarian; Roma; other

Religious mix
Romanian Orthodox Church 86.7%, Roman Catholic 4.7%, Protestant
3.7%, Pentecostal 1.5%, Romanian Greek-Catholic Church 0.9%

Major sights
Romanian Athenaeum, People's House, Cismigiu Garden, Peasant
Museum

Insiders' tips
Visit the Sunday flee-market in the courtyard of Bucharest City Museum,
buy local fruit and veg from the Piata Amzei market, in summer explore
the terraces in the backyards of old houses in the Gradina Icoanei area

Where's the buzz?
The bars, clubs and restaurants in the Lipscani quarter; the Peasant
Museum's Club; jazz, theatre and drinks at Green Hours Club; live
performances at Kisseleff

First mentioned under its present name
20 September 1459 as a residence of the Walachian Prince, Vlad Tepes
(Vlad the Impaler)

Legendary figure
Vlad the Impaler. A blood thirsty prince who inspired Bram Stoker's Dracula

Became capital of Romania
1862

Communist dictatorship
Nicolae Ceausescu led the Romanian Communist Party from 1968-1989.
In 1989, a popular uprising supported by the military, led to the arrest and
execution of Ceausescu and his wife, Elena, on Christmas Day 1989

Percentage of central Bucharest razed for the construction of
Ceausescu's palace and Centrul Civic
20%, leaving just one historic district, Lipscani

Romania joined the EU
2007

Patron of Saint
Saint Dimitrie of Basarabov

Budapest

HUNGARY

Rekindling the glamour of the Golden Age

Pályaudvar! Forgalom! Repülőtér! The signs for seemingly universal words ('train station', 'traffic', 'airport') in Hungary's capital can appear utterly alien. A little background reading instructs you that the natives responsible for them were fearsome warriors, the blood-drinking Magyars who conquered this otherwise tranquil patch of the Carpathian Basin just over a millennium ago. Legend has it they were guided here by the mythical grandmother-raping, dynasty-siring, eagle-like turul bird, whose statue guards the Royal Palace atop Castle Hill. And it is from here, reached by funicular railway, that the stunning cityscape is best appreciated: hilly Buda on one side; busy, grid-patterned Pest on the other, panoramically divided by the Danube. The view's as impressive as any in Europe.

In reality, Budapest is neither fearsome nor alien (airports, main roads and metro stations now bear English renditions). In fact, to those relaxing over a post-spa coffee and gooey cake at the historic Gellért Hotel, Budapest can seem remarkably accommodating. Vistors are tempted to extend their stay to Tuesday, next weekend, mid September, a lifetime. The city is easy and cheap to get around, its grand Habsburg façades hide courtyards lined with ornate, high-ceilinged flats; its shops are retro and friendly. And Budapest gives you time: spa-soaked mornings, lingering lunches, wine-sodden evenings… days fly by satisfyingly.

At the same time, Budapest houses a savage drinking culture, partly driven by party-minded expats of post-'89 vintage, boozing in bohemian bars and crumbling courtyards. An art scene thrives in a similar atmosphere. Live music is back – here folk is not a four-letter word but a living, changing culture. Classical musicians earn the same as bus drivers but fill auditoria once graced by Mahler

Architecture	8
Arts & Culture	6
Buzz	5
Food & Drink	4
Quality of Life	5
World Status	2
Total	30/60

Rank

51

Left: Gellért baths. Above: top left, Citadella statue; top right, Matthias Church; bottom left, celebrating Hungarian National Day (15 March)

the same as bus drivers but fill auditoria once graced by Mahler and Liszt. Chefs no longer churn out slightly spicy stodge but inventive recreations of the Hungarian cuisine that defined Budapest's Golden Age.

The grandiose metropolis you see from Castle Hill was created then, in the late 1800s. As twin capital of the Austro-Hungarian empire, Budapest erected broad boulevards, sumptuous palaces and pretty bridges. Its parliament, taller than Westminster, ruled over Bratislava, Zagreb and other since-independent cities still easily reached by train from palatial stations, one designed by Gustave Eiffel. Between the wars, the Silver Age of the Grand Tour and the Orient Express saw the Gellért Hotel and the Gundel restaurant fill with moneyed visitors.

And now, in the third millennium, its five-star hotels revamped and reopened for a new generation of lower-budget tourists, grand, weird old Budapest has much the same attraction. The age has yet to be named – hopefully something long, exotic and unpronounceably Hungarian will emerge.

Instant Passport

Population
1,825,000

Area
702sq km

Where is it?
Central Europe, past a bend in the Danube on its journey from
Vienna to Belgrade

Climate
Continental. Freezing winters, sweltering summers

Ethnic mix
Magyar, Roma (Gypsy)

Major sights
Royal Palace, Parliament, Basilica of St Stephen, National Museum,
Museum of Fine Arts, Citadella statue

Insiders' tips
Római fürdö riverbank near Aquincum, lined with bars and fish eateries;
all-night DJ Cinetrip parties every month at the revamped Rudas Baths;
Jewish Quarter walking tours

Where's the buzz?
District VII, the old Jewish Quarter, for nightlife; Király utca – no longer
dilapidated haunt of pedlars and pawnbrokers

Historical milestones
Conquest by the Magyars in 895, 1896 Millennium celebrations, Treaty
of Trianon, liberation by the Soviets in 1945, fall of Communism in 1989,
EU accession in 2004

Local flavours
Halászlé (fish soup), gulyás (goulash), fözelék (purée), lángos (fried dough),
palacsinta (pancakes), somlói galuska (rum sponge pudding), turós táska
(cheese-filled pastry), túró rudi (cream-cheese bar dipped in chocolate)

Local drink
Unicum – a dark, bitter and syrupy alcoholic drink

Number of road accidents caused by drunk people (drivers or pedestrians)
2,855 in 2007

Stock of cars
66,304 Trabants, 39,602 BMWs and 24,198 Volvos in 2007

Average life-expectancy for men in Pest
63.81 in 1990; 69.49 in 2007

Festivals
Sziget rock festival every August

Number of natural thermal springs
118

Sporting rivalry
Ferencváros v Újpest, competing in football, ice hockey and waterpolo

The Chain Bridge

The Chain Bridge was built in 1849, on the eve of the revolution that would eventually grant Hungarians the political and economic freedom to assemble their capital, and has huge symbolic importance as the first permanent span to connect Buda and Pest across the Danube. Instigated by diehard anglophile and political reformer Count István Széchenyi, whose foresight brought huge civic benefits to Hungary through the 19th century, the suspension bridge is guarded by stone lions and lit up at night like a bright necklace. The bridge's creator never saw it completed, having withdrawn from public life in 1848 after a nervous breakdown. William Tierney Clark, an English engineer, was responsible for the design, while a Scottish engineer Adam Clark – no relation – not only supervised the construction but preserved the structure from being blown up by Hungarian and Austrian armies. The square between the bridgehead and the Buda Tunnel now bears Adam Clark's name, as well as containing the milestone from which all distances across Hungary are measured.

Opposite: Parliament. Left: Városliget (the City Park)

Architecture	5
Arts & Culture	8
Buzz	10
Food & Drink	5
Quality of Life	6
World Status	5
Total	39/60
Rank	**16**

Buenos Aires

ARGENTINA

A sad soul and a party spirit

It would be unjust to suggest that all porteños, as BA residents are called, are born pessimistic – some acquire the trait during childhood or adolescence. However, most of the inhabitants of this gorgeous, enchanting city have deduced that their town has either gone to the dogs or is on its way to the dogs in the not-very-distant future. Such, at any rate, is the stereotype. But how accurate is it?

The cited-ad-nauseum fact that Buenos Aires contains more psychiatrists per capita than any other city in the world has led many to conclude that porteños must be more-than-averagely screwed-up. But it could just as easily mean that porteños are more-than-averagely analysed – and saner for it. And then there's tango, which many regard as the acme of miserabilism; sad songs played on sad-sounding instruments by sad-looking people for sad people to shuffle around sadly to. But most of BA's canonical tangos were written during the city's belle époque, when grain was shipped out as fast as it could be harvested, and gold bars deposited in the country's bank vaults as fast as they could be stacked.

Beyond its chaotic and frenetic exterior, the city is beautified by grandiose buildings, world-class art galleries, fine restaurants and a thriving fashion industry. It has been saddled with the wince-inducing 'Paris of the South' tag, but Buenos Aires is undoubtedly a Latin city, as neighbourhoods such as Once and Retiro demonstrate.

It is also a city of barrios, some unofficial (if you ask someone where they're from and they reply with a number, you're probably talking to a shantytown, or villa, dweller), others, like Recoleta, long established and world-renowned. Most of the affluent

Left: Plaza del Congreso. Top: left, Monumento de los Españoles; right San Telmo. Bottom: San Telmo

Monumento a las Víctimas del Terrorismo de Estado

It took 25 years, numerous hold ups and the usual rounds of internecine wrangling, but Buenos Aires now has a fitting memorial to the thousands of people who 'disappeared' – that is to say, were murdered – during the military dictatorship that ruled Argentina between 1976 and 1983. The Monument to the Victims of State Terrorism was unveiled in November 2007 and is now the centrepiece of the Parque de la Memoria, a sculpture park on a spit of reclaimed land in the north of the city, surrounded by the Río de la Plata.

The rather nondescript location is inconvenient but appropriate. Of the perhaps 30,000 people who were tortured and killed in one or other of the junta's mini-gulags, many – either already dead, or drugged – were dumped into the river from planes. The names of those known to have died are engraved on a black granite monument which has been laid out so as to represent a scar in the earth: a twisted, running wound symbolising pain and a breach of natural law. It is a memorial that glorifies nothing; that in its jagged discontinuities suggests the absence of 'closure' for the families. Nearby, placed in the water but visible from a small viewing station, is the most moving sculpture in the park: a statue of Pablo Miguez, at 14 years old the youngest known victim.

The park is still a work in progress. More sculptures are due to be installed and there is space for more names to be added, as investigations continue, to the 9,000 already inscribed.

Instant Passport

Population
10,800,000 (core city 2,956,000)

Area
1,580sq km

Where is it?
East-central Argentina, on the western bank of the Río de la Plata estuary

Climate
Mild year-round – extremely hot or cold days are rare, though summer days are often humid

Ethnic mix
97% white (of European descent), 3% native Indians and other

Major sights
Cementerio de la Recoleta, El Abasto, Plaza de Mayo, Palacio Barolo, Palacio del Congreso, San Telmo, Alvear Palace

Where's the buzz?
San Telmo, Palermo Viejo

BA's ranking in list of world's noisiest cities
4th (Corrientes and Madero is the loudest street corner)

Percentage of porteños who define themselves as 'unhappy'
20%

Ratio of psychoanalysts to population in Argentina
1:30

Number of Argentinians who have undergone plastic surgery since 1970
1 in 30

Percentage of Argentinian population living below the poverty line in 2005
40%

Percentage of city streets still cobbled
20%

Number of left-wing dissidents 'disappeared' under military rule from 1976 to 1983, according to official reports
14,000

Number of left-wing dissidents 'disappeared', according to most human rights groups
30,000

Argentina's world ranking for soy meal and soy oil exports
1st

Argentina's world ranking for beef exports in 2007
4th

Amount of beef consumed per year per capita in Argentina
60kg

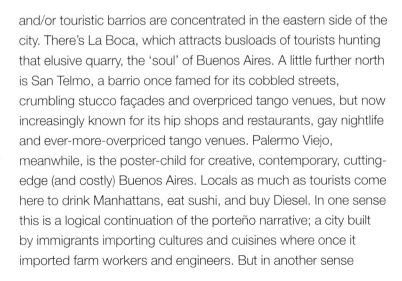

Clockwise from top left: Centro Cultural de los Artistas; San Telmo; Palermo Viejo; Azema Exotic Bistró

and/or touristic barrios are concentrated in the eastern side of the city. There's La Boca, which attracts busloads of tourists hunting that elusive quarry, the 'soul' of Buenos Aires. A little further north is San Telmo, a barrio once famed for its cobbled streets, crumbling stucco façades and overpriced tango venues, but now increasingly known for its hip shops and restaurants, gay nightlife and ever-more-overpriced tango venues. Palermo Viejo, meanwhile, is the poster-child for creative, contemporary, cutting-edge (and costly) Buenos Aires. Locals as much as tourists come here to drink Manhattans, eat sushi, and buy Diesel. In one sense this is a logical continuation of the porteño narrative; a city built by immigrants importing cultures and cuisines where once it imported farm workers and engineers. But in another sense

the efflorescence of 'creative capitalism' represents an important break with the past.

The challenges still faced by BA are daunting: poverty, poor housing, underfunded public hospitals, dilapidated public schools. But porteños love their city and, in a manner that is hugely charming, want everyone else to love it too. They never tire of hearing newcomers tell them how sensational their buildings/women/steaks/footballers are. In BA, you never know what's around the next corner: a spontaneous tango display, a flash mob from the exciting theatre scene, an all-night party, or maybe another protest. Despite all its problems, Buenos Aires was, is and probably always will be one of the world's great cities.
Matt Chesterton and Daniel Neilson

ALL YOUR FINANCES IN ONE PLACE WHEN YOUR FAMILY ISN'T

UK – Lymington: 50°N

Architecture
3

Arts & Culture
8

Buzz
9

Food & Drink
1

Quality of Life
5

World Status
7

Total
33/60

Rank
39

Cairo

EGYPT

Crumbling charisma held together by history

Supersized flyovers and alleyways too narrow for cars; Tahrir Square's Stalinist-style Mogamma building – hub of Egyptian bureaucracy – and the glorious symmetry of the Ibn Tulun mosque; marble shopping malls and medieval markets; the feat of ancient architecture that is the pyramids, and the traffic-clogged, built-up road that takes you to them. All are part of this contradictory, exasperating, yet somehow still-functioning megacity, Africa's largest urban area.

Sitting at the crossroads between Africa and the Middle East, and with historical influence from Europe, Cairo underwent radical social change in the wake of the 1952 revolution. The departure of Egypt's minorities of Greeks, Italians and Jews brought along with it the slow demise of the capital's old cosmopolitanism. In subsequent decades, increased economic inequality and religious conservatism, mass migration from the countryside and cars have also changed the face of the city – and few would say it has all been for the better. Once-fine 19th century buildings in the city centre are dilapidated; fin de siècle villas have been pulled down to make way for blocks of flats; informal, illegal housing in its many ingenious forms (including the use of mausoleums as homes in the City of the Dead) proliferates around the city's edges.

Yet, in the heart of the modern city, the core of medieval Islamic Cairo remains relatively intact – there has been a move to recognise and preserve the mosques, madrasas, mausoleums and other aspects of Islamic heritage found here (it's a UNESCO World Heritage Site). Begun in the tenth century, Cairo became the centre of the Islamic world; it is home to the mosque and

Instant Passport

university of Al-Azhar, founded in 975 and still the world's foremost centre of Sunni Islamic learning. It is also the location of the Khan El-Khalili market – part emporium for tourist tat, part market for essentials, and certainly an economic and cultural hub.

Egypt's Christian heritage has also been preserved. In the area of Old Cairo known as Coptic Cairo are the city's oldest Coptic Orthodox churches, including St Mary the Virgin, or the Hanging Church. A church has stood on this site since the seventh century – parts of the current structure date to the 11th century. But Egyptian churches are not just historic monuments – around ten per cent of Egyptians are Christians, many keen churchgoers, devoted to their church's distinctive iconography and ancient liturgy.

Previous page: Feshawi café in the
Khan El-Khahili souk. Left: Sultan
Hassan mosque. Above right: Khan
El-Khahlili souk

This overcrowded metropolis may be hanging on to sanity
by the skin of its teeth, but it hasn't abandoned hope. Amid a
built environment that is sometimes dehumanising, and levels
of poverty that can be debilitating, social and family structures
remain strong in all levels of society, crime is low, kindness is
respected (rogues who bother tourists excepted) and
resourcefulness is a byword among the poor. A strong sense
of identity may be one explanation: Cairo and Egypt share the
same name in Egyptian Arabic – Misr. And Cairenes, whatever
their background, are aware that they are citizens of somewhere
with a culture and history that's worth talking about.
Abdoulie Sey and Ros Sales

Cape Town

SOUTH AFRICA

European sophistication dancing to an African beat

Architecture	6
Arts & Culture	4
Buzz	4
Food & Drink	4
Quality of Life	5
World Status	3
Total	26/60
Rank	**65**

The Mother City, Cape of Good Hope, Tavern of the Seas, Cape of Storms, Cape Town: it doesn't matter what you call this vibrant, cosmopolitan city at the southern tip of Africa, as long as you're able to call it home – whether it's for a day or a lifetime. Cape Town is a city blessed with spectacular natural bounty, a diverse floral kingdom, an unusually flat mountain and an expansive, icy ocean. While its roots are firmly in Africa, giving it an eclectic energy and funky vibe, European influences are palpable in its fabulous wines and gourmet food, as well as the contemporary design, architecture and art.

Even Cape Town's bitter history is now mapped out in tourist attractions. Colonial rule left the pentagonal fortification of the Castle of Good Hope; more recent oppression under apartheid made Robben Island prison famous as the place where Nelson Mandela was incarcerated for 18 years. The Cape's legacy of slavery is remembered in the Cape Minstrel Carnival on 2 January, traditionally the only day slaves were allowed off, and the slaves' architectural prowess can be admired in the historic Bo-Kaap area.

Some divisions persist from the days of apartheid – leafy suburbia remains mostly 'white', less affluent neighbourhoods are mostly 'coloured' – and violent crime, although it is decreasing, remains a problem in some parts of the city. Yet modern Cape Town is also a fusion of the best the world has to offer: from the French-speaking Congolese trader in a flea market to a beach-front ice-cream seller punting his wares in colourful Cape patois, the city is a crucible of languages, people and culture.

Capetonians and visitors indulge in activities as diverse as whale-watching from the coastline, wine-tasting in the majestic Cape winelands, hunting for antiques in laid-back Kalk Bay,

March of the Penguins

No one needs a refresher viewing of *Happy Feet* or *Surf's Up* to be convinced that penguins can be entertaining, and the jackass penguins that nest on sheltered little Boulders Beach never fail to raise a smile. There are over 3,000 in residence, ducking under brush and over boulder to slide into the surf.

Named for its distinctive donkey-like honk, the jackass is more accurately known as the African penguin (*Spheniscus demersus*): although certain South American penguins also bray, this is the only species to breed in Africa. The African penguin grows to about 70cm tall, usually lives for ten years and weighs up to four kilos. For all its Charlie Chaplin gait on land, in water it is impressive: an average swimming speed of 7kph isn't bad (roughly the same as Michael Phelps), but their top speed is nearer 20kph. They swim with such grace and vigour you'd swear they're enjoying themselves.

Calm, warm-ish waters and the opportunity to swim with wild animals – the penguins let you approach to within a few feet – have made Boulders as popular with locals as with tourists, and since 2004 the Simonstown Penguin Festival has been a firm fixture on Cape Town's conservation calendar in mid September (which is spring here).

Previous page: Table Mountain, seen from across the city. Opposite: one of the superb beaches at Clifton. Above: top V&A Waterfront; left, the town hall; right, Cape wines sold at the hole-in-the-wall shop Vino Pronto

soaking up the sun at the fashionable Camps Bay beachfront bars, sourcing fresh, organic produce at a local market, hiking up Table Mountain or lazing under the trees at Kirstenbosch Botanical Gardens as a band plays on the stage. A walk up mad, bad Long Street entertains with cutting-edge shops, lively bars and great after-hours bites. Further along, up Kloof Street, the mood is more lattés and lace, with high-end boutiques, trendy coffee shops and fine interior finds. Wherever you go, there's something cool, quirky and idiosyncratic to experience.

And even the locals never tire of the city's iconic attraction – Table Mountain – a view best enjoyed with glass of the Cape's finest, of course.

Lisa van Aswegen

Instant Passport

Population
2,700,000

Area
686sq km

Where is it?
At the south-western tip of Africa

Climate
Hot, dry summers (with a temperamental south-easterly wind) and cool, wet winters

Ethnic mix
The Cape Coloured account for almost half of the population, followed by Africans at 31%, Whites at 18.75% and Asians at 1.43%

Major sights
Robben Island, Cape Point Nature Reserve, Table Mountain, Kirstenbosch, V&A Waterfront and Aquarium

Insiders' tips
Old Biscuit Mill in Woodstock for trendy design and a buzzing Saturday food market, old-fashioned cinema The Labia, penguins at Boulders Beach at Simonstown, Sunday summer sunset concerts at Kirstenbosch Botanical Gardens in Newlands

Where's the buzz?
Long Street, Kloof Street, Camps Bay, Kalk Bay

World's first successful heart transplant
Performed on 3 December 1967 by Professor Christiaan Barnard at the Groote Schuur Hospital in Cape Town

UNESCO World Heritage Sites
Robben Island and the Cape Floral Kingdom

Number of plant species found in the Cape Peninsula
2,285 – more than in the whole of Great Britain, which is around 5,000 times bigger

Number of cyclists that take part in the 109km annual Argus Cycle Tour
40,000 – the world's biggest individually timed cycle race

The world's best mayor
Helen Zille. As voted by citymayors.com in 2008, in part for 'questioning corruption within the South African police and opposing the disbanding of the anti-corruption Scorpions unit'

Largest township (living area set up for non-whites under apartheid)
Khayelitsha, 50km from the city centre with at least 600,000 residents

South Africa's oldest tradition
The firing of the Noon Gun, situated on Signal Hill – since 1806

Most celebrated wine
Vin de Constance, from Klein Constantia Wine Estate. It enamoured King Louis Phillipe, kept Napoleon Bonaparte company during his exile on St Helena, and features in novels by Charles Dickens and Jane Austen

Chicago

USA

Down-to-earth star of the Midwest

Architecture	9
Arts & Culture	8
Buzz	7
Food & Drink	7
Quality of Life	7
World Status	6
Total	44/60
Rank	5

For a relatively young city (it was only incorporated in 1837), Chicago lets its iconography hang over it heavily, like a billboard erected on a skyscraper: tommy gun-toting gangsters, weeping blues guitars, the Daley Machine, 'Da Bears' jokes, rioting hippies of '68 and deep-dish pizza. Toss in the indelible 'windy city' and 'city of big shoulders' subtitles, and the clichés form a dense fog that can be suffocating – or just flat-out annoying. National newscasters even refer to Chicago as the big city in 'the country's mid-section', unconsciously insinuating that all of us residents have got beer-and-brat bellies. The thing is, some of us do. And there's just no use in discarding these visions of Chicago.

Those clichés do reveal something about the city, but not everything. Gang violence remains a fact of life in some parts, Donald Trump has a new skyscraper, live music (be it indie rap, indie rock, blues or free jazz) still beats strong. Eating one's way through Chicago's taco joints and concept restaurants is a pleasure on any budget, and local politics in this Democratic Party bubble tend to be somewhere between colourful, idealistic, scandal-ridden and just plain sad. Chicago has character.

But Chicago's raison d'être in the post-industrial America has yet to be spelled out – another slogan, 'The City that Works', doesn't quite suffice. Once a place where immigrants settled in enclaves and toiled in massive industrial zones, Chicago is still about working hard and making things, even as it continues to haemorrhage manufacturing jobs. It's hard not to drive through a former factory corridor and think of trainloads of musical instruments, pinball machines, candy, meat, furniture, that used to be shipped out by the tonne every day.

One constant is that Chicago remains a mosaic, rather than a melting pot. The romanticised enclaves of the city-gone-by might be shadows of their former selves (notably Little Italy), but newer ones – the Mexican, Puerto Rican, Indian-Pakistani (Devon Street) areas and Eastern European villages on the north-west side – comprise a patchwork of communities that can be by turns dazzling, beguiling and inspiring. A great deal of this sprawling, stretched-out city is still reserved for modest living – quaint small houses in residential areas. It's also dramatically segregated. While it may be gentrifying near its centre, it's worth noting that Chicago is sorely underpopulated by many planners' standards – it has a million fewer people than at its peak in 1950.

Main picture: Marina City, with Sears Tower in the distance. Below: Jay Pritzker Pavilion, designed by Frank Gehry, in Millennium Park

'Chicago has this unassuming quality where you can find yourself back where you started without really realising it'

Billy Corgan singer/guitarist with the Smashing Pumpkins

Instant Passport

Population
8,308,000 (core city 2,896,000)

Area
5,498sq km

Where is it?
South-west tip of Lake Michigan, on the St Lawrence Seaway

Climate
Extreme and seasonal, with long cold winters and warm summers

Ethnic mix
European American, African American, Latin American, an Asian minority

Major sights
Art Institute of Chicago; Millennium Park; Grant Park; MCA (the Museum of Contemporary Art); Wrigley Field ballpark; Frank Lloyd Wright's home, studio and Robie House; Second City; Lincoln Park Zoo; Marina City; Pullman Historic District; Water Tower; Magnificent Mile; Ida Bell Wells' house; Lake Michigan path; Sears Tower; Architectural Boat Tour

Insiders' tips
Mies van der Rohe's Illinois Institute of Technology Campus, contemporary art at the Renaissance Society, the medieval collection at the Loyola University Museum of Art, Arts Club of Chicago, discount shopping on State Street, dining on Devon Street, Garfield Park Conservatory, New Apartment Lounge, Diversey River Bowl, Boom Boom Room, Rainbo Club, Music Box Theatre, Hot Doug's

Where's the buzz?
The boutiques and bars of Wicker Park; Oak Street shopping district; North Avenue beach; nightclubs of River North; Fulton Market restaurants, clubs and galleries; loft parties on Lake Street; West Loop galleries

Historical milestones
Fort de Chicago founded, Fort Dearborn founded, Chicago Fire, Haymarket Riot, World's Columbian Exposition, Eastland Disaster, Al Capone found guilty, Dillinger shot, Fermi tests nuclear energy, Second City founded, riots at the 1968 Democratic Convention, Harold Washington elected mayor, Michael Jordan retires, Barack Obama elected US President

Hot dog consumption
Chicagoans spent $43,885,180 on hot dogs in 2007

Sport
Chicago Cubs and White Sox (baseball); Chicago Bears (American football); Chicago Bulls (basketball) and Blackhawks (ice hockey), who play at the largest arena in the USA, the United Center

The only river that flows backwards
The Chicago River was reversed to take pollution away from Lake Michigan in 1900, and every St Patrick's Day it is dyed green

Immortalised in
Dark Knight, Ferris Bueller's Day Off, The Blues Brothers, High Fidelity, The Untouchables, Medium Cool, Running Scared, The Fugitive, ER, Barbershop, The Coast of Chicago, Division Street, Devil in the White City

It's a city of compromise where the charms outweigh the challenges. Choosing to live in Chicago involves calculated trade offs – a winter that can be fierce and long comes with a civilised cost of living; higher taxes versus an extensive parks system; neighbourhoods with unique flavour against a struggling school system; Midwestern close-mindedness comes with Midwestern generosity; cultural amenities versus a culture of sports worship. Chicago is imperfect, but far from full of itself, and that makes its drawbacks easily tolerable.

Chicago – big, bold and optimistic (the ebullient dance genre house music began here), but also ruthless – epitomises the authentic, everyman American metropolis. And now Chicago can boast an era-defining president, it may get more attention. That's not a bad thing; we could do with a new image for this millennium.

John Dugan

Left: Cal's Liquors, in the Loop, at South Wells and East Van Buren. Below: Gene Siskel Film Center. Right: top, the 'El' – CTA's elevated railway; bottom, drinking in the blues at New Checkerboard Lounge

Copenhagen

DENMARK

Quintessentially cosy

Architecture	6
Arts & Culture	6
Buzz	5
Food & Drink	6
Quality of Life	10
World Status	4
Total	37/60
Rank	**20**

Compact and incredibly easy to navigate on foot or by bicycle, Copenhagen exemplifies the notion that 'small is beautiful'. What it lacks in landmark buildings, epoch-defining contemporary culture, wild nightlife and raw urban energy, is made up for by *hygge* (cosiness), stylish design, beautiful people, and lots and lots of bicycles. It is common to see a father riding home in his work suit after a hard day (at 4.30pm!), with blond children sandwiched between grocery bags on his 'station wagon bike'. Copenhageners cycle everywhere – on dates, going clubbing (you can get a ticket for being drunk in charge of bicycle, but the law is rarely enforced), and shopping for groceries or even DIY supplies.

Strolling along today's car-free streets and into lively squares with vibrant café life, it's hard to tell that most of the public spaces in the town centre were parking lots in the '50s and early '60s. Cleared of vehicles in 1962, Strøget – the main shopping street – was one of the first pedestrianised streets in the world. At the time, shop owners argued that removing cars would kill business because no one was going to walk in this climate – there are 300 days of overcast skies a year and 180 days of rain. They couldn't have been more wrong.

Copenhagen, which translates as 'merchant harbour', supported a Danish empire that formerly encompassed present day Norway, parts of Sweden, northern Germany and Iceland. Today, the once bustling channel to the Baltic is largely quiet, dotted with a series of iconic buildings that are high profile but rarely used. The Royal Library, Opera House (controversially donated to the Queen by Denmark's richest man) and Theatre Playhouse are an attempt to redefine the harbour front as a prime cultural playground, yet it is the simple Harbour Bath lido and community-designed Islands

Main picture: Opera House. Bottom: left, Dansk Design Center; right: view from the top of Vor Frelsers Kirke

Brygge park that truly provide an opportunity for people to enjoy the abundance of water that runs around and through the city.

Even arriving at the CPH Airport is a pleasure. How many other airports offer hard-wood floors and a painless 12 minute ride to the central train station? This is the essence of Danish design: simple, easy to use, elegant and finely detailed. But how does the city function so well? Watching drunk Copenhageners wait patiently at vehicle-free street corners until the red 'Don't walk' sign turns green provides some insight: they are obsessive about following certain rules, notably traffic legislation and paying for public transport (so much so that Copenhagen's transport operates on an honour system). About some other issues, however – especially graffiti and smoking (the controversial 2008 indoor smoking ban made an exception for any bar smaller than 35sq m) – they are pleased to remain stubborn Vikings.
Jeff Risom

Harbour Bath

Copenhagen's ambition is to become, by 2015, the capital city with the best urban environment, and the Harbour Bath illustrates how close the city already is to achieving this. Built out into the harbour in the old industrial area of Islands Brygge, it is a key part of the city's 'Blue Plan', a strategy for revitalising 42 kilometres of former docklands with houseboats, promenades, watersport facilities, playgrounds and recreation areas. Wastewater from sewers and factories – as well as pollution from the port's traffic – has been reduced and controlled so that, for most of the summer (bar a few days of closure when heavy rainfall reduces the water quality), the water of Harbour Bath is clean enough to swim in.

Designed by young local architects PLOT (now disbanded and practising as JDS and BIG) and divided into five separate pools, the Harbour Bath embraces the urban environment that surrounds it with dry docks, piers for sunbathing, boat ramps, cliffs, playgrounds and pontoons imaginatively incorporated into the space. As soon as it opened in 2002, as part of the Havneparken, it was an instant hit. It has become the hub of the city's summer social activity, attracting families, teenagers, even businessmen and -women looking for some post-work refreshment.

Instant Passport

Population
1,525,000

Area
816sq km

Where is it?
Copenhagen occupies the easternmost tip of Denmark, on the islands of Zealand and Amager

Climate
Coastal and windy with mild winters and summers. Despite the northerly location, average daytime temperatures rarely get above 22°C or below 2°C

Ethnic mix
Mostly Scandinavian, with small numbers from Turkey and the Middle East

Major sights
Amalienborg Palace, Nyhavn, Louisiana Modern Art Museum, Rosenborg Palace, Christiania, Tivoli Gardens, Harbour Bath

Insiders' tips
Vernaedamsvej, Halvandet beach bar at Refshaloeen, a free peek at the Zoo through Frederiksberg Park, Bankeråt café on Nansensgade, Bopa Plads, Blaagaardsgade, the kitch but fun Absolut Ice Bar, Library Bar near the train station

Where's the buzz?
Kødbyen, the old meat-packing district, for trendy bars and galleries; Istedgade for small bars; Sankt Hans Torv along Elmegade and Birkegade for boutiques and cocktail bars; Vega for music; Custom House for cutting-edge trendiness

Percentage of inner-city commuters who ride their bicycle to work
38%

Amount of pedestrianised space in the inner city
71,000sq m

Number of outdoor café seats in the inner city
7,025

Construction cost of each seat in Denmark Radio's new concert hall
470,000 dkk – the only auditorium in the rest of the world that was more expensive was the Disney Concert Hall in Los Angeles

Length of the Øresund Bridge
1,092m main span – the longest cable-stayed bridge in the world – plus 3,739m eastern approach and 3,014m western approach bridges. The structure connects Copenhagen with Malmö in Sweden

Tivoli Gardens opened
1843. The second oldest amusement park in the world (and inspiration for Disneyland), with one of the oldest working rollercoasters

Immortalised in
Peter Høeg's *Miss Smilla's Feeling for Snow*, Michael Frayn's *Copenhagen*, Rose Tremain's *Music and Silence*

Top: centre, Edvard Eriksen's Little Mermaid; right, Frederiksberg. Centre: left, Christianshavn; right, Café Zeze. Bottom: left, Black Diamond concert hall; centre & right, Christianshavn

Architecture
5

Arts & Culture
4

Buzz
8

Food & Drink
1

Quality of Life
5

World Status
1

Total
24/60

Rank
67

Dakar

SENEGAL

The Paris of Africa

Pumping the lifeblood through Senegal's commercial and administrative activities, Dakar manages to combine the trappings of early 20th-century western capitalism with a cultural and spiritual personality that is uniquely African.

Fashioned after Paris by the vanguard of France's 'civilising mission' to the African continent, Dakar is at the same time an African restatement of French architectural ingenuity and a testament to the successes and failings of the French colonial policy of assimilation. The city's equivalent of the Champs-Elysées is Place de l'independence, where the city's major landmarks, important government offices, private banks, hotels, restaurants and coffee shops are concentrated. On the streets of this cosmopolitan district, sharp suits make a colourful contrast with the lavish robes of those who favour indigenous fashions.

The contrast between affluent, tree-lined neighbourhoods and the squalid congestion of the ghettoised slums is, however, far from appealing. Like most African cities, poverty, destitution and filth are a frequent counterpart to the arrogant glamour of the smart buildings and flash cars.

Africa's population boom put immense pressure on Dakar's infrastructure, especially a road network that was planned and built back in colonial times. Even on the outskirts of the city, traffic jams can now stretch for miles, which at least gives enterprising hawkers an opportunity to exploit the frustrated occupants of stationary vehicles, suffocating in their own exhaust fumes. This is a town in which even a traffic jam can become an excuse for a bazaar. Still, he main transport system – the Indian-made TATA buses and minivans that work the major metropolitan arteries – is surprisingly

reliable. One of the city's characteristic sights is the *car rapide*, rusting, overcrowded Renault vans that remain a fully functional symbol of daily life in Dakar.

The city has a buzzing night life. The handsome residential and business area of Almadies boasts world-class casinos and fully air-conditioned nightclubs, in which the dancers seduce pleasure-seekers with sexually suggestive dances, swaying their hips to the frantic *mbalax* beats of home-grown talent such as Youssou N'Dour, Omar Pen, Thione Seck and Titi.

Dakar is rich in history, with its many tourists descending on such sights as the Catholic Cathedral, the Marché Sandaga (full of exquisite leatherwork, paintings, sculpture and clothing made locally from woollen fabrics) and, a couple of miles offshore on the island of Gorée, the harrowing Slave Museum.

Despite the widening gap between the haves and the have-nots, the people of Dakar find common ground in two things: the thieboudienne, a traditional dish of fried fish, rice and vegetables that no one is too rich to disdain, and the tchourie, a sweet-scented incense that is almost magical in its effect on men. Every evening, the streets fill up with its intoxicating aroma, as houswives burn it to welcome their husbands back home.
Ebrima Sillah

Les cars rapides

The cheapest means of transport is the *car rapide*, Renault vans first manufactured and introduced to the city in the early 1950s. Dirty, habitually overcrowded, rusty and completely out of date in almost any other country, they are synonymous with the roads of Dakar. Their endurance and ubiquity has led some to call them 'the face of Dakar'. They generally operate along the main arteries to suburbs, though routes can change daily.

Instant Passport

Population
2,400,000

Area
550sq km

Where is it?
The western-most city in Africa, at the tip of the Cape Verde peninsula, surrounded by the Atlantic

Climate
The dry season (December to April) is dominated by the hot, dry, Harmattan wind that blows sand from the Sahara into the Gulf of Guinea. When the Harmattan blows hard, it can push dust and sand all the way to North America

Ethnic mix
Wolof, Pular, Serer, Jola, Mandinka, Soninke, European, Lebanese, other

Major sights
Catholic Cathedral, Marché Sandaga, the museum of the Institut Fondamental d'Afrique Noire (IFAN), Soumbédioune fishing beach, the Grande Mosque, Gorée Island

Port traffic
The city is the busiest port in west Africa, thanks to a deep natural harbour. The port exports 368,405 tonnes of wheat each year, out of an annual total of 2,192,890 tonnes of solid cargo

Main exports
Peanuts, fish, refined sugar, textiles

Education
Home to the Institut Fondamental d'Afrique Noire, which promotes scholarly research into the linguistics, history, anthropology and archaeology of west Africa

Famous musicians
Youssou N'Dour, Baaba Maal, Orchestra Baobab, hip hop singer-songwriter Akon (who gives his full name as Aliaune Damala Bouga Time Puru Nacka Lu Lu Lu Badara Akon Thiam)

Slave trade history
The port of Dakar was the largest slave-trading centre on the African coast from the 15th to the 19th century. The island of Gorée, three kilometres off Dakar, was designated a UNESCO World Heritage Site for the key role it played in the Atlantic slave trade. Tens of thousands of men, women and children were locked up in tiny cells here, prior to being shipped to Europe or the Americas. Gorée is famous for its 'Door of No Return': located in the outermost wall of the slave house, opening to the sea, it was the last thing the slaves would ever see of their homeland

Football
Patrick Viera, who played club football for Inter Milan and Arsenal, as well as winning the 1998 World Cup and Euro 2000 with France, was born in Dakar. The city's most successful team is ASC Jeanne d'Arc, which has won Senegal's Premier League ten times. The team is based in the Stade Léopold Sédar Senghor

Delhi

INDIA

Charging ahead in opposite directions

Architecture	6
Arts & Culture	6
Buzz	5
Food & Drink	2
Quality of Life	4
World Status	7
Total	30/60
Rank	51

If India's story is the tale of how a modern democracy of more than a billion citizens deals with the accumulated weight of millennia of recorded history, then Delhi is where its authors are currently sitting.

Delhi is a microcosm of its parent country, simultaneously heaving with possibility and burdened by the past. It will bulldoze a slum in order to build gleaming new high-rises, and then raise a new slum to house the people who are building them. People make offerings to the river, the holy Yamuna, in a plastic bag. Shiny new SUVs sit marooned in the traffic. Everyone loves the incredibly expensive Metro system, even though it will never come anywhere near their own doorsteps, but the city won't pay up for a few air-conditioned buses. Delhi, like the rest of India, isn't for someone who likes their experiences easily encapsulated.

The city itself has a recorded history of about a thousand years, though myth places the *Mahabharata*'s ancient capital of Indraprastha here. It's been a capital for kings and emperors, been invaded by men like Tamerlane, ravaged and left for dead and then rebuilt, time and time again. Certain things define it, then. Resilience. A love of politics, for Delhi's only happy when it's a capital. A quest for physical immortality (for how else can you explain Delhi's most famous erection, the absurdly tall Qutab Minar?) leavened with a love of the 'small things': music, dance and, always, poetry.

Delhi's the seat of the government of India, with a new set of symbols that emphasises its centrality to the nation: the President's home, India's Parliament and the broad leafy avenues that British architects Edwin Lutyens and Herbert Baker imagined, lined with the homes of cabinet ministers. But here as well, subversion and

Previous page: Connaught Place.
Left: top, the boat club at India Gate;
centre, Jantar Mantar; bottom, Jama
Mazjid. Above: Nehru Place. Facing
page: Galleria market in Gurgaon

Instant Passport

Population
14,300,000 (core city 7,206,000)

Area
1,295sq km

Where is it?
In northern India, on the banks of the Yamuna, within a few hours of the foothills of the Himalayas and the Rajasthan desert

Climate
Hot dry summers, a monsoon, a distinct autumn (and spring) and a short sharp winter, with temperatures falling almost to zero

Ethnic mix
Indians from everywhere. Predominantly Punjabi, with large helpings of Bengalis, Tamils, Malayalees and North-easterners, as well as a growing expat population

Major sights
The Qutab Minar, Humayun's tomb, Akshardham temple, Bangla Sahib Gurudwara, the Mutiny Memorial, National Museum, National Gallery of Modern Art, Dilli Haat, INA market, Red Fort, Jama Masjid, Purana Qila, Lodhi Garden

Insiders' tips
Art at Gallery Nature Morte and arts.i, music at Turquoise Cottage, shopping at Shahpur Jat, drinking surrounded by Qin warriors at Bar SaVanh or by broke artists at the 4S bar

Where's the buzz?
Connaught Place (Rajeev Chowk), Sunday sales at Khan Market, bargains at Lajpat Nagar

Languages spoken
Hindi, Urdu, Punjabi, English

Became capital of India
1911, taking over from Calcutta (as Kolkata was then called), with the administrative centre – New Delhi – built to the south of the old city. Delhi had previously been capital of the Mughal Empire from 1649 to 1857

Height of the Qutab Minar
73m. The tallest brick minaret in the world, completed in 1386

Oldest temple
Digambar Jain temple, built in 1526

Number of rickshaws
Approximately 10,000, 85% of them unlicensed

Mass Rapid Transit System opened
2002

Number of districts
Nine, of which New Delhi is just one

Number of call-centre workers in the city
1,300,000

'Delhi is never satisfied – it's a huge, varied and ever-growing city. That's what makes it exciting'

Laila Tyabji artist

sedition skulk along in power's wake. India's gay movement is powered from here. Five major universities and countless colleges pump out informed, socially aware graduates every year. Protests and rallies are a feature of the cityscape, and everything from workers' rights to longer bar hours finds an impassioned advocate. The moral crusade in South India against women going to clubs, by a fringe political group, garnered a riposte that could only have been born in Delhi: thousands of young women mailed the group their pink underwear.

Now, as the sleepy colonial city wakes up to find itself one of the largest urban agglomerations on earth, with a population that's hurtling towards 20 million, Dilliwalas seek to join history's legacies to the promise of the past few years. Naturally, a few questions remain. Are the call-centre tower blocks of Gurgaon and Noida where we'll all end up? Why can't an Indian-built Mercedes cost as little as any other car? Why must every Delhi nightclub play electronica? And what, finally, is the deal with vegetarian sushi?
Avtar Singh

Architecture	**6**
Arts & Culture	**2**
Buzz	**3**
Food & Drink	**7**
Quality of Life	**5**
World Status	**6**
Total	29/60
Rank	**56**

Dubai

UNITED ARAB EMIRATES

Built on sand and oil

Mention that you live in Dubai and you'll always provoke a reaction. Often, it's one of wonder ('Are the motorways really paved with gold?'); sometimes, it's one of revulsion ('Does that building site have any soul?'); but it's consistently one of interest. The world hasn't quite got its head around Dubai yet. Compared to London, Paris and New York, Dubai has only had a short time to become a true city. Now it's relentlessly morphing, rising taller, even stretching itself out into the ocean. Yet, a few decades ago, it was nothing but a desert port. Then the 'father of Dubai', Sheikh Rashid, realised it might be wise to invest the emirate's oil riches in creating somewhere that would catch the attention of the world.

Living here, rather than reading about it in magazines, is rather like taking part in a colossal social experiment. With a population made up of hundreds of different nationalities – only around 25 per cent of residents are citizens of the UAE – life involves a constant culture clash, as contradictory mindsets and religions attempt to align. Rules are vague, blind eyes are turned and everyone does their best to get along.

But whether residents hail from India, Russia, Africa or beyond, everyone has one thing in common: they've all come looking for a better life. Whether it's the Burj Dubai – which became the tallest tower in the world in 2007 – or the seven-star Burj Al Arab hotel that stands proudly over the city's coast, people here don't want to settle for second best (or second biggest, or tallest, or whatever record is being broken that week). Indeed, many residents don't settle for long, but instead squeeze the place for everything they can before heading elsewhere. Thus, along with the never ending construction, Dubai has a perpetual, disconcerting transience.

'Sometimes I love Dubai, sometimes it's hard. I've lived and worked here for 25 years – my family is back in Pakistan. Everybody here is so busy; none of us ever stop working. But it's good!'

Mohammed **taxi driver**

Of course, many new arrivals see the gleaming towers and imagine they're in a Western city. When they encounter Dubai's idiosyncrasies, they get angry. They fume about terrible traffic, lack of expat rights, a rigid social hierarchy in which race appears to determine salary. They're bitter at the ridiculous rents, now among the highest in the world. They're flabbergasted that it's acceptable for the Sheikh to close the entire city for a day just because the American president wishes to drive down the main road.

But later they will wander along one of the free beaches at sunset, passing dozens of Filipinos enjoying picnics, perhaps share a moment of understanding, a joke or a meal with someone from the other side of the world. It's then that they'll feel proud to have integrated themselves into such a unique, challenging place – without getting too sucked into to the shallow merry-go-round of five-star hotels, beachside bars and fleeting friendships.

Dubai may well be amazing when it's finished. Right now it's fascinating to be part of its progress.

Becky Lucas

Previous page: main picture,
Palm Jumeirah; bottom right, Dubai
Creek Golf & Yacht Club. Above: the
'billowing sail' of Burj Al Arab. Below:
traditional *abra* crossing Dubai Creek

Instant Passport

Population
1,500,000

Area
1,287sq km

Where is it?
On the southern coast of the Persian Gulf on the Arabian Peninsula,
one of the seven emirates that make up the UAE

Climate
Hot and humid from May to September, but warm and sunny from
October to April. Temperatures exceed 40°C in August

Ethnic mix
60% Indian, Pakistani and Filipino; 25% Emiratis; 12% Arab;
3% Western expats

Major sights
Burj Al Arab, Burj Dubai, Emirates Towers, Ski Dubai in Mall of the
Emirates, the Creek, the aquarium in the Dubai Mall, Atlantis hotel
at the Palm Jumeirah, the desert

Insiders' tips
Bastakiya's quaint galleries and alleyways; Khan Murjan, the underground
'souk' restaurant underneath Wafi mall; yacht and dhow trips; authentic
Indian and Pakistani food at bargain prices in Karama; the tailors in Satwa;
cheese manakeesh at Diyafah Street's Al Mallah street café

Where's the buzz?
The multicultural streets of Satwa, Bur Dubai and Karama – the few
areas of the city with a bit of street life, as well as some of Dubai's
cheapest shops and services; Jumeirah Beach Residence in the Marina,
a new and popular community with its own beach, parade of shops and
Friday flea market; Madinat Jumeirah, where the crowds speed around
the faux-Venetian waterways on *abras* (motorboats, that literally buzz)

Average monthly rent for a two-bedroom apartment
$3,300

Height of the Burj Dubai
818m

Most ostentatious building
Atlantis hotel

Cars owned per 1,000 people
451

Traffic offences committed in 2006
1,445,000 – in a population of roughly the same number

Average speed of a racing camel
40kph

World records achieved at the Dubai Shopping Festival 2009
The biggest shopping bag (180cm high and 120cm wide), the most
people with the same name in the same place (2,000 Mohammeds
congregated), the longest chopsticks (22ft)

Architecture
6

Arts & Culture
5

Buzz
4

Food & Drink
5

Quality of Life
6

World Status
3

Total
29/60

Rank
56

Dublin

IRELAND

Moving beyond the pastoral idyll

Far from conforming to the romantic notion of farmers, fairies and little people, Dublin's brash urbanity doesn't sit comfortably within the idyllic rural stereotype of Irish national identity. The 'Celtic Tiger' years of economic plenty transformed the city into a dynamic European capital, ending decades of stagnation, unemployment and emigration. Dublin's new-found vitality is in evidence everywhere – from the gleaming modern apartments and office buildings of the regenerated docklands, to the bustling cafés, restaurants and street markets of Temple Bar. Some argue that its economic good fortune has made Dublin less 'Irish', but while the city has certainly been affected by the homogenising forces of globalisation, its warmth and character have survived intact.

Dublin is a largely unplanned city, without the wide straight boulevards, civic squares and triumphal arches found in many other European capitals. These grand imperial gestures have never been part of the Irish psyche. Rather the city is a collection of villages that have, over the years, gradually merged together around a medieval core, giving Dublin an intimate character. The city centre is compact and well used: the streets are as busy at two o'clock in the morning with people spilling out of pubs as they are at two in the afternoon when they are populated with shoppers. And while many of the shops are generic European high-street chains, the pubs are truly unique to Dublin, and one of the best places to get to know the city and sample its most famous export – Guinness.

The city's other principal export has traditionally been people. Dublin has long been a point of departure for Irish emigrants seeking their fortune abroad. It is only since the late 1990s that

Previous page: Ha'penny Bridge.
Top: left, General Post Office; right,
the Monument of Light. Centre: left,
Malahide Castle; right, Gallery of
Photography. Bottom: JJ Smyth's

the trend has been reversed and the recent influx of immigrants
from Eastern Europe, Asia and North Africa has given the city a
distinctly cosmopolitan flavour.

It's not always easy to see contemporary Dublin in the mind's
eye. Cultural depictions have yet to catch up with the complex
reality of the modern city. The place described in the writings of
Yeats, Beckett and Joyce; the romantic Ireland of Hollywood
imagination; the image of Dublin taken away by the departing
emigrants and held sacred throughout the vast international Irish
diaspora – these are all visions of somewhere that no longer exists.
Paul McGann

Instant Passport

Population
1,187,176 (core city 505,739)

Area
921sq km

Where is it?
At the mouth of the River Liffey on Ireland's east coast, opening on to Dublin Bay and the Irish Sea

Climate
Maritime temperate: cool and very rainy

Ethnic mix
Predominantly Irish, but now attracting Poles, Lithuanians, Chinese, Spanish, African

Major sights
Trinity College, Dublin Castle, St Patrick's Cathedral

Insiders' tips
Science Gallery on the Trinity campus, coffee at Lemon and Crêpe Coffee Company, catching an art-house film at the Light House cinema, the docklands

Where's the buzz?
Temple Bar, Grafton Street, Market Bar, the Liberties

Foundation of Trinity College Dublin
1592

Number of people killed during the 1916 Easter Uprising
64 rebels, 132 from the security forces and over 300 civilians

Year Eire proclaimed a sovereign, independent and democratic state
1937

Ban on divorce lifted in Ireland
1995

Year the Euro replaced the Punt
2002

Number of pints of brewed daily at the Guinness brewery
3,000,000

Owners of the Clarence Hotel
Bono and the Edge, U2's vocalist and lead guitarist

Number of players in a Gaelic football team
15

Where to catch a hurling match
Parnell Park, Croke Park

Famous Dublin writers
Jonathan Swift, Oscar Wilde, George Bernard Shaw, WB Yeats, JM Synge, James Joyce, Samuel Beckett, Brendan Behan, Colm Tóibín, John Banville, Roddy Doyle

Guinness

There can be few images as iconic in the world of brewing as the swirling black-and-white cloudscape of a pint of Guinness settling in its glass. Even the name is synonymous with a certain kind of twinkly-eyed nostalgia for the vanishing glory days of 'Old Dublin'. The Dublin brewery was founded in 1759 by Arthur Guinness, although it was his great-grandson, Edward Cecil Guinness, who built up the Guinness empire and family fortune.

The dark stout, sometimes referred to as 'the black stuff', gets its distinctive colour and rich flavour from the roasted barley included in the brew. In the past, a portion of the beer was aged to give a sharp lactic taste, but whether or not this still occurs is a closely guarded secret. The thick, creamy head is created by nitrogen being added to the mix as it is being served. Pulling the perfect pint of Guinness is considered an art form and takes at least two minutes to complete. Barstaff will pull just two-thirds of a pint then allow it to settle before finishing it off. In some bars, the pint is topped off with a shamrock drawn in the foam.

Claims have also been made (though not by its current brewer, Diageo) for the health benefits of Guinness, based on claims that it contains both a high proportion of iron and cholesterol-busting antitoxidants. From the 1920s, iconic advertising carried the slogan 'Guinness is Good for You' and during the '60s and '70s pregnant women in the UK were advised to drink it (sadly, this is no longer recommended). Although wine now accounts for a fifth of all alcohol consumed in Ireland, it is estimated that every other pint of beer drunk is a Guinness.

Edinburgh

UK

Brooding literary capital

Architecture	9
Arts & Culture	5
Buzz	5
Food & Drink	4
Quality of Life	7
World Status	4
Total	34/60
Rank	**34**

Behind the squat confidence of St John's Episcopalian church at the west end of Princes Street sits St Cuthbert's, its Presbyterian neighbour. There has been a place of worship here since the Dark Ages – easy to believe in a falling winter dusk when walking in the atmospheric cemetery with the Castle directly above. Various people of note have been interred at St Cuthbert's including the writer Thomas de Quincey, best known for his 1822 book *Confessions of an English Opium-Eater*. First millennium faith, two strains of Protestantism, the Castle and a blow-in English junkie all in one neat location – but that's Edinburgh for you, the city of stories.

The city's headline attractions are excruciatingly well known. That Castle up on its high volcanic rock along with the medieval Old Town and the elegant Georgian New Town together constitute a UNESCO World Heritage Site. The annual jamboree in August, comprising several huge and concurrent arts festivals, makes Edinburgh the world's cultural capital for those weeks while its status as Scottish capital creates a natural home for major galleries and museums. Add royal palaces, Michelin-starred restaurants, dramatic geology and all the rest, and you have a compelling tourist destination.

Not everyone who comes here, or even comes from here, just stands and stares. Some absorb what Edinburgh has to offer then confect tales and entertainments – the major talents are celebrated with due reverence. Off the Lawnmarket is the Writers' Museum, dedicated to regular city visitor Robert Burns, as well as residents Sir Walter Scott and Robert Louis Stevenson. Princes Street has the Gothic spire of the Scott Monument – surely the most outlandish ever memorial to a novelist – while anyone can walk through the New Town to see where the young Stevenson grew up. There is more evidence of Edinburgh's literary associations down the Royal Mile with the Scottish Storytelling Centre, a statue of acclaimed 18th-century poet Robert Fergusson and the Scottish Poetry Library.

More recently, Ian Rankin's Inspector Rebus series has made a huge contribution to modern detective fiction, scratching the city's dark underbelly; Irvine Welsh's drug-fuelled *Trainspotting* exposed the world the tourists never see; and JK Rowling famously started and finished the Harry Potter series here over a dozen years. Science-fiction luminaries Iain M Banks and Ken MacLeod are now joined by newcomer Charles Stross, whose *Halting State* is set locally, promising that the city's relationship with the written word will continue well into the 21st century.

Keith Davidson

'Edinburgh – stony, grey-faced Edinburgh, where every route you walk seems to be uphill: one of the strangest, most entrancing cities I've ever seen. Watch the confused tourists wonder why they can't turn left from North Bridge on to the Cowgate. Explore the crescents and drawbridge-fronted houses of the New Town. Drink in the innumerable small watering holes, from dusk until dawn in August (not that there's much more than an hour of darkness). Edinburgh is small but perplexingly complicated: it could take you the rest of your life to explore it'

Charles Stross sci-fi author

Top left: looking down Princes Street to Calton Hill. Above: the Heart of Midlothian on the Royal Mile – it is traditional to spit on its centre, whether for luck or, in the case of Hibs football fans, to mark opposition to Hearts

Top: left, a 21st-century kilt on the Royal Mile; centre, Edinburgh Castle. Bottom: left, Enric Miralles's Scottish Parliament building; right, Beltane Fire Festival on Calton Hill

Instant Passport

Population
468,070

Area
262sq km

Where is it?
East-central Scotland, on the Firth of Forth

Insiders' tips
Stockbridge, Bruntsfield, Marchmont

Where's the buzz?
Cowgate, George Street, Lothian Road, Broughton Street

Climate
Temperate maritime climate, but very windy due to its position between the sea and mountains. In January, it rarely gets above 7°C, while 26°C constitutes a very warm day in August

Ethnic mix
Almost entirely white European, with 1.80% South Asian, 0.78% Chinese, 1.57% all others

Major sights
The five National Galleries of Scotland, Edinburgh Castle, the National Museum of Scotland, the statue of Greyfriars Bobby

Nicknames
'Auld Reekie', 'the Athens of the North', 'the Empress of the North'

Made capital of Scotland
1437

New Town created
Grid street-plan designed in 1766 by James Craig

Cost of the Scottish Parliament building
Over £400 million, ten times the original budget. Designed by Catalan architect Enric Miralles, it was opened in 2004

Number of shows staged during the annual Edinburgh International Festival and Edinburgh Fringe Festival
2,000. The first year of the Fringe, in 1947, hosted just eight companies

Latitude
About 55°N. Edinburgh is around the same latitude as Copenhagen and Moscow – on the longest day, the sun rises at 4.30am and sets at 10pm

Amount of haggis made by Bruntsfield butcher MacSweens every year
370 tonnes. Most of it is eaten on St Andrew's Day (30 November) and Burns' Night (25 January)

First human settlement
Solid evidence from Cramond of human habitation 10,500 years ago

Immortalised in
The Prime of Miss Jean Brodie, *Trainspotting*, *Shallow Grave*, *Heart of Mid-Lothian*

Florence

ITALY

Birthplace of the Renaissance

Since the early days of the Grand Tour, when this cradle of the Italian Renaissance was an obligatory stop-off for any self-respecting young man of means with time to burn, Florence has been attracting tourists. Today, with around six million visitors pouring into its small *centro storico* every year to admire some of the greatest artistic achievements ever produced by man, there is no doubt that this Tuscan city owes much of its present success to its past glories. In the 15th and 16th centuries, Florence was on the cutting edge of artistic, cultural and scientific achievement, with luminaries such as Michelangelo, Leonardo da Vinci, Galileo, Brunelleschi and Machiavelli among its residents.

The same cannot be said today of a city that views innovation with a degree of hostility and is often criticised for living in the past. However, Florence's world-class museums and art galleries, its fine gastronomic tradition, its increasingly interesting shopping scene and its accessible size, still make it one of Italy's most appealing cities. While the locals grumble about the *degrado* (degradation) of their beloved city and the administration battles with contentious issues such as the city's overwhelming traffic problems, a controversial new tramline and the much-needed new opera house that it can ill afford, most visitors soak up the art and the atmosphere in blissful ignorance.

A gesture towards modernity has been made by the choice of A-list international architects to design new showpieces such as Arata Isozaki's highly controversial new entrance to the Uffizi Gallery and Norman Foster's underground terminal for the new Milano-Roma high speed train link. But the battles to get such projects approved are long and bloody.

Florence's overpowering beauty caused French writer Stendhal to swoon when he first visited in 1817. These days you are just as likely to be overcome by exhaust fumes, but the concentration of treasures packed within the medieval walls remains unrivalled. Visits to museums, galleries and churches should be generously interspersed with cappuccino, gelato and aperitivo breaks, and time needs to be set aside for just wandering. Peer behind heavy carved doorways into hidden courtyards. Look into lit-up windows at night to admire gilded, coffered ceilings and frescoes. Crane your neck to catch a glimpse of Florence's secret roof-gardens. Pop into tiny churches to admire glowing, unsung alterpieces.

The city is often overrun. In March and April, the streets are clogged with school groups; in May, June and September, by

Previous page: the Ponte Vecchio over the Arno. Above: from left, Ghirlandaio's *Last Supper*; Boboli Gardens; views of the Duomo, which was designed by Arnolfo di Cambio and begun in 1296

tourist hordes. But in November, January and February, they are returned to the Fiorentini for a much-needed respite.

Even when the tourists are lapping it all up in their millions, the Florentines continue to live their very Florentine lives; cappuccino (never after 11am) and a catch up with the gossip in the local bar in the morning; an aperitivo and dinner at one of the growing number of contemporary restaurants serving creative food in the evening; maybe some live music or dancing afterwards. There's not a huge choice, but it's not bad for a small city.

Nicky Swallow

David

It's barely fanciful to see Western art since the beginning of the 16th century as having all been in the shadow of *David*. Created behind a shuttered scaffold over three years, the sculpture exemplifies the beauty and strength of the human body. Carved from a 16ft-tall single slab of Carrara marble, *David* was intended by Michelangelo for the top of the Duomo – he gave it a slightly oversized head and hands so that those looking up from below would get the best viewpoint. However, in 1873, when the statue was moved from piazza della Signoria (where this copy stands, literally overshadowing the statue of Adam), the authorities decided to keep the plinth low so visitors could see it close-up; hence it's a little out of proportion.

Instant Passport

Population
381,762

Area
102sq km

Where is it?
Regional capital of Tuscany, located on the river Arno in central Italy

Climate
Hot, humid summers and cold, damp winters

Ethnic mix
90% Italian, plus some Chinese, Albanians, Romanians, North Americans

Major sights
Galleria degli Uffizi, Galleria dell'Accademia, Museo Nazionale del Bargello, Galleria Palatina, Santa Croce, Santa Maria Novella, Duomo, Museo di San Marco, Cappelle Medicee, Cappella Brancacci

Insiders' tips
Museo dell'Opera del Duomo, Boboli Gardens early in the morning, Ghirlandaio's *Last Supper*, Gregorian chant at the church of San Miniato, artisan workshops in the Oltrarno

Where's the buzz?
Piazzas Santo Spirito and Santa Croce, and the surrounding streets

Firsts
Masaccio 'invented' perspective in painting, Dante Alighieri 'invented' the modern Italian language, Galileo Galilei discovered that the earth is not the centre of the universe, the first city to mint its own coins (the florin in 1252), the first city to pave all its streets, the first city (as capital of the Grand Duchy of Tuscany) to ban the death penalty in 1786

Percentage of the world's major art treasures located in Florence
Around 30% (as estimated by UNESCO)

Most famous paintings
Botticelli's *Primavera* and *The Birth of Venus* in the Uffizi

Most terrifying sculpture
Donatello's gnarled and withered Mary Magdalene, carved out of poplar wood and on display in the Museo dell'Opera del Duomo

Famous residents, past and present
Michelangelo Buonarotti, Leonardo da Vinci, Galileo Galilei, the Medici clan, Florence Nightingale, Robert Browning, Salvatore Ferragamo, Roberto Cavalli

Lucky colour
Unlike the rest of Italy, Florentines believe violet brings good fortune – it's the colour worn by their football team, ACF Florence

Highest concentration of designer clothes shops
Via Tornabuoni

Immortalised in
A Room with a View, *Tea with Mussolini*, *Up at the Villa*, *Hannibal*

Glasgow

UK

Sharp-edged and culturally assertive

Glasgow is not for the faint-hearted. It's a gallus, raunchy, in-your-face city, where shopping and socialism live vibrantly alongside each other, but where the contrast between wealth and poverty is more obvious than perhaps any other city in northern Europe. Glasgow, despite its weather, is a place that feels more like Barcelona than Manchester or Liverpool. Its grid plan echoes Barcelona's, and its Charles Rennie Mackintosh buildings evoke the same love-hate relationship that Barcelona has with Gaudí. Each architect is central to his city's tourist agenda, but at the same time their dominance of the cultural agenda masks great achievements by others. Glasgow has famously ignored the work of classical architect Alexander 'Greek' Thomson, several of whose great churches lie abandoned and rotting, and until recently it looked as though the fine modern buildings by Gillespie, Kidd & Coia would suffer the same fate. Up on the hill to the East of the centre, the Necropolis – probably Glasgow's finest moment – bristles with monuments and gravestones for the wealthy Victorian merchants of what was then the 'second city of the Empire'. This is the place to marvel at the Glasgow that proudly played host to some of the wealthiest tradesmen in Europe. It's been a long and steady decline since then.

The city may have lost its merchants, but it has to some extent replaced them with a vibrant cultural community. Glasgow has spawned contemporary artists such as Douglas Gordon and Simon Starling, Jenny Saville and Peter Howson, and generations of collectable names from the famous (Mackintosh-designed) School of Art. Its rock and pop successes stretch back decades; from the feisty independent scene that centred around Postcard Records in the early 1980s, styling itself 'the sound of young

Architecture	6
Arts & Culture	6
Buzz	7
Food & Drink	3
Quality of Life	6
World Status	3
Total	31/60
Rank	**48**

Top: *Waverley* in front of 'the Armadillo', Lord Foster's Clyde Auditorium. Bottom: left, Old Fruit Market; right, Kelvingrove Art Gallery & Museum

Scotland', to stadium bands such as Simple Minds and, more recently, the angular guitar-pop of Franz Ferdinand.

Unlike its Catalan counterpart, Glasgow has not yet completed the job of revitalising its post-industrial waterfront. Only a stone's throw from the city's main shopping streets, now surprisingly strong on alfresco dining, the River Clyde slides past a patchwork of derelict spaces, speckled with new apartment blocks and spec office buildings. Most of the shipyards are gone. Valiant attempts are being made to turn the city back to face the river again, and new buildings such as Zaha Hadid's River Museum, the BBC Scotland building by David Chipperfield, and the recently restored Titan Crane in Clydebank, are a testament to the efforts being made. Nevertheless, the river is surprisingly resistant to the city's post-industrial overtures. If all goes to plan, Glasgow's 2014 Commonwealth Games will finally do for the city what the Olympics did for Barcelona, and allow it to fulfil its ambition to become a world-beating city of contemporary culture.
Nick Barley

Instant Passport

Population
1,200,000 (core city 600,000)

Area
368sq km

Where is it?
In the Central Belt of Scotland, on the west coast

Climate
Mild, but wet

Ethnic mix
96.5% white, 2.5% Asian; the rest are black, Chinese or other

Major sights
Kibble Palace, Barras Market, Botanic Gardens, Burrell Collection, Kelvingrove Art Gallery & Museum, Mackintosh House, People's Palace, Necropolis

Insiders' tips
Lighthouse, Tenement House, Tramway theatre

Where's the buzz?
Byres Road, Buchanan Street, Gallowgate on a Sunday

Percentage of Scots living in Glasgow or its region
41%

Glaswegian bands
Glasvegas, Belle & Sebastian, Biffy Clyro, Franz Ferdinand, Travis, Orange Juice, Altered Images, Lloyd Cole & the Commotions, Teenage Fanclub, Primal Scream, Simple Minds

Famous alumni of Glasgow School of Art
Charles Rennie Mackintosh, John Byrne, Robbie Coltrane, Peter Capaldi, Joan Eardley, Carol Smillie, Fran Healy, Peter Howson, Pam Hogg, Liz Lochhead, Bruce McLean, Jenny Saville

Inventions from Glasgow
Waterproof coat (Charles McIntosh, 1824), Kelvin scale (Lord Kelvin, 1847), paraffin oil (James Young, 1850), beta-blocker (Sir James Black, 1988)

First long-distance television transmission
John Logie Baird in 1928, from Glasgow's Central Hotel

First international football match
Scotland versus England in Partick in 1872

Sporting rivalry
Celtic versus Rangers – the 'Old Firm' game – is one of the world's most fiercely contested football derbies. Both clubs are working to eradicate sectarian chanting between Protestant Rangers and Catholic Celtic fans

Nickname for the Glasgow underground railway
The Clockwork Orange

Longest echo of any building in Europe
Hamilton Mausoleum, dating from the 1850s, has a 15-second echo

Far left: a footbridge over the Clyde.
Top: centre right, Mackintosh House;
right, Royal Exchange Square.
Centre left: Necropolis. Bottom
left: Provand's Lordship

Architecture
7
Arts & Culture
4
Buzz
8
Food & Drink
6
Quality of Life
4
World Status
4
Total
33/60
Rank
39

Hanoi

VIETNAM

A 1,000-year-old city with irrepressible rickshaws

Hanoi is a city a thousand years old that has gone by many names over the centuries. Emperor Ly Thai To named it Thang Long (Soaring Dragon) when he founded it in AD 1010. More recently, as both the political and cultural capital of the Socialist Republic of Vietnam, this dragon's influence reaches every part of the country and, at times, its neighbours as well.

The Vietnamese capital is rich in ambience: here ancient architecture, refined culture and shrewd conservativeness blend harmoniously with modern Asian chic. Hanoi has a much slower pace than its rival, Ho Chi Minh City, Vietnam's southern centre of industry, commerce and pop culture. Men and women rise early for t'ai chi and relaxing walks around the city's many lakes, such as the legendary Hoan Kiem. Elderly men in berets pass the afternoon in peaceful parks or on shaded street corners, playing Chinese chess and sipping green tea. In the evenings, the city's youth flock to myriad trendy Vietnamese and Western bars, cafés, restaurants and nightclubs.

During the Vietnam War, Hanoians suffered constant hardship; the Christmas Bombings of 1972 did considerable damage to the city. However, the Old Quarter and central city survived, and though it suffered a sharp decline during the initial isolated years of the current communist government, Hanoi has emerged into the 21st century as one of Southeast Asia's premier cities.

The Old Quarter, originally known as '36 Streets' after the 36 ancient merchant guilds that settled there, dates back to the 13th century, although the current incarnation is only 100 or 150 years old. The streets are no longer so strictly organised by craft, but the area remains the centre of activity. Narrow alleyways heave with honking motorbikes, old women in conical hats selling tropical fruit,

Above: Downtown nightlife. Below: fowl market near Long Bien Bridge. Right: top, Quan Thanh pagoda; bottom, junks sailing between the limestone peaks of Ha Long Bay

young women selling sesame doughnuts stuffed with sweet green bean filling, pho noodle stands, shoe-shiners, hawkers of hats and T-shirts with Vietnam's solitary gold star in a sea of red, and mobs of foreign and local shoppers. Although *xich lo*, or rickshaws, are now officially banned, their stubborn drivers typify the defiant Vietnamese spirit, still managing to clog the city streets.

Hanoi also has an elegant and complex array of unique local cuisines. French colonists gifted the Vietnamese a love for baguettes and strong coffee, but the best French pastries are found in Hanoi – at a fraction of the price you'd pay in Paris. Bia hoi (fresh draught beer) outlets occupy many street corners, a cheap place to meet friends and soak up the atmosphere. Hanoi also lays claim to Vietnam's signature dish, pho, a rice-noodle soup served most commonly with beef. Unfortunately, it's Hanoians' love of dog meat and snake (most famously served in Le Mat village) that garner most attention from outsiders.
Adam Bray

'Hanoi is a beautiful city, where many talented singers and musicians were raised. Hanoian music has a long history. Everybody knows Trinh Cong Son, and other famous musicians: Quoc Trung, Anh Quan, Huy Tuan, or singers Tran Thu Ha, Hong Nhung and Thanh Lam. I like to hear them at Ho Guom Xanh'

Le Hieu pop singer

Instant Passport

Population
6,232,940 (core city 3,400,000)

Area
186sq km

Where is it?
On the Red River Delta in northern Vietnam. Hanoi occupies a 'rolling dragon and sitting tiger' position with its back to a mountain and facing a river, a sign of a city where art and science may flourish

Climate
Temperate and mild, although summers are usually humid and hot (averaging 31°C or 32°C)

Ethnic mix
Kinh (ethnic Vietnamese), Hoa (ethnic Chinese), various hill tribe minorities

Major sights
Ho Chi Minh Mausoleum Complex and One Pillar Pagoda; Museum of Ethnology; Temple of Literature; Thanh Long Water Puppet Theatre; Museum of Vietnamese History, Military History Museum and Citadel Flag Tower; Hoa Lo Prison (the 'Hanoi Hilton'); Ha Long Bay (outside the city)

Insiders' tips
Home by Restaurant Bobby Chinn; Highway 4; late at night on the food streets at Cam Chi, Thuy Khue and Tong Duy Tan; Café Pho Co; Bia Hoi Corner (Luong Ngoc Quyen and Ta Hien); Minh's Jazz Club; Forest (Rung) Restaurant; the Russian circus at Lenin Park

Where's the buzz?
The Old Quarter, around Hoan Kiem lake, around St Joseph's Cathedral, around the Opera House, New Century Nightclub, Vincom Tower

Livestock living within the city limits
13,847 water buffalo, 39,142 oxen, 338,950 pigs

Number of motorbikes on the road
More than 1.36 million

Number of sizeable lakes within the city
At least 25

Number of high-rise apartment buildings
488

Number of art objects on display at the Museum of Fine Arts
Over 2,000 Stone and Bronze Age artifacts, Buddhist statues, lacquer paintings and other culturally significant pieces

Number of temples and pagodas
More than 600, with 130 of them recognised as being historically and culturally significant

Number of significant traditional markets
25 inner-city markets, with at least another 40 in the suburbs

Proportion of the population working for the government
Over 10%

Architecture	8
Arts & Culture	8
Buzz	9
Food & Drink	2
Quality of Life	4
World Status	5
Total	36/60
Rank	25

Havana

CUBA

A blast from 1959

When Fidel Castro took over Cuba in 1959, he effectively pressed the 'Pause' button, and little has changed since. To this day, old American cars – the only type that can be bought and sold freely here – trundle around Havana's empty roads. Extravagant, if fading, architecture is an ever-present reminder of the pre-revolution days when Havana was the playground of the rich and famous, and Cuba had an economy six-times that of Spain. Here, the modern international brand names and billboards that are a feature of most other modern capitals are conspicuous by their absence – no Starbucks, no McDonald's, no Coca-Cola.

International tourism was reluctantly restarted in the early 1990s to raise badly needed hard currency to replace the huge vacuum left by the collapse of the Soviet Union. Fidel told his people that this influx of capitalist visitors was 'a necessary evil' and would help the Cuban economy. Now Cuba boasts 3,000,000 visitors a year.

Havana has the history, depth and artistic refinement of a European city, with the pace and climate of the Caribbean. The 16th- and 17th-century architects of Old Havana were the same ones who built Seville. Every day there are concerts of myriad styles of music from classical to Flamenco, and salsa to rock 'n' roll. There are 37,000 registered professional musicians in Havana, and everyone else can play something pretty well. Music wafts from the doorways of every café, bar and restaurant in Old Havana. Colourful galleries sell everything from paintings to wood carvings and metal work. The National Ballet, which performs in the spectacular Lorca Theatre in the Parque Central, is of the same high standard and discipline as the Bolshoi in Russia, but with more Latin heart and soul.

Instant Passport

Population
2,192,000

Area
727sq km

Where is it?
At the north-western end of the Carribean island of Cuba, on the Straits of Florida

Climate
Tropical, with hot, wet summers and cool, dry winters. The Gulf Stream warms the waters, while *la brisa* (a trade wind) cools the city throughout the year. August to October is hurricane season

Ethnic mix
66% white, 22% mulatto, 12% black, less than 1% Asian

Major sights
La Habana Vieja, Museo de Bellas Artes, Plaza de Armas, Plaza de la Revolución, Museo de la Ciudad, Fundación Havana Club, Cementerio Colón, Partagás Factory, Ballet Nacional de Cuba, El Capitolio

Insiders' tips
Parque Lennon in Vedado (the John Lennon statue has its own guard who, famously, takes the statue's glasses home with him every night to prevent them being stolen); Union Francesa restaurant; the Prado; Coppelia ice-cream parlour; Danza Contemporánea de Cuba; gigs, festivals and book fairs at the Fortaleza de San Carlos de La Cabaña, across the canal from the old town

Where's the buzz?
Calle Obrapía and Calle Obispo in La Habana Vieja, the Malecón, Café Cantante Mi Habana and La Madriguera for cutting-edge music

Distance from the USA
144km (90 miles)

Number of times the CIA attempted to kill Castro between 1961 and 1965
Eight

Castro's age when he ceded power to his brother, Raúl
80

Literacy rate
95% (on a par with Australia and Sweden)

Ratio of doctors to population
One for every 175 people. (In Britain it is approximately one to 435)

Life expectancy
76 years (men); 80 years (women)

Year Cuba signed a trade agreement with the USSR
1960

Famous musicians
Buena Vista Social Club, Issac Delgad, Irakere, Pablo Milanés, Orishas, Compay Segundo, Los Van Van, Silvio Rodríguez, Yusa

Previous page: classic cars outside the Capitolio.
Opposite, top left: Monumento a Ernest Hemingway.
Bottom: left, Edificio Bacardí; right, Café Taberna

Despite this cultural feast, Cuba is still a communist country. Most business – including shops, restaurants, hotels, galleries – is 'official', and therefore 'owned' by the government, though some habaneros open up their homes as *paladares* (small restaurants with, generally speaking, the best food and atmosphere) and *casa particulares* (bed and breakfasts). There is also a black market of *jineteros* who will sidle up to tourists with offers of great cigars or lobster to be had in their houses, or other services, though the cigars usually turn out to be sub standard and are certainly not what their labels imply.

For the native habanero, life can be hard. There are few shops, blackouts are common, the infrastructure is crumbling and the

media is fully censored. Most Cubans do not have access to the internet or any international news. However, since Raúl Castro took over, there have been significant and very noticeable investments in public transport, electricity and water systems, and road resurfacing. For the first time in 20 years there are now lines, arrows and signs on the roads of Havana.

For the Cubans, Havana is a place of simple pleasures – buying an ice-cream from the famous Coppelia Gardens in Vedado, sipping mojitos, listening to rumba, going to live concerts, or strolling down the Malecón with friends. How much longer Havana will remain in this picturesque time warp is, however, uncertain.

Toby Brocklehurst

Architecture	8
Arts & Culture	5
Buzz	7
Food & Drink	6
Quality of Life	6
World Status	8
Total	40/60
Rank	**12**

Hong Kong

CHINA

Reaching for the stars

The man-made world does not get more spectacular than this. The sky twinkles and glistens, not with stars in the smog-filled sky, but with the luminous glow of skyscrapers. The air is perfumed with an aromatic cocktail of curry fish balls, car fumes, ocean breezes and general grit. Anorexic antique double-decker trams rattle past, rare reminders of the colonial past. And every inhabitable slope of this craggy isle grows a high-rise forest.

This is the tallest city in the world, a city with a Chinese heart that has embraced the West like no other – more dense than New York, more intense than London, more of a melting pot than any other Asian city.

Despite the emergence of Shanghai in recent years, Hong Kong remains a financial hub of the East, continuing in its strong fiscal traditions even after the handover to China in 1997. There are those who would say that Hong Kong is all about money.

Previous page: bottom right, drinking at Felix and shopping at the Landmark. From left: trams in Sheung Wan; the Big Buddha on Lantau Island. Bottom left: Star Ferry

'I love the liveliness and energy of Hong Kong. There are always new things to visit and try, and there's no time to get bored as the city is always moving. You can see it in the way people move, walk, eat and do business. Food is such a huge part of the culture here that it's always exciting for a chef. We Hong Kongers say that eating is the most important part of life!'

Chan Yan-tak head chef at the triple-Michelin-starred Lung King Heen restaurant

Indeed, per capita, Hong Kongers drive more Mercedes and Rolls-Royces, turn over more money on horseracing, and drink more cognac than people in any other country in the world. In many respects, it is an ode to capitalism, but – behind all this – there is a far less superficial side to the city.

Hong Kong, 'fragrant harbour', is a city for romantics. The sweeping view from Tsim Sha Tsui and the Peak, with the famous Star Ferry bobbing across Victoria Harbour below, is one of the best in the world. Hong Kong is a city for nature-seekers, with picturesque beaches just a stone's throw from Central and rugged trails over the dramatic, craggy landscape of the country parks. It is, with its sheer density of bodies and constant wall of noise, a city for those who adore a frenetic metropolis. An unrelenting combination of squealing bus brakes, the patter of pedestrians and raucous market-stall bargaining fill this city with life.

Most of all, it is a city for food lovers. There's a strange sense of assurance in knowing that you're never far away from deep-fried squid on a stick when an acute craving hits. Hong Kong is full of culinary wonderment, catering for those with the taste for exotic adventure (snake soup), traditional street food, Spanish tapas and cosmopolitan Michelin-starred dining. Not forgetting, of course, the institution that is dim sum.

Hong Kong is the gateway to China: the country's richest city – Shenzhen – lies just across the border. The question is whether Hong Kong, physically or spiritually, will ever be part of China proper.
Mark Tjhung

Instant Passport

Population
7,034,100 (estimated)

Area
1,092sq km

Where is it?
Off the southern coast of China, covering Hong Kong Island, the Kowloon Peninsula and the New Territories

Climate
Subtropical, with temperatures dropping below 10°C in winter and exceeding 31°C in summer

Ethnic mix
Chinese, Filipino, Indonesian, Indian, Pakistani, Nepalese, Vietnamese, Thai, Japanese, Korean, North American, Australian, Canadian, European

Major sights
Victoria Peak, Tsim Sha Tsui Promenade and Avenue of the Stars, Temple Street night markets, Stanley Market, Ngong Ping 360, the Giant Buddha, Ocean Park

Insiders' tips
Hiking along Dragon's Back ridge to Shek O, chicken's feet dim sum, hidden alley bars in Soho, seafood in Sai Kung

Where's the buzz?
Lan Kwai Fong at the weekend, the markets of Yau Ma Tei and Mong Kok, the street bazaars and boutiques of Causeway Bay, Chungking Mansions and its surrounds in Tsim Sha Tsui

Number of buildings over 90m high
3,069, the most in the world. New York, in second place, has only 886

Most densely populated district
Ap Lei Chau – 66,755 people per sq km

Number of US$ millionaires
95,000, plus 28 billionaires

Area of Hong Kong covered by Country Park
38%

Average number of tropical cyclones per year
2.5

Famous dishes
Jah dai cheung (pig's intestine stuffed with whole spring onions), ho jai jook (rice congee with preserved vegetables and small oysters), xiao long bao (Shanghainese dumplings)

Historical milestones
Sovereignty handed from Britain to China (1997), opening of Hong Kong Disneyland (2005)

Immortalised in
Chungking Express, *A Chinese Ghost Story*, *In the Mood for Love*, *A Better Tomorrow*

Istanbul

TURKEY

Centuries and continents collide on the Bosphorus

Architecture	7
Arts & Culture	7
Buzz	9
Food & Drink	7
Quality of Life	6
World Status	7
Total	43/60
Rank	8

It takes just one sunset to fall for Istanbul. You may be sipping tea among canoodling couples along the Bosphorus in Üsküdar with a backdrop of skyscrapers and minarets, or smoking a hookah in Tophane as freighters glide by on their way to the Black Sea, when the sun dips down low and sets the whole city afire. Just as the lights of the modern metropolis begin to sparkle, the muezzin rises from a nearby mosque, filling the streets with plaintive wailing. The effect is narcotic.

Istanbul is one of those accidents of geography where there will always be a city. For millennia, poets have been scrambling for new clichés to express how this city links past and present, Europe and Asia. Napoleon referred to it as the 'capital of the world'; two empires were inclined to agree. In the simplest terms, Istanbul is a place of fusion and transition, a land that boasts a glut of history and Europe's youngest population, home to a people who fast over Ramadan and gobble up Prada and iPhones.

Istanbul is truly gargantuan: with a population of nine million, it is one of the biggest metropolises in the world. From the rooftop club 360 in Beyoglu, the city is a whirlpool, rising and falling on hillsides, broken only by water. The sheer slopes can make for teeth-grinding frustration when you're trying to slither your way through a crowded market in Fener or dodge dozens of solicitous cabbies in Taksim Square. The essential sights and experiences are straight from the pages of *National Geographic*: browsing mountains of produce fresh from Anatolia among legions of head-scarved old women at the bazaar; chilling out along the railing of an Asia-bound ferry while hovering gulls beg for scraps of simit, the traditional pastry; a wiry teenager winding through the crowds with 80 of those simit balanced expertly on top of his head.

Main picture: inside the Hagia Sophia. Above: top left, Üsküdar ferry crossing the Bosphorus; top right, the Grand Bazaar; bottom left, the intricate designs at Topkapı Palace, former centre of Ottoman power

A city with so much can only be uncovered by degrees. The sites in Sultanahmet never fail to astound first-timers. Return visitors might find their way to Beyazit Square – home to a breathtaking mosque, a university and the Grand Bazaar. Experienced travellers might venture out to the city's thousand-year-old walls and nearby Chora Church, within it the world's greatest collection of Byzantine frescoes. Even some residents have yet to see Dolmabahçe Palace or ride the cable car up to Pierre Loti café for the exquisite view and Turkish coffee.

Not to be outdone by the wonders of the past, the Turks have built a canyon-shaped shopping mall, a restaurant floating in the Bosphorus, and are working on the first intercontinental tunnel. As Turkey regains its place among the global players, Istanbul will join the shortlist of the world's most vibrant cities.
Rich Carriero

'I think there's a kind of soul-bond between cities like Istanbul, Barcelona, London, New York and Cairo, but I know what it is like to long for this city. Whenever I'm abroad I miss Istanbul dearly'

Elif Šafak author

Instant Passport

Population
9,000,000 (core city 8,260,000)

Area
1,166sq km

Where is it?
Straddling the Bosphorus Strait, which links the Black Sea to the Mediterranean and separates Europe from Asia

Climate
Hot and dry Mediterranean summers and cool, rainy winters

Major sights
Hagia Sophia, Blue Mosque, Topkapı Palace, Basilica Cistern, the Grand Bazaar, the Spice Bazaar

Where's the buzz?
Cihangir, Etiler, Moda

Insiders' tips
The Bosphorus neighbourhoods Bebek and Arnavutköy, Prince's Islands for a summertime getaway, Kadıköy for the Asian side at its edgiest

Earliest evidence of civilisation
While excavating around Yenikapı for the Marmaray Tunnel Project in 2008, archaeologists uncovered a Neolithic settlement dating to 6500 BC. The previous oldest settlement – in Fikirtepe – dates to 5500 BC

Previously called
Byzantium, Constantinople, Stamboul, Tsarigrad. In 1930 the Turkish authorities ensured Istanbul was recognised under its new name by returning mail sent using any of the others

Capital status
Istanbul has been capital of the Roman, Byzantine, Latin and Ottoman empires, yet Ankara is the capital city of modern Turkey

Early plumbing
Under the Ottomans, Istanbul had over 1,400 public toilets, far ahead of other European cities. Over the last 80 years, internal plumbing has seen Turkey's 2,500 *hammams* (bath-houses) fall to only about 100

Biggest covered bazaar in the world
The Grand Bazaar, founded by Sultan Mehmed II in 15th century. Slippers, mirrors and fur have been sold here for over 500 years

Diameter of the dome of the Hagia Sophia
31.24m

Number of commercial vessels passing through the Bosphorus
53,000 each year

Football teams
Beşiktaş, Fenerbahçe, Galatasaray

On familiar terms
Yogurt, pilaf, coffee, baklava, shish kebab, pitta, kilim, sherbet and caviar are all words of Turkish origin now used in ordinary English

SİPAHİ SK. ↑
TERPUŞÇULAR SK. ↑
KOLTUK KAZAZLAR SK. ↑
PÜSKÜLCÜLER SK. ↑
FERACECİLER SK. ↑
YAĞLIKÇILAR CAD. ↑

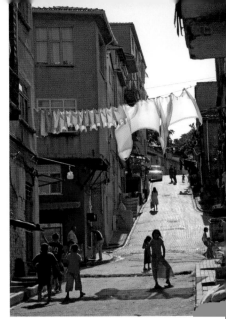

Left: Sultanahmet Mosque. Top: left, Lokal; centre, the Grand Bazaar; right, the Jewish Quarter. Bottom: left, the Grand Bazaar; centre, Fatih market; right, Erenler Çay Bahçesi

Jakarta

INDONESIA

Mall culture

Eight million people inhabit the capital of Indonesia, yet it's rare to see as many as a hundred of them outdoors at the same time. Instead, armies of their motor vehicles create havoc on the city's streets. Jakartans don't like to use their feet – at least, not outside. They prefer to meander around the ubiquitous air-conditioned malls, hundreds of thousands of Jakartan consumers supporting the country's economy. While the rest of the world reels from the recession, Jakarta has welcomed the opening of Harvey Nichols and Indonesia's fifth Louis Vuitton boutique (the biggest in the country to date). Yet the capital was deemed the second worst place in the world for expats to work by an ORC Worldwide survey. Admittedly, the traffic is terrible – and the city is often paralysed come rush hour – but the fact that people can't get home straight after work means white-collar workers, most of whom live in the suburbs, have developed a post-work habit of shopping, eating and drinking while waiting for the traffic to subdue. Come the weekend, the malls are still full, providing an air-conditioned playground for all the family.

At a glance, present-day Jakarta looks as if it's made of concrete, steel and sin. It's ugly and sexy in equal measure – certainly not a place for sightseeing. Historical museums are legion, but only a handful are visitor-friendly. And while any Jakartan can point you to two of the city's major theme parks, none will ever be an international destination.

Designer clubs and lounges complement their million-dollar decor with rows of Ferraris parked outside, while in the underground, punk, rock, electronica and many other scenes keep hipsters happy in the knowledge that their doing their part in deconstructing the mainstream.

Architecture	4
Arts & Culture	5
Buzz	6
Food & Drink	3
Quality of Life	4
World Status	6
Total	28/60
Rank	**58**

Outside the glittery city centre, the middle-class Jakartans celebrate life differently. Family and community are key: martini brunches are replaced with a round of thick black coffees served in transparent glasses, and wine tasting evenings are substituted with arisan (social gatherings involving money and lottery). Here, the closest they come to hedonism is going to a traditional dance performance or a *dangdut* (traditional Indonesian music) concert. For many, city centre life is as real as the life portrayed in *sinetron* (Indonesian soaps) that they religiously watch on TV.

Often referred to as The Big Durian, Jakarta carries as distinctive smell of *kretek* (clove cigarette). For some, it's pleasant and tasty; for others, it's repulsive. When it comes to the capital of Indonesia, there is no middle ground.

Unggul Hermanto

Previous page: Jalan Sudirman. Top left: cocktails at vodka bar Red Square. Bottom left: Rawa Belong flower market. Above and right, Old Jakarta, known as Kota

Instant Passport

Population
14,250,000 (core city 9,373,000)

Area
1,360sq km

Where is it?
At the mouth of the Ciliwung River on Jakarta Bay on the north-west coast of Java island

Climate
Hot and humid with short, heavy bursts of rain all year (it rains almost daily from late October to May)

Ethnic mix
Javanese, Chinese-Indonesian and others from the Indonesian archipelago

Major sights
Sunda Kelapa (old port), Kota (old Jakarta), Presidential Palace, Istiqlal Mosque, Taman Mini Indonesia Indah, Ancol Dream Park, Pasar Ikan (fish market), Monas (National Monument), Museum Nasional

Insiders' tips
Salihara art complex in Ragunan, the late night street food vendors in Menteng, the art galleries in Cikini

Where's the buzz?
Loewy in Mega Kuningan, the bars in Kemang, Plaza Indonesia

Dutch recognise Indonesian independence
1949 (after four years of guerrilla warfare)

Also known as
The Big Durian (a fruit famed for its pungent smell and acquired taste)

Year protests and rioting topple President Suharto
1998

Number killed during the May 1998 riots
1,200

Number of rivers flowing through the city
13

Number of people made homeless during floods in 2007
340,000

Number of people dead or missing in Indonesia after the 2004 Tsunami
More than 220,000

Number of *bajaj* (three-wheeled vehicles) in Jakarta and its surrounds
Approximately 14,000

Local flavours
Gado-gado (a salad with peanut sauce), soto (clear soup with slices of beef, veal or chicken), sate (skewered meat served with soy or peanut sauce), sop kaki (soup made from beef or goat shank), sop buntut (oxtail soup), sambal terasi (hot dried fish or shrimp paste), bakmie Goreng (Chinese-style fried noodles)

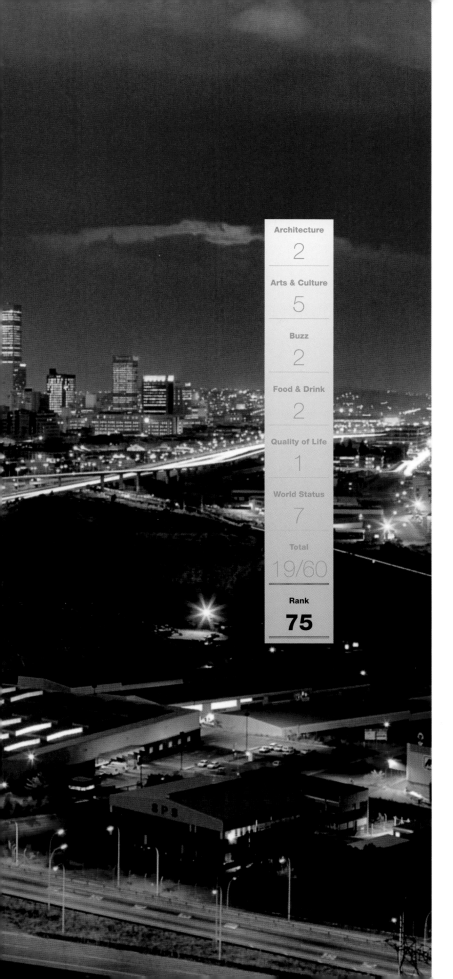

Architecture	2
Arts & Culture	5
Buzz	2
Food & Drink	2
Quality of Life	1
World Status	7
Total	19/60
Rank	75

Johannesburg

SOUTH AFRICA

The now factor

Johannesburg is, above all, a working town – a magnet for dreams. Since the first gold strike in 1886, it has evolved from a tented mining camp into the world's largest city not situated on a body of water. No lakes or rivers inform its geography or layout. Instead, you'll find millions of trees planted by its original inhabitants to offer respite from the dusty Highveld. The end-result is a city that's also the world's largest urban forest visible by satellite.

As a teenager among world cities, Johannesburg has always been a bit rebellious, if not schizophrenic. It exploded on to the global stage in less than a decade, attracting speculators, capitalists, prostitutes, labour, refugees and – above all – dreamers. Hundreds of thousands of gold-struck souls poured in from every corner of the globe, all in search of El Dorado: African and Chinese miners; Jewish refugees escaping pogroms in Russia; hard-working, hard-drinking miners from America and Australia; Boers from the Cape; Indian traders and European immigrants – united in their hunger for success, divided by a competitive spirit. Dream maker, dream breaker.

That tangible sense of duality still exists. Today, Johannesburg is a city of blinding contrast. It is relatively rich when it might be poor. It's considerably white when it might be black. It's decidedly cosmopolitan when it might simply be African. It's green when it should be arid. It's a symbol of the good life on a notoriously hard continent. And it's a surprisingly back-slapping friendly city for a place notorious for danger.

While other global cities are simmering stews, with flavours and nuances that have evolved through centuries of slow-cooking, Johannesburg is a packet of microwaved instant soup. Its

> *'Whenever I return to Jozi from wherever I've been, it just feels right. There's something in the air'*
>
> **Tselane Tambo actress**

Instant Passport

Population
6,000,000 (core city 3,800,000)

Area
2,396sq km

Where is it?
In north-eastern South Africa, on the Highveld (plateau) 1,753m above sea level (more than 100m higher than Denver, the 'Mile High City')

Climate
Dry and sunny, with summer rains

Ethnic mix
73% black, 16% white, 6% mixed-race, 4% Asian

Major sights
Gold Reef City, Apartheid Museum, Carlton Centre, Constitution Hill, Hillbrow Tower, Nelson Mandela's home, Munro Drive, Soweto

Insiders' tips
44 Stanley for shopping and dining, Moyo at Zoo Lake for Sunday lunch, hi-tech displays at the Origins Centre at the University of Witwatersrand

Where's the buzz?
Parkhurst, Rosebank, New Chinatown, Greenside

Languages spoken
English, Afrikaans, Ndebele, Northern Sotho, Southern Sotho, Swati, Tsonga, Tswana, Venda, Xhosa, Zulu

Nicknames
Joburg, Jozi, Egoli (City of Gold), Joeys

Year Raymond Dart discovered the Taung Child
1924. The fossil was discovered at a lime quarry at Taung, south-west of Johannesburg, and is thought to be approximately two million years old

Date of the Soweto riots
16 June 1976. The violent student protests against the Apartheid administration are now commemorated each year by Youth Day

Number of trees
10,000,000

Percentage of the world's gold found in the Johannesburg area
40%

Percentage of population over 60 years old
6%

Indigenous dance music
Kwaito

Host of FIFA World Cup
2010

Immortalised in
Cry Freedom; *Long Walk to Freedom*; *Tsotsi*; *Cry, the Beloved Country*

Opposite: Hillbrow Tower. This page: clockwise from top left, Emmarentia Dam, cricket fans, Melrose Arch hotel, a Ndebele design, a Xhosa bride in Lesedi Cultural Village

underclass, business leaders, socialites, intelligentsia, counter-culture, criminals and police force all arrived in the same year.

As an 'instant' city, it has little interest in next week. Johannesburg is always about today, perhaps tomorrow, at a push. Time is compressed: 50 years in another city is 10 years in Jo'burg. Its city centre has been rebuilt four times in less than a century: first as a tented camp; then as an Edwardian masterpiece which, over three decades, gave way to art deco-meets-Brasilia modernism; followed by an American-inspired high-rise interpretation, earning a tepid tagline as 'the New York of Africa'.

Like its original inhabitants, Johannesburg excels at reinventing itself. A collective attention deficit disorder prevails. Its inspiration shifted from New York to Los Angeles, seemingly overnight. Why build upwards when it can build outwards? Indeed, why rebuild when everything can be built from scratch all over again? Today, an endless expansion of freeways and Tuscan-inspired townhouses, malls and office parks devour the outlying Highveld at an alarming rate.

The end-result is a city that feeds on itself, hungry for reinvention and success. Johannesburg's new-generation immigrants – this time from other parts of Africa, China, India and Eastern Europe – continue to dream and scheme: 'Today I'm going to hit the big time! Or maybe tomorrow… latest.'
Josef Talotta

Architecture	2
Arts & Culture	5
Buzz	8
Food & Drink	2
Quality of Life	3
World Status	1
Total	21/60
Rank	73

Kingston

JAMAICA

Non-stop reggae party town

Kingston is a global city in a small island nation. Its allure flows from its status as the HQ of reggae, Bob Marley and Sean Paul. It is the city where the revolutionary ideas of Marcus Garvey and Rastafari took root, ideas now dispatched across the world by the international success of reggae.

It is also party central, a city of all-night raves. On 'Passa Passa Wednesdays' you can experience the raw energy of throbbing dancehall rhythms and the spectacle of dancers whose dazzling hip gyrations and costumes are so sexual they leave little to the imagination. It's party, street theatre and performance art merged into one, heady, spontaneous mix.

But there is much more to Kingston culture than hedonism. The city boasts a vibrant poetry, literary and theatre scene. It nurtures cutting-edge film-makers and video directors such as Storm Saulter (*Betta Mus' Come*) and Ras Kassa (Damien Marley's *Welcome to Jamrock* video), who capture the city's movement, drama, colour and grace in creative ways. Kingstonians are famed for their sense of style, celebrated in Caribbean Fashion Week, an internationally recognised showcase of Caribbean couture. There is a long, rich history of fine art, as well. The brilliant work of Edna Manley, Oswald Watson, Karl Parboosingh and Dawn Scott is on show at the National Gallery, and for those whose taste runs to the experimental and contemporary, there are pieces by Khepera Oluyia Hatshepwa, Ebony Patterson, O'Neil Lawrence and others at the Mutual and Cage Galleries.

Kingston began life as an outgrowth of Port Royal. When that wicked pirate port of the Caribbean was devastated by the 1692 earthquake, its refugees moved inland. Eighty years later it became Jamaica's capital city. It now spreads from Kingston Harbour in the

This page: clockwise from right, boys diving off Kingston Harbour, Devon House, girls' night at St Christopher's Jazz Bar. Opposite: Channel 1 Recording Studio

south to the hills and mountains in north St Andrew, from Portmore in the west to Harbour View in the east. Downtown is home to government institutions and working-class residents; uptown is the financial nerve centre and home to the upper-middle-classes. Landmarks are as diverse as the British colonial architecture of Devon House, music memorabilia at the Bob Marley Museum and the National Stadium where Olympic champion Usain Bolt trained.

Food is crucial to Kingstonians. While there is a variety of cuisines, they will seek out indigenous dishes at takeaway shops, fine-dining restaurants and Rastafarian vegetarian cafés. On Sunday mornings after church, they indulge in 'fish and festival' at Hellshire beach.

Admittedly, crime in Kingston is a problem, albeit one that the government is tackling. Fortunately, the random shootings that grab all the headlines are rare, and most of the violence is confined to particular downtown neighbourhoods. The Kingston we know is rather a place of gorgeous tropical beauty, of majestic fruit trees, flowers splashed with bright colours and lush green grass. If the fear does ever grab you, you simply head up to the mountain-top mansion of Strawberry Hill – 3,000 feet above sea-level in the Blue Mountains – and take in a breathtaking view of the entire city that makes you feel soothed again.

Dionne and Klive Walker

'Kingston is a fireball of excitement! There is always something happening: wicked sessions, good music, great vibes. It's a true metropolis, always busy and on the move, with food galore. Energy and creativity ring in the air. It's the heartbeat of the Caribbean, nowhere else comes close! And then St Andrew island suburbia gives you a cool hillside breeze and the lush green slopes as your daily drop. A great escape from the hustle and bustle, a true experience of chillaxation'

Ebony G Patterson artist

Instant Passport

Population
555,800 (core city 96,052)

Area
450sq km

Where is it?
On the south-eastern coast of Jamaica, between the Caribbean Sea to the south and the Blue Mountains to the north

Climate
Tropical, with temperatures of around 30°C all year

Ethnic mix
African, South Asian, Chinese, Middle Eastern, European

Major sights
The Blue Mountains, Port Royal, Ward Theatre, Devon House, the art at the National Gallery, the Institute of Jamaica museum, the Bob Marley Museum, Strawberry Hill

Insiders' tips
Lime Cay beach, Earl's Juice Bar, Christopher's Jazz bar, Bembe dancehall, St Andrew Island

Where's the buzz?
Hellshire Beach, the nightclubs of New Kingston, Caribbean Fashion Week, Emancipation and Heroes Park

Historical milestones
Founded in 1692, became the nation's capital in 1872, University of the West Indies founded, revolutionary movements including Rastafari and Michael Manley's democratic socialism, independence from Britain in 1962, hosted the Commonwealth Games, reggae created, home to Bob Marley

Sport
Cricket, football (the 'Reggae Boyz' qualified for the 1998 World Cup)

Exports
Reggae, rum, coffee

Highest point
Blue Mountain Peak at 2,256m

National fruit
Ackee

National dish
Ackee and saltfish

National motto
Out of many, one people

Number of recording studios
50 – one of the highest concentrations per capita in the world

Immortalised in
Bob Marley and the Wailers 'Trench Town Rock' on *Kingston 12*, *The Harder They Come*, *Life and Debt*, Dawn Scott's *Ghetto/Zinc Yard*

Architecture	8
Arts & Culture	5
Buzz	8
Food & Drink	4
Quality of Life	5
World Status	3
Total	33/60
Rank	**39**

Kolkata

INDIA

Colonial creation now proud to be Bengali

Everyone who has been to or lived in the first capital of British India has a quintessential Kolkata experience: sunset from a tinny barge bobbing between the Howrah Bridge and Vidyasagar Setu on the muddy waters of the Hooghly river; pancakes and tea at the Tollygunge Club, where a round of golf is accompanied by yelping foxes who either celebrate, or protest the landing of little white balls near their foxholes; saving the world and arguing about postmodernism over tea at the Coffee House; Christmas Eve at the 300-year-old Armenian Orthodox Holy Church of Nazareth in north Kolkata; a meal at the dirty little Chinatown called Tangra where Chinese food is a fusion of China's and Bengal's culinary styles; walking around Victoria Memorial where the gardens have been the site of fumbled and rushed liaisons for generations. Leafing through books in College Street before stepping into Paragon for a sherbet; crossing over the Mallickbazar graveyard to Shiraz Restaurant whose biriyani and chicken *chaap* are the stuff of legends.

Put your eye to the kaleidoscope that is Kolkata, and its curious neighbourhoods and varied histories fall into myriad colourful patterns. Kolkata – long stress on the first 'a' and a soft 't' – is the Bengali pronunciation of the anglicised Calcutta, which was officially dropped in 2001 but continues to linger in English conversations. The city was lovingly built out of swampy villages by the East India Company in the 17th and 18th centuries. Following in British footsteps, the Bengali aristocracy and the ambitious middle class settled in the now-crumbling neighbourhoods of north Kolkata with their gorgeous, palatial bungalows. The Armenians came here, as did the Jews and the Chinese, and all of them left their imprint upon the city. From the other end of the

Instant Passport

Population
12,700,000 (core city 4,339,000)

Area
531sq km

Where is it?
Along the eastern bank of the Hooghly River in West Bengal

Climate
Subtropical, with humid summer monsoons and pleasant winters

Ethnic mix
Bengals, Ghotis, Biharis, Marwaris, Anglo Indians, Punjabis, Parsis, Jews, Tibetans, South Indians, Europeans, Chinese, Armenian

Major sights
Fort William, Eden Gardens, Victoria Memorial, St Paul's Cathedral, Howrah Bridge, Indian Museum, Birla Planetarium, The Maiden

Insiders' tips
Take a boat across the Hooghly River from Outram ghat or Princep ghat, buy *rosogolla* or *mishti doi* from Balaram Mallick sweetshop

Where's the buzz?
Someplace Else – the Park Hotel's music bar

Founded 300 years ago by incorporating three villages
Sutanati, Gobindapur and Kolikata

Capital of British India
1772-1912

Bengal Famine
1943-1944 (between 3 and 5 million people starved)

Year Mother Teresa opened the Nirmal Hriday Home for Dying Destitutes
1952

Number of universities
Nine

Nobel Laureates
Ronald Ross, Sir CV Raman, Rabindranath Tagore, Mother Teresa, Amartya Sen

Languages spoken
Bengali, Hindi, English, Bhojpuri, Urdu, Maithili

Regional dishes
Rasgolla (sweet white balls of paneer), sandesh (flavoured paneer paste cooked with sugar), jhaal (fish with ground mustard seeds and chillies), luchi (chicken or mutton in gravy), misthi doi (sweetened curds)

Length of Kolkata's metro railway system
16.45km

Nicknames
City of Palaces, City of Joy

country, swathes of *Marwaris* from Rajasthan migrated to Kolkata and made it their home. Perhaps it's this historical layer cake of cultures that makes Kolkata both gregariously welcoming of outsiders and yet fiercely proud of the local Bengali culture that has birthed greats like Nobel laureate Rabindranath Tagore, film maker Satyajit Ray and economist Amartya Sen.

Adda – a Bengali word for chatter, debate and any conversation whose central purpose is to waste time – is a tradition in Kolkata, along with left liberalism, eating well and partying hard. Chairman Mao and Che Guevara make Calcuttans weak around the knees, as do Jacques Derrida, Gabriel García Márquez and Kryzstof Kieslowski. If the references sound dated, it's because Kolkata teeters between quaint and passé, despite the mushrooming malls with glass fronts and neon lights. The Naxalite uprisings of the late 1960s and early 1970s resulted in a brain drain that left the city in something of a time warp, losing some of the polish that made it the cultural capital of India for decades. Still, Kolkata is one of the few places in India where the party begins at 7.30 in the evening and ends at 5.30 in the morning (followed by breakfast at a roadside restaurant). And the best part is, everyone's invited.
Deepanjana Pal

Opposite: Flower Market. Top: Hindu ritual bathing in the Hooghly river at Armenian Ghat. Bottom: Metropolitan Building on Chowringhee Road (officially Jawaharlal Nehru Road)

Architecture	
9	
Arts & Culture	
6	
Buzz	
6	
Food & Drink	
2	
Quality of Life	
8	
World Status	
1	
Total	
32/60	
Rank	
45	

Krakow

POLAND

A stunning snapshot of Poland's past

M odern times have been hard for Poland. For much of living memory, it was just somewhere floating around on the wrong side of the Berlin Wall. Probably near Russia, maybe in it. But Poland is misunderstood: this was once a great commonwealth that swept from the Baltic to the Black Sea, author of Europe's first constitution and home to Copernicus and Chopin.

To see Krakow is to see Poland in its historic heyday, to understand Poles at their proudest. The show-stopping Old Town, a brassy parade of palaces and churches, provides a lasting testament to a time when the country and its then capital were one of Europe's premier powers. This city of kings and queens is a strutting model on a runway who knows she's being watched. Yet there is weight to the claim that this is the most beautiful city centre in Europe.

But it's more than bricks and mortar. It's the melancholic strains of the *Hejnal*, a bugle call played on the hour to commemorate the eagle-eyed guard who spotted Genghis Khan's Mongol hordes sharpening their swords at the city gates and sounded the alarm. It's eating in Wierzynek, a restaurant that dates back 600 years, when its namesake served up a feast for three European kings. It's even the cellar pubs, now stuffed with gleaming Buddhas, shabby couches and Americans trying to find themselves, but almost all set in the earthy bowels of historic townhouses.

Even faith here feels historic. The city's devotion to Catholicism is red-blooded and raw, almost fundamental. You only need to turn around to find a church. Pope John Paul II cut his teeth in Krakow as Archbishop and when he died, nearly a million people turned out to weep. The uglier streak of this fundamentalism is its intolerance to difference. The annual gay pride parade regularly

Previous page: Sukiennice (Cloth Hall). Top: Wawel castle from Jubilat shopping centre. Right: art nouveau window in the Franciscan Church. Far right: Church of Sts Peter & Paul

Instant Passport

Population
740,000

Area
327sq km

Where is it?
In southern Poland on the Vistula river, 300km from Warsaw and 100km from the Tatra Mountains

Climate
Temperate and changeable, with cold winters and warm summers

Ethnic mix
White European

Major sights
Market Square, the Cloth Hall, St Mary's Basilica, Wawel Castle, Czartoryski Museum, Collegium Maius, the synagogues of Kazimierz, Wieliczka Salt Mines, milk bars, Old Town cellar pubs

Insiders' tips
Soviet style in Nowa Huta, Wajda's Manghha Centre, Schindler's factory in Podgorze, eating zapiekanka (a halved baguette, usually topped with mushrooms and ham) on plac Nowy

Where's the buzz?
Kazimierz, although it's slowly shifting across the river to Podgorze

Historical milestones
Golden Age of the Jagiellons, union with Lithuania, the Royal Court moves to Warsaw, partitions, the Kosciuszko uprising, independence, World War II and Auschwitz, Pope John Paul II

Best communist-style milk bar in town
Pod Filarkami

Largest medieval square
Rynek Glowny (the Market Square), which dates from 1257, is the largest medieval square in Europe. It is 200sq m in area

Number of churches
22

Number of synagogues active in 1939
Around 90

Number of synagogues active now
2

Number of pubs
An estimated 700

Famous inhabitants
Karol Wojtyla, later Pope John Paul II; film directors Roman Polanski and Andrzej Wajda; Lenin; Nigel Kennedy

Exports
Film, the *mloda polska* art movement, the bagel

descends into scenes from Saigon, as bigots and thugs turn out to ambush those flying the rainbow flag.

Yet, on the other side of town, tolerance and history are encouraging a rebirth. Kazimierz, the city's once influential Jewish district, was little more than a crumbling collection of bullet-scotched buildings 20 years ago. Today, there is major restoration and gentrification is in full swing. Synagogues have reopened, flyers for Hebrew classes hang from the lamp posts, and klezmer music spills out from period piece restaurants.

The area is also home to a growing crowd of dishevelled counter-culture bars, a magnet for Krakow's legion of students. Hailing from the hallowed halls of Jagiellonian University, they're the brightest in the country and help inject some much needed vitality into the city. Kazimierz is their playground, where they debate Nietzsche, down vodka and fall under tables, at the same time earning Krakow its reputation for unchecked hedonism.
Rory Boland

Kuala Lumpur

MALAYSIA

Shared experience

Architecture	3
Arts & Culture	3
Buzz	3
Food & Drink	6
Quality of Life	7
World Status	3
Total	25/60
Rank	**66**

By government decree, every guide to the country must at least once use the phrase 'Malaysia, Truly Asia', and its capital – Kuala Lumpur – certainly showcases the best and worst of the region with honour. The city is as steamy, noisy, physical, oppressive, raw, polluted, inexpensive and sexually deviant as Bangkok, Jakarta, Singapore, Manila and their like, in spite of being much smaller.

It isn't size, however, that makes KL more accessible than the behemoths over the Causeway, the Malacca Straits or the Thai border. The reason people feel at home in Kuala Lumpur – on the face of it, a pretty uninspiring concrete skyscrapered jungle painted a drab grey by the hot, damp tropics – is the eccentric yet welcoming folk who live therein. That, and the price of a hot meal at a hawker stall.

The proliferation of street-side diners and the fact that everyone, absolutely everyone, eats at them, says as much about Malaysia's love of food as its passion for gossip and the great outdoors (at least by comparision to the air-con obsessed Singaporeans). KL-ites are never backward about coming forward; they think nothing of making a comment to even the briefest acquaintance if they notice they've put on weight – but it is aways done with disarming innocence.

Kuala Lumpur fancies itself as a 'melting pot' despite the recent (just prior to and since the 2008 General Election) tensions emanating from the aggrieved Indian community and supporters of controversial opposition leader Anwar Ibrahim. For a proud Muslim city with huge Chinese, Indian and expatriate contingents, as well as a pro-Bumiputra (Malay) bent, there is next to no serious trouble in KL. In fact, Malaysia is arguably the most tolerant Muslim

Previous page: Petronas Towers, as seen from the SkyBar. Top right: Wei-ling Gallery. Centre right: Sutra Odissi dancers. Opposite: Yot Kee, an old-style *kopitiam* (coffee shop)

Instant Passport

Population
4,400,000 (core city 1,145,000)

Area
1,606sq km

Where is it?
On the west side of the central Peninsular Malaysia, at the confluence
of the Gombak and the Klang rivers in the heart of the Klang Valley

Climate
Equatorial. Hot and sunny with regular monsoon storms. Haze caused
by forest fires from Sumatra can cause visibility and health problems

Ethnic mix
Malay, Chinese, Indian, Eurasian, indigenous Kadazan and Iban, as well
as an estimated 100,000 legal and illegal expatriates from neighbouring
countries such as Indonesia and Thailand

Major sights
Petronas Twin Towers, Menara KL (KL Tower), Masjid Negara, Tugu
Negara, Petaling Street (Chinatown), Batu Caves, Lake Gardens, Sepang
International Motor Racing Circuit, Petrosains, Aquaria KLCC

Insiders' tips
Eat at the busiest hawker stall; always carry an umbrella; don't wear
shoes you are attached to; when haggling in Chinatown, expect to pay
30-50% of the price originally quoted (if you begin to negotiate you are
expected to buy the item)

Where's the buzz?
Bukit Bintang, Changkat Bukit Bintang, Asian Heritage Row, Desa Seri
Hartamas, Jalan Telawi, Bangsar, Mutiara Damansara, Jalan Alor (for
24/7 hawker cuisine), the area around The Beach Club

Languages spoken
Bahasa Malaysia, English, Cantonese, Mandarin, Tamil

Length of the KL Monorail
8.6km. It opened in 2003

Height of the flagpole at Dataran Merdeka (Independence Square)
95m – the tallest free-standing flagpole in the world

Oldest virgin city forest
Bukit Nanas jungle reserve. It dates back millions of years

Twinned with
Casablanca, Osaka, Ankara, Delhi

Number of Malaysians who will be offered a youth contract with Chelsea
Football Club following a reality television show based in KL
2

Mega-sales
March, May and December

International home of halal food
Global Halal Food Forum is held in Kuala Lumpur every year

Malaysia is one of the most tolerant Muslim countries in the world.
Though the religion is always evident, it never seems divisive or
intrusive. KL is not to everyone's taste, of course. After all, no one
wants to be told they have a fat arse.

Thanks to a dire public transport system and clogged roads,
travelling in KL in the rain or during rush hour is hugely frustrating.
Yet even in the midst of a storm there are heart-warming moments
to be shared, such as waiting for the rains to abate from the shelter
of a semi-covered stall, cupping a mug of kopi ais (iced coffee). As
lightning strikes the tin roof and thunder bounces off the buildings
either side of you, look around. Dozens of people are stuck, just
like you, grinning with friends and sharing their own kopi ais or
teh tarik (pulled tea), complaining about work, the weather, the
government, reality TV and everything else that other nations
tend to moan about behind closed doors.
Matt Bellotti

Above: the red *torii* that mark the path to the inner shrine of Fushimi Inari. Right: the superb gardens of Kinkakuji, a Rinzai Zen temple.

Architecture	8
Arts & Culture	7
Buzz	2
Food & Drink	8
Quality of Life	8
World Status	2
Total	35/60
Rank	28

Kyoto

JAPAN

Where the old envelops the new

In eastern Kyoto, an apprentice geisha clip-clops down a cobbled street to meet her patrons in a nearby teahouse. Out west, a Zen monk slowly rakes his gravel into precisely the same pattern as always. Throughout the city, chefs and their kimono-clad staff stand outside their restaurants holding deep bows until their departing customers have disappeared from view. All are icons of a city that doesn't believe in gratuitous change.

While most cities face the conflict of old versus new, Kyoto has proven adept at synthesising the two. Wooden townhouses that long ago ceased to be practical as living quarters are finding new lives as restaurants, art galleries, coffee shops and hair salons. A one-time kimono warehouse has become a stylish cocktail bar, and a former backstreet bathhouse is now a café furnished with plush sofas and tiled walls. The kimono, a garment as impractical as it is beautiful, is still a normal, everyday sight in Kyoto. The only difference is that these days it might be emblazoned with a Marimekko-style print and paired with split-toe sneakers. On Shijo Street, a dowdy shopping thoroughfare that generates little local affection, the one modern architectural eye-popper is home not to the high-end fashion of a Prada or a Dior, but to Fukujuen, a venerable supplier of finest green tea since 1790, repositioning the hallowed foodstuff for the 21st century.

Kyoto has good reason to be measured in its modernisation. As Japan's capital for over a millennium, it was – and is – the cultural heart of the nation. It is the spiritual home of the tea ceremony, of calligraphy, of both Kabuki and Noh theatre. It is also home to an astonishing 1,600 temples, 400 shrines, an emperor's palace, a shogun's castle and more snap-worthy gardens than anyone has been able to count. Back in 1994,

UNESCO regarded 14 sites in Kyoto as being worthy of World Heritage status; since then, they've found another three. And the only wonder is how they managed to keep the number of designations so low.

This city is the feudal-era fantasy of which visitors to Japan dream, but it is much more than just an archive of old Japan, it is an enviable example of a 21st-century city that's modernising without homogenising.

Nicholas Coldicott

Instant Passport

Population
1,461,000

Area
829sq km

Where is it?
In the midwest of Honshu, Japan's largest island

Climate
Winters are bitterly cold and summers are humid

Ethnic mix
Japanese, Chinese, Korean

Major sights
Kiyomizudera temple, the silver and golden pavilions, Ryoanji's Zen garden, the geisha and maiko (apprentice geisha) of Gion, Fushimi Inari shrine's corridor of vermillion *torii*

Insiders' tips
The bar inside Zen temple Kanga-an, Funaoka Onsen bathhouse, Honke Daiichi Asahi ramen (noodle soup), Ukai Shoten sake shop

Where's the buzz?
Kiymachi, Pontocho, Gion

Proportion of Japan's population
1.2%

Proportion of Japan's National Treasures
20%

Sister cities
Boston, Cologne, Florence, Guadalajara, Kiev, Prague, Zagreb

Oldest restaurant
Honke Owariya soba restaurant, since 1465

Priciest lunch
Kaiseki (formal, multi-course grande cuisine) at Kitcho Arashiyama costs 35,000 yen

UNESCO World Heritage Sites
17

Famous foods
Yodofu (silky tofu), yuba (soy milk skin), vegetables and soba (buckwheat noodles)

Number of years as Japan's capital
1,200

Environmental impact
The 1997 Kyoto Agreement set the first international emissions targets

Major industries
Tourism, kimonos, computer games, cars (both Nintendo and Daihatsu have their headquarters here)

Left: Heian Shinto shrine. Top: left,
Nishiki Market; right, Gion district.
Centre: left, Sanjusangendo temple;
right, Kyoto Tower. Bottom: left, Chi
on-in temple; centre, Kinkakuji

Lisbon

PORTUGAL

A harbour that's in love with its river

Lisbon has always been defined by the River Tagus. The gargantuan estuary into which the Phoenicians sailed almost three millennia ago dwarfs even the sprawling modern city. Even when you're well away from its broad expanse, it remains an unseen presence: its reflections create Lisbon's unique light, and if you travel around town during the day you are likely to see it, even if from a distance, at least once. Tourists who lose themselves in the alleys of the ancient Alfama quarter know they only need head downhill and catch sight of the water to be able to pinpoint their location on a map. Even on the modern avenues inland, the Tagus rules, with the house numbers starting at the end nearest to it.

Dotted around this picturesquely hilly city are *miradouros* – designated lookout points offering dramatic vistas. But even in the most densely packed neighbourhood, a Lisboeta taking a break from dusting can lean out of an upper-floor window and catch a glint of gold in the distance. Bar hoppers in the hilltop Bairro Alto, emerging from its tight grid, let the moon's silvery gleam on the water guide them towards dockside nightclubs.

For centuries, Lisbon prospered thanks to its access to the Atlantic. Caravels set sail from the district of Belém to 'discover' the coast of Africa, Brazil, the sea route to India, and beyond. In the 20th century, as the empire declined, Lisbon remained a busy port – and troop ships carried conscripts off to fight in doomed colonial wars. Over the decades, bustling wharves, ferry stations and container terminals ate up ever more land, Lisbon living 'with its back to the river' as the locals say. The port authority – answerable to national government, not the city – came to control most of the riverfront.

'Lisbon would be nice today, if it weren't a nightmare. My favourite time in Lisbon was 1974 – the second half, of course, after the Portuguese democratic revolution on 25 April'

Jorge Silva Melo filmmaker

Instant Passport

Population
2,250,000

Area
881sq km

Where is it?
On the western coast of Portugal, where the River Tagus flows into the Atlantic Ocean

Climate
Mediterranean: sunny for most of the year with cool, rainy winters

Ethnic mix
Portuguese and other European, Brazilian, Cape Verdean and other African

Major sights
Praça do Comércio waterfront, Miradouro de Santa Luzia, Castelo de São Jorge, Elevador de Santa Justa

Insiders' tips
Eating and drinking at COP'3, Adega dos Lombinhos, chocolate cake at Vertigo, cocktails at Cinco Lounge, poetry at Poesia Incompleta

Where's the buzz?
Cabaret Maxime, Fábrica de Braço de Prata, LX Factory, Fábrico Infinito

Reason the pavements are chequered
Black represents the holy attire of Vincent, Lisbon's patron saint, while white is for the battle dress of the Crusaders who vanquished the Moors

Percentage of population who are Roman Catholic
97%

Symbol of the city
A ship with crows, supposedly following the remains of St Vincent here

Number of people killed in the Lisbon earthquake of 1755
40,000 (it measured 8.9 on the Richter scale)

Roman remains
Roman corridors, bridges, rooms and galleries were discovered beneath the streets of the downtown shopping district after the 1755 earthquake

Most famous export from Olisipo (Roman Lisbon)
Garum, an expensive paste made of fish

Major current industries
Textiles, footwear, leather, furniture, ceramics, cork

Most expensive street
Avenida da Liberdade, 35th most expensive in the world

Named European City of Culture
1994

Longest suspension bridge
25 April Bridge, the third longest in the world, stretching 1,013m

Left: Torre de Belém. Above, top:
Olaias Metro; bottom, Cerve Jeiria
Trinidada. Right: top, Parque das
Nações; centre and right, fado at
Tasca do Chico, Benfica fans

Towards the end of the 20th century, foreign visitors began to discover Lisbon, the only capital on mainland Europe that borders open water; tourism boomed; and it dawned on the authorities that riverside promenades could generate big money, too. Now Lisboetas are eagerly reacquainting themselves with the river. Each summer a fashionable new esplanade opens and alfresco concerts are staged on long-silent wharves. The Cais das Colunas, or 'quay of columns', where travellers used to disembark at the grand Praça do Comércio, re-emerged after years of work on the Metro system, and was instantly mobbed by courting couples and passersby stopping to gaze at the Tagus.

The Portuguese have a word, *saudade*, which means a sad yearning for the return of something that is gone, something that is needed to make one whole. It captures a flavour of Lisbon's relationship with its river.

Alison Roberts

Architecture
7
Arts & Culture
10
Buzz
9
Food & Drink
9
Quality of Life
6
World Status
9
Total
50/60
Rank
2

London

UK

Centre of attention

L ondon is a city that exists on arrogance. A small Roman settlement right at the edge of the continent, it somehow made itself the centre of the world: culturally in 1811, when it was the first Western city to top a million inhabitants; quite literally in 1884, when Greenwich was designated the official Prime Meridian.

People with ambition have always been drawn to London. Global financial institutions fight for a foothold in the City. Retail brands are not considered contenders until they have a flagship in the West End. International talent comes to join theatres, dance companies, orchestras, galleries, football teams. Collectors spend millions through art fairs and private dealers. Students crowd universities and vocational colleges. In return, the city and its suburbs export designs, actors, artists, comedy, films, fashion, TV and rock stars to the rest of the world, while international magazines repeatedly proclaim London the coolest city on earth.

Received wisdom is that Londoners are reserved and unfriendly – avoiding eye contact in public places and brushing dawdlers out of the way in a hurry to get to their next appointment. Yet the city has a history of welcoming outsiders. The area of Whitechapel alone has, over the centuries, assimilated incoming waves of Huguenots, Jews and Bangladeshis, all now bona fide Londoners themselves. As the traditional London of cosy boozers and greasy caffs fades out, a new, equally indigenous culture is evolving where kids of all backgrounds mix Caribbean vowel sounds with Asian slang, where every local high street has a curry house and Vietnamese noodle bar, and where the whole city celebrates Chinese New Year, Diwali and the Notting Hill Carnival.

The city's size allows for anonymity. You can, broadly speaking, be who you want, which has made London fertile ground for youth

PHOTOGRAPHING BRITAIN AT TATE BRITAIN TAKE THE TATE BOAT

Instant Passport

Population
8,278,000 (core city 7,074,000)

Area
1,623sq km

Where is it?
The south-east of England, on the River Thames

Climate
Mild but wildly unpredictable

Ethnic mix
Approximately 77% 'white', 9% Afro-Caribbean, 9% Indian/Pakistani/
Bangladeshi, 5% of other ethnic origin. There are strong Irish, Cypriot,
Vietnamese, American, Antipodean, French, Chinese, Turkish and Polish
communities

Major sights
The London Eye, Tate Modern, Houses of Parliament, Westminster
Abbey, Trafalgar Square and the National Gallery, South Kensington
museums, the British Museum, St Paul's Cathedral, the Tower of London
and Tower Bridge, Royal Botanic Gardens at Kew, National Maritime
Museum and Royal Observatory at Greenwich, Hampton Court Palace

Insiders' tips
Cheshire Street, Marylebone Hight Street, East End art galleries, Geffrye
Museum, stand-up comedy clubs, Bankside and the Southbank Centre,
Battersea Arts Centre, Sir John Soane's Museum, Wellcome Collection,
many free museums and galleries

Where's the buzz?
Brick Lane, Hackney, Hoxton, Camden and New Cross for indie bands,
Vauxhall and Camberwell's gay scene

Theatre box-office receipts
£401 million in 2006

Households officially homeless
21,140 in 2005

Proportion of London that is open space
30%, including 147 public parks or gardens and the eight Royal Parks

Number of black cabs
21,000

Number of pubs
3,800

Number of CCTV cameras a Londoner will be seen by in a day
300. Estimates claim there are close to 4.2 million closed-circuit cameras
watching London

Average distance travelled per person on public transport in a year
2,282 miles

Side of escalator to stand on
Right, and walk down on the left. Only tourists to do otherwise

Experience London like a Londoner

Over 15 inspirational London guides available

TIME OUT GUIDES
WRITTEN BY
LOCAL EXPERTS
visit timeout.com/shop

'This is the best city in the world for music and parties. We've got fantastically creative people who get inspiration from living here and go on to change the world. London's built on a vibrant street culture. Fashion, music, art… it's unrivalled'

Norman Jay DJ

culture and street styles. It is the natural home of eccentrics, resonating with their creative energy.

But London has no right to be so popular. It is an inefficient sprawl of villages, bound together by Victorian terraced housing and concrete estates. Unadventurous clients and planning officials have ensured that, while many of the world's most fêted architects live here, London itself sees little of their work. It has its own muddled beauty, but not the obvious good looks of European capitals such as Paris, Rome or Stockholm. Pride in London's iconic Tube system is crushed by daily evidence that it can no longer cope with demand. Living costs are high, working hours and commutes long, and Londoners stressed.

Arrogance, attitude, ambition. They allowed the city to rebuild itself after the Great Fire of 1666 destroyed 80% of the city, and again after the devastating Blitz bombings of 1940-41. They allowed it to reinvent itself from a shabby, post-industrial town in the 1970s, to become a cultural touchstone for the new millennium.

Around the world, London makes sure it still grabs all the attention. No wonder the rest of Britain resents it.

Jessica Cargill Thompson

Opening page, main picture: the London Eye and South Bank from the air. Previous page, far left: Turbine Hall, Tate Modern. Main group, clockwise from top left: Dublin Castle, Spitalfields Market, Whitechapel Market, Waterloo Bridge, The Big Chill House, London's iconic Tube; Borough Market. This page: Columbia Road flower market

Los Angeles

USA

Hollywood and hidden depths

Los Angeles. To some, the city's name invokes images of Hollywood glamour, jobbing actors, plastic beauties and fame seekers. But there's so much more to this glorious sun-drenched (and smog-ridden) paradise. Those who claim LA is 'superficial and shallow' have never properly immersed themselves in this adult playpen.

As everyone knows, life in LA revolves around the entertainment industry, but it is also a city built on dreams, which gives it the imagination and depth that many accuse it of lacking. Chance upon the Bodhi Tree Bookshop in West Hollywood and you'll find people seeking spiritual solutions. Walk along the beach at sunset and you'll spot people meditating or practising yoga. In a city so filled with celluloid aspirations, the flip side is a populace seeking sanity amid all that fantasy.

LA attracts people from all round the world. People move here attracted by the idea of a better life in blazing sunshine. Among just short of 12 million residents, more than 220 different languages litter the streets, making LA one of the most diverse counties in the United States. This has sometimes been the source of cultural tensions, especially between the Latino and black communities, and full-blooded, born and bred Angelenos can feel like a rarity.

Naturally, some of the clichés are still realised. The coffee shops are filled with Apple Macs and dreaming script-writers. The shift-like nature of the service industry means most waiters genuinely are would-be actors just waiting for a casting. Nearly everyone drives (though there is a much-derided public transport system) and the idea of walking a few blocks is often met with scorn.

Such is the spread-out nature of the city that Los Angeles as a whole lacks a focus. Cruising around in your car, it can be difficult

to get a handle on where things are. There's Santa Monica, Malibu, Venice, Los Feliz, West Hollywood, Koreatown, Hancock Park, Downtown, Hollywood, Studio City, Pasadena, Sherman Oaks, Silverlake, Echo Park… through your tinted windshield, the neighbourhoods roll on and on. En masse they can begin to feel daunting, but appreciate each for its individual vibe and suddenly LA feels like home.

Noam Friedlander

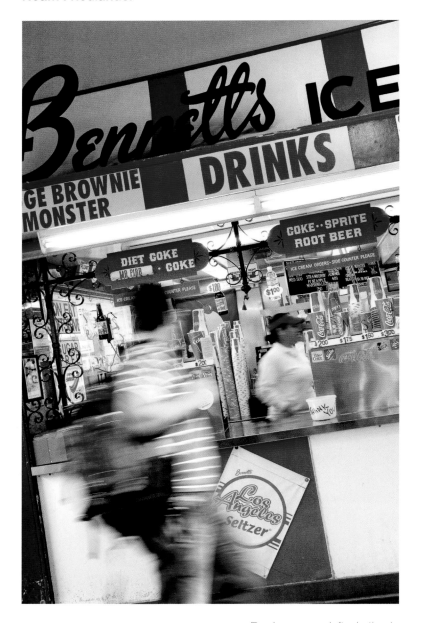

Previous page: left, skating in Santa Monica; right, top, Rodeo Drive. Opposite: top left, drinking on Mulholland Drive; bottom right, hanging in Hollywood

Instant Passport

Population
11,789,000 (core city 3,694,000)

Area
4,320sq km. If the five-county Los Angeles area were a state, it would be the fourth largest in the USA

Where is it?
The south-west corner of North America, in southern California, bordered by the Pacific to the west. There are mountains to the north and east

Climate
The annual rainfall is only 15 inches (38cm), while the average temperature climbs from 9°-20°C in winter to 21°-28°C in summer

Ethnic mix
45% Latino/Hispanic, 31% Caucasian, 12% Asian-American, 10% African-American, 1% Native American

Major sights
Hollywood Walk of Fame, the J Paul Getty Center, the Hollywood sign, Rodeo Drive, Grauman's Chinese Theatre, Sunset Strip, Venice Beach, the Grove, the La Brea Tar Pits, Disneyland, Malibu, the Museum of Contemporary Art, Huntington Library, Griffith Observatory

Insiders' tips
Bodhi Tree bookshop, Franklin Canyon, Mulholland Drive, the view from Skybar at the Mondrian Hotel, the hidden beaches in Malibu, night hikes in Griffith Park, Museum of Jurassic Technology

Where's the buzz?
The vibrant gay scene in West Hollywood, near the intersection of Santa Monica and Robertson; the clubs of Hollywood; a chilled-out hippy environment along Venice Beach; Downtown's modern edge

Founded
1781

Oldest building
Avila Adobe, built as recently as 1818

Money
LA County is the world's 18th largest economy. LA is the largest retail sales market in the United States, making $75 billion in sales in 1996

Airports
Los Angeles International Airport (LAX) is the third largest airport in the world by passenger traffic: more than 61 million travel in or out each year

Sports teams
Clippers and LA Lakers (basketball), Dodgers and Angels (baseball), LA Galaxy (football), LA Kings (ice hockey). It is, however, the largest US city without an American football team in the NFL

Immortalised in
LA Story, *Mulholland Falls*, *Crash*, *The Big Sleep*, *Sunset Boulevard*, *Grease*, *Blade Runner*, *Beverly Hills Cop*, *Dragnet*, *Lethal Weapon*, *Boyz n the Hood*, *White Men Can't Jump*, *Pulp Fiction*, *Clueless*, *Boogie Nights*, *LA Confidential*, *The Big Lebowski*, *City of Angels*, *Laurel Canyon*…

'*Los Angeles. The City of Angels. A beautifully flawed social dichotomy in which Addiction lives next door to Celebrity. Wealth beyond most people's imagination shares real estate with a gang culture born out of desperation. Where Fame and Obscurity discuss the latest screenplay over coffee. Add a few palm trees and blue skies, and you have the wonderfully eclectic melting pot of opportunity that I call home*'

Billy Morrison rock musician with the band Camp Freddy

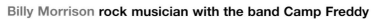

Madrid

SPAIN

Energy, optimism and attitude

Architecture	7
Arts & Culture	7
Buzz	7
Food & Drink	6
Quality of Life	7
World Status	6
Total	40/60
Rank	**12**

Wild-eyed gypsy singers wailing and stomping downstairs at Candela. Matador-of-the-moment José Tomás being carried through the Las Ventas gates on the shoulders of the crowd. Downing brown bottles of manzanilla and tucking into plates of plump green olives at La Venencia. One of the most charming things about Madrid is that the romantic stereotypes have life beyond the tourist trail. The thing is, they're barely a fraction of the story. For that you'd need to add Asturian cider bars, Basque Country pintxo joints, Arab city walls, Latin American grocery shops, Chinese-run convenience stores, Irish pubs, an ancient Egyptian temple – just for starters.

It's a state of affairs to which globalisation is only the most recent contributor. Madrid is a largely artificial city. Though founded by the Moors in the 9th century, it only became the Spanish capital in 1561, after Philip II decided he wanted an administrative centre at the very heart of his kingdom.

The decision utterly transformed the sleepy Castilian hilltown: people flooded in from all over Spain and what little indigenous culture there was got swept away by new mass entertainments, such as public theatre performances and the Inquisition's grisly *autos de fe* (trials of heretics).

Today, there may no longer be ritual public humiliation in the Plaza Mayor (unless you count the street performer statues), but the madrileño habit of doing things en masse endures, whether it's attending the huge Epiphany or Carnival parades down Paseo de la Castellana, taking to the streets in their thousands to mourn the victims of the 2004 bombings, or all choosing the same day to drive off on their summer holidays. It's a big city, but it often feels very small.

Left: view across the Plaza de Cibeles of Madrid's post office, Palacio de Communicaciones, built between 1904 and 1918 by architect Antonio Palacios

Instant Passport

Population
4,900,000 (core city 2,823,000)

Area
945sq km

Where is it?
The centre of the Iberian peninsula, 667m up on the Castilian plateau, the Meseta Central

Climate
Temperate Mediterranean, but the altitude can make winters extremely cold. Summers range from hot to unbearably hot, despite the relative lack of humidity

Ethnic mix
European, Latin America, Asian (mainly Chinese and Filipino), North African, West African, Basque

Major sights
Museo del Prado, Museo Nacional Centro de Arte Reina Sofía, Museo Thyssen-Bornemisza, Palacio Real, the Retiro, Plaza Mayor, Estadio Santiago Bernabéu, Las Ventas bullring, El Rastro flea market, Casa del Campo, Gran Vía, La Latina

Insiders' tips
The gardens of Capricho de la Alameda de Osuna, the 2,200-year-old Templo de Debod from Egypt, La Casa Encendida, Herzog & de Meuron's CaixaForum, the village of Chinchón, El Escorial

Where's the buzz?
The chic bars and boutiques between the boarded-up storefronts and fly-postered walls of Malasaña, the gay bars and clubs of Chueca, multicultural Lavapiés

Historical milestones
Moorish beginnings, Christian conquest, Philip II makes Madrid his capital, the War of Spanish Succession, Napoleonic occupation, Carlist Wars, First Republic, Primo de Rivera's dictatorship, Second Republic, the Spanish Civil War, the Franco years, return to democracy, the Movida Madrileña, the Madrid bombings

Foreign population
1,060,606

Number of visitors a year
6,000,000

Number of rooms in the Palacio Real
More than 3,000

Most famous work of art
Picasso's *Guernica* in the Museo Reina Sofía

Football teams with fervent support
Real Madrid, Atlético Madrid, Getafe, Rayo Vallecano

Immortalised in
Paintings by Goya and Velázquez, *The Hive*, almost every Almodóvar film

'If Madrid has a specific characteristic that differentiates it from other cities of a similar size and importance, it would have to be its inhabitants: the madrileños. From every part of the peninsula or the farthest reaches of the planet, they "Madridify" themselves instantly. Arranged in groups of friends, they are sociable, carefree and vibrantly optimistic. They reckon life begins when they leave work and they devote their lives to having a laugh. They are the soul of this otherwise unimportant city'

Borja Casani former editor of *La Luna* magazine, bible of the Movida

All this helps give the place a vibrant, can-do attitude. The heady days of the Movida, the post-Franco arts movement which took new-found freedoms to their extremes – when magazine editor Borja Casani could hire out the entire chandelier-clad Hotel Palace and host a party for 3,000 hard-drinking, joint-smoking movidistas – may be gone, but the same sense of boundless possibility has now taken more grown-up forms. The vast Richard Rogers-designed airport terminal, the business district's shiny Cuatro Torres ('Four Towers') development and the subterranean road network beneath the River Manzanares are just some of the ambitious building projects that have reshaped the city in recent years. Meanwhile the legendary nightlife raves on around Plaza Santa Ana, grungy Malasaña and gay district Chueca.

Also providing inspiration is that Madrid sky. On more days than not a brilliant cobalt blue, it's influenced Velázquez, Goya and many others whose works now line the Prado walls; sometimes it seems so close you could climb a stepladder and touch it. *De Madrid al cielo* ('after Madrid, there's only heaven'), they say around here, and gazing up into the cloudless blue, an ice-cold caña cradled in your palm, it's hard to disagree.
Nick Funnell

Above: top, Corral de la Pacheca; bottom, tapas bar La Torre del Oro

Manchester

UK

The original industrial city

People – Mancunians and others – talk a lot about Manchester's rebirth after the IRA bomb of 1996. Without it we might never have had Urbis, the glass wedge-shaped museum of urban life. Also, it might not have occurred to anyone to stick a huge outdoor TV screen on the exterior of the Triangle shopping centre, once the Corn Exchange. And we might have had to wait a lot longer for anyone to have a decent crack at redesigning the Arndale Centre, once among the ugliest and least-loved buildings in Europe. The Arndale remains for the most part an undistinguished shopping mall, with an airy and attractive new wing on the north side where you'll find Apple, Waterstone's and a bunch of fashion outlets. Exchange Square, with its outdoor telly, is more of a triangle really, hence the Triangle nomenclature. If you'd tried telling anyone growing up in Manchester in the 1970s that one day they'd be able to sit and watch a TV set the size of a bus in the open air outside the Corn Exchange, you'd have most likely received a two-word answer. But that's precisely what you can do these days, weather permitting, and if it does start to precipitate, for Manchester's reputation as a rainy city remains intact, you can just toddle indoors to spend an hour or two in Harvey Nicks or Selfridges. Or Urbis, for that matter.

Partly as a result of the bomb, Manchester, birthplace of the industrial revolution, now looks and feels like a 21st-century city. It could have been very different. Had the opportunity to rebuild not happened to coincide with the opening of out-of-town retail mecca the Trafford Centre in 1998, it might have been spurned. Furthermore, without the vision of architect Ian Simpson – responsible for much of the new skyline, including landmark buildings such as No.1 Deansgate and Beetham Tower – the city

Architecture	5
Arts & Culture	6
Buzz	5
Food & Drink	2
Quality of Life	7
World Status	3
Total	28/60
Rank	**58**

'I like Manchester. It's a friendly place. An honest and proud, industrious city that's not afraid to embrace change. And yet it's near some of England's most beautiful and unspoilt countryside'

Alex Poots Manchester International Festival Director

could have entered a period of terminal decline. Instead, it's a vibrant centre for shopping and living and dining out and even craning your neck to look up at tall buildings.

The architectural delights of Deansgate notwithstanding, the most interesting part of 'town', as Mancunians call the city centre, is the Northern Quarter. In the 1970s, the Northern Quarter didn't exist. Or it did, but it wasn't called the Northern Quarter. You'd go to Tib Street for the pet shops. Or up Oldham Street to Affleck & Brown's, a posh department store that closed when the Arndale opened and whose name lives on in Affleck's Palace, a three-storey warren of novelty and second-hand clothes stalls, founded in 1982. In the same year across town, the Haçienda, the club that made Manchester officially cool, opened its doors for the first time. Now, with the Haçienda having become a block of flats, you can spend your spare cash on CDs from Vinyl Exchange or on drinks at Night and Day while watching Performance, the best Manchester band since Joy Division. Or you can blow it on vintage threads from Rags to Bitches and catch live jazz at Matt & Phred's.

At the same time it's in the alleys and side streets of the Northern Quarter that you can find traces of the dirty old town of the pre-bomb years. Old ragtrade warehouses fallen into disuse and not yet transformed into loft-style apartments. Extendable iron fire escapes climbing walls that turn these streets into a low-rise New York. It's an interstitial area; businesses sprout but fail to take root. Buildings remain empty. Every city needs its scruffy, ungentrified districts. This is Manchester's most vibrant.

Nicholas Royle

Instant Passport

Population
2,245,000 (core city 430,818)

Area
558sq km

Where is it?
North-west England, in a bowl between the Pennine hills and the Cheshire Plain

Climate
Temperate maritime climate. It rains on average 140 days a year

Ethnic mix
White, South Asian, Indian, Pakistani, Black, Black Caribbean, Black African, East Asian, Chinese

Major sights
Museum of Science and Industry, Manchester Art Gallery, Lowry, Imperial War Museum North, Urbis, Beetham Tower, Town Hall and Central Library

Insiders' tips
Rags to Bitches for vintage clothes, then Bread and Butter tea shop next door; drinks at the Castle Hotel; Band on the Wall; the People's History Museum in Spinningfields; John Rylands Library, for over-the-top Victorian Gothic and priceless treasures; Cornerhouse for independent cinema, contemporary art and a cool vibe

Where's the buzz?
Northern Quarter, Canal Street, Spinningfields, Chorlton

Student population
85,000, the largest in the UK as a percentage of city residents

World's biggest football club
Manchester United

World's richest football club
Manchester City

Famous bands
Joy Division, New Order, the Smiths, Happy Mondays, the Stone Roses, Buzzcocks, Oasis, Elbow, the Tings Tings, Badly Drawn Boy, the Fall

First…
…industrial city in the world (by 1816 it had 86 steam-powered mills), passenger railway station (Liverpool Road, 1830), commercial computer (developed in 1948 at Manchester University by Tom Kilburn and Fred Williams), split the atom (Ernest Rutherford, 1919), test-tube baby born (Oldham General Hospital in 1978), meeting of the Vegetarian Society (1847)

Tallest building
Beetham Tower, Europe's tallest residential building, a 47-storey skyscraper, 168.87m high, completed in 2006

Immortalised in
The Condition of the English Working Class, *24 Hour Party People*, the poetry of John Cooper Clarke, the paintings of LS Lowry, *Hobson's Choice*, *Queer as Folk*, *Shameless*, *The Royle Family*, *Coronation Street*

Previous page: bridges at Castlefield. Opposite: Palace Hotel (formerly the Refuge Assurance Building). This page: top left, Manchester 235; top right, Imperial War Museum North. Above: left, Northern Quarter; centre, Peveril of the Peak. Left: Canal Street. Right: Old Trafford, home of Manchester United

Manila

PHILIPPINES

Chaos made glorious

Architecture	7
Arts & Culture	2
Buzz	4
Food & Drink	2
Quality of Life	3
World Status	3
Total	21/60
Rank	**73**

Manila is a chaotic and spiritual place, dirty and divine, gritty and gorgeous all at once. If you don't find beauty and poetry here, you will never find it anywhere. It's a city that reflects your state of mind, and living here often becomes an intense experience.

Named after a riverside flower and founded by the conquistador Miguel López de Legazpi, Manila – one of the world's largest cities – was once, hard though it may be to believe, just a tiny Muslim village. During three centuries of Spanish rule from 1571, Manila, then known as Intramuros ('within the walls') in Latin, became the seat of Spanish power in the archipelago. Grand government offices controlled the state, while its majestic cathedrals controlled the soul of the islands christened Filipinas (after King Felipe II). The city's wooden walls were replaced by volcanic tuff and its bamboo mosques acceded to seven baroque Catholic churches made out of limestone, hardwood and seashells.

A $20 million treaty following the Spanish-American War transferred the islands to American rule in the late 19th century, causing more major changes in both the size and spirit of Manila. American city planner Daniel Burnham revamped Manila's central core and filled it with government buildings, sprawling lawns, fountains and grand residences. Eventually telephones, ice-cream, toothpaste and Coca-Cola would be introduced to society and Intramuros' southern districts of Ermita, Malate and Pasay would be converted from a row of seaside huts into a civilised collection of art deco and neo-classical structures, connected by wide roads and accented by parks and rotundas.

Then, just as quickly as new buildings and beliefs replaced the old ones, Manila was in transition again. This time it would never

Jeepneys

New York cabs, London double-decker buses, the Tokyo bullet train, Mexico City's green VWs... many cities have distinctive public transport, but nothing can compete with the jeepney. Initially an informal and pragmatic means of re-establishing the public transport infrastructure after it had been destroyed during World War II, the first jeepneys were converted US military jeeps, extravagantly decorated and always overcrowded, the backs of the vehicles having been stripped down to cram in more passengers. The name speaks for itself, once you know that a 'jitney' is an unlicensed taxi. Modern jeepneys are made locally – and subject to increasingly stringent fare regulation and pollution restrictions – but their freewheeling spirit remains, most evidently in the magnificent abundance of chrome and lamps. Today, there are 56,000 operating in Metro Manila.

Instant Passport

Population
14,750,000 (core city 1,654,000)

Area
1,399sq km

Where is it?
On the western side of the largest island in the Philippine archipelago, Luzon, at the mouth of the Pasig River

Climate
Tropical climate, with the wet season lasting from June to November and the dry season lasting from December to May

Ethnic mix
Filipinos (subdivided into Tagalog, Visayan, Ilocano, Bicolano, Kapampangan, Pangasinan and Moro ethnic and ethnolinguistic groups), Chinese, Japanese, Indian, Spanish, American, Korean

Major sights
National Museum of the Philippines, Bahay Tsinoy Museum, Cultural Centre of the Philippines, San Agustin Church, Quiapo Church, Flaming George National Recreation Area, Cuneta Astrodome, Chinatown

Where's the buzz?
Malate for nightlife, Divisoria for market hubbub

Nicknames
Perla del Oriente (Pearl of the Orient), Queen of the Orient, City of Our Affections, City by the Bay, Insigne y Siempre Leal Ciudad (Distinguished and Ever Loyal City)

The country's oldest church
San Agustin Church, built 1607

Languages spoken
Tagalog, English, Hokkien Chinese, Spanish

National hero
José Rizal, a doctor, linguist and writer, executed by the Spanish colonial forces in Manila on 30 December 1896

Number of pairs of shoes owned by Imelda Marcos, widow of former president Ferdinand Marcos, who governed from 1965-1986
About 2,700

Number of municipalities that make up Metro Manila
17

Number of islands that make up the Philippines
7,107

Local cuisine
Dinuguan, kare-kare (oxtail stew), kilawen, pinakbet (vegetable stew), pinapaitan, sinigang (tamarind soup with a variety of pork, fish or shrimp), balut (fertilised egg, boiled with embryonic duckling inside), halo-halo (shaved ice with sweet beans, custard and ice-cream), puto (little white rice cakes), bibingka (rice cake with butter or magarine and salted eggs), ensaymada (sweet roll with grated cheese on top)

Opening picture: Greenbelt Square in Makati District. Right: Fort Santiago in the Intramuros

recover: in 1945 the city's centre – and its soul – were destroyed. More than 120,000 people were killed here during World War II, only the San Agustin Church left standing inside Intramuros.

After the madness of the fighting between the Americans and the Japanese came the madness of reconstruction. From the 1950s onwards, Manila grew at a radical rate. Today, Metro Manila has nearly 15 million inhabitants and sprawls 636 square kilometres across 16 districts. Despite this tremendous growth, Manila has managed to maintain its identity and unique heritage.

It is said that the Jeepney – gaily decorated leftover World War II army vehicles that are still the most popular form of transport here – is a good metaphor for Manila. Are they beautiful or bizarre? Are they inefficient or entrepreneurial? Are they an everyday utility or a progressive work of art?

Maybe Manila is more like halo-halo, the local dessert made from sweet beans, custard, shaved ice and ice-cream. This city is a reflection of how different flavours can make up a greater whole, and how sometimes too much can be a very good thing.
Carlos Celdran

Architecture
6
Arts & Culture
3
Buzz
6
Food & Drink
4
Quality of Life
4
World Status
1
Total
24/60
Rank
67

Marrakech

MOROCCO

Delight in the everyday

Marrakech is, even more than most cities, changing all the time. One old man remembers when there was nothing but an empty stretch of road between the old Post Office in Guéliz and the Koutoubia mosque; now the road, Ave Mohammed V, is the main artery of the new town, lined with buildings and parks. Another woman speaks of how, when she first arrived in town 23 years ago, the roads of the Medina were unpaved, and there were no tourists, just a few straggling travellers.

Since the end of French collonial rule in 1956, but accelerating since the accession of King Mohammed VI in 1999, Marrakech has seen dramatic change. Gated communities are springing up in the outskirts of the city; golf courses are appearing in outlying areas where there were once shanty towns; the shanty towns, in turn, have been pushed even further out.

Moroccans who lived for generations in the Medina, the medieval walled city, have moved out. With them, some older Moroccans say, has gone the life and soul of the city, making the new neighbourhoods busy and bustling, while the smartened up Medina caters to the tourist industry and European incomers buying up the bigger houses.

A so-called refinement of Moroccan life also seems to have taken place. *Hammams*, the traditional public bath houses, were once something of an institution in a city where private houses have little if any running hot water; now many are being converted to spas. *Riads*, townhouses built around a central courtyard and inhabited by large extended families, are becoming boutique hotels; travel outside the Medina is by air-conditioned SUV, though the narrow roads of the Medina itself are still crowded with bicycles, scooters and even donkeys.

Top: left to right, Ksar Es Saoussan, Bahai Palace, Jnane Tamsna, Café des Epices. Bottom: scenes from the souks; right, traditional mint tea

But it is still possible to find the everyday pleasures of living in this city. It may be taking your *tanjia* (a deep clay pot used for cooking lamb an chicken) to the basement shop where there are glowing embers; baking your first bread in the public ovens or *farram*; watching tiles being made; buying cows milk fresh from the pail.

Eating out in the over-priced restaurants is far less satisfying than getting to know the stalls and vendors you like best, stopping and having the best panache (like a smoothie, but better) at Souk Khmiss, or eating great food at some unobtrusive café. Eating great food without all the distracting frills.

Driving around the city on a scooter is also thrilling. Though the traffic at first appears wild and disorderly, you soon learn to work with its ebb and flow, filtering off from main roads, tearing through souks at high speed, taking shortcuts along pavements and across public squares… the anarchy just part of the excitement.

Still the most quintessential Marrakech experience is visiting the local *hammam* in winter. After a week at home without hot water, the sensation when it hits your cold body is a joy: the warm humid air rising up to suffuse you; the vaulted rooms carrying the soft, dull echo of other bathers. It is a ritual of calm and spritual well-being, one of Marrakech's genuine old-fashioned pleasures.
Anna Mzwena

Instant Passport

Population
1,036,500

Area
6.4sq km

Where is it?
South-western Morocco, on a plain 40km from the Atlas mountains

Climate
Sunny year-round, hot summers with little humidity and mild winters with cold nights

Ethnic mix
Arab and Berber, with a large European community consisting mainly of French, Germans, Italians, English, Spanish and Swiss

Major sights
Jemaa El Fna, Ben Youssef Merdersa, souks, Koutoubia Mosque, Saadian Tombs, Badii Palace, traditional tanneries at Bab Debbagh

Insiders' tips
For fresh produce, Sidi Youssef souk; grills in the kasbah, often serving until 3am; seafood at the Bab Doukkala restaurant behind the fish shop

Where's the buzz
The souks, Jemaa El Fna, upmarket shops and fashionable cafés on the rue de la Liberté in Guéliz

Also known as
El hamra ('the red city'). The whole town is a rich salmon pink colour, the mud walls made of the ruddy local soil. Any new building must be coloured the same way

Founded
1062

Came under French rule
1912

Number of mosques
Over 500. A local saying has it that 'at every step there is a mosque'

First female Muslim guides
Mourchidats were introduced in Morocco in 2006. They are permitted to conduct religious discussions, but cannot lead prayers

Typical produce
Leather goods, *babouches* (slippers), carpets, ceramics, lanterns

Superstition
Belief in evil spirits or *jinn* is widespread. Spirits are blamed for a range of ills including bad luck, sudden antisocial behaviour or illness

Traditional dishes
Tagine, couscous, *briouettes* (ouarka pastry filled with meat, rice or cheese and fried), *pastilla* (ouarka pastry filled with pigeon or chicken dusted with cinnamon and sugar), rhgiaf (Moroccan thick pancakes), panache (smoothy-type drink), mint tea

Food stalls at Jemaa El Fna

Early evening in the square sees the arrival of massed butane gas canisters, trestle tables and tilly lamps to form an array of food stalls that together form probably the world's biggest outdoor eaterie. Most stalls specialise in one dish, and between them they offer a great survey of Moroccan soul food.

Several places serve bowls of harira (a thick soup of lamb, lentils and chickpeas flavoured with herbs and vegetables). Similarly popular standbys are grilled brochettes, kefta (minced, spiced lamb) and merguez (spicy sausage; stall no.31 apparently sells the best in Morocco). Families perch around stalls selling boiled sheeps' heads, scooping out jellyish gloop with plastic forks. Elsewhere are deep-fried fish and eels, bowls of chickpeas drizzled with oil, and mashed potato sandwiches, while stalls along the west side have mounds of snails, cooked in a broth flavoured with thyme, pepper and lemon. Humblest of all is the stallholder selling just hard-boiled eggs.

Menus and prices hang above some stalls, but it's easy enough to just point, and prices are so low that they're hardly worth worrying about. Etiquette is basic: walk around, see something you like, squeeze in between fellow diners. Discs of bread serve instead of cutlery. For the thirsty, orange juice is fetched from one of the many juice stalls that ring the square.

Food is fresh and prepared in front of you. Few germs will survive the charcoal grilling or boiling oil, but the dishes are a different matter. The same water is used to wash up all night, so it's safest to ask to be served on paper.

Marseille

FRANCE

Loud, proud and on the up

Born more than 2,000 years ago of a love affair between a young Greek captain and a Ligurian princess, or so the legend goes, Marseille's Vieux Port has all the trappings of a seaside stage where centuries of drama have unfolded under vivid blue skies.

The port has welcomed waves of immigrants fleeing heartbreak in their homelands or simply seeking a better life, the effervescent cultural mix now fuelling a revival on a scale that even the fiercely proud football-loving, pastis-swilling Marseillais can't exaggerate. Long forgotten are the post-war badlands when films such as drug-trafficking blockbuster *The French Connection* shot the city's reputation to pieces. Visitors no longer turn up their noses at this Mediterranean metropolis, where a kaleidoscope of characters declare themselves *fier d'être Marseillais* (proud to be from Marseille).

Hard to beat for sheer authenticity is the hot-blooded *cagole*, the local woman who takes her name from the apron worn by her turn-of-the-century sister, who packed dates for a pittance and sold her charms for a song. Today she can be seen – short skirt, high heels and dripping with jewellery – on the arm of a *cake* (her preening fancy man, fond of gold medallions and open-necked shirts), frequenting the bling-bling cafés of the Vieux Port around the Quai des Belges. She is not to be confused, of course, with playwright Marcel Pagnol's marvellous trio *Marius*, *Fanny* and *César*, who brought everlasting fame to the atmospheric Bar de la Marine on the Quai de Rive Neuve.

In the play, Fanny's mother Honorine sold fish at the market on the Quai des Belges, the setting for the city's superb cuisine. Seagulls circle and fishwives shriek above the traffic, while locals

Above: top, Vieux Port; bottom, a garlic stall on the main boulevard, La Canebière. Right: the huge, gilded Virgin Mary and Child above Notre-Dame-de-la-Garde cathedral

Architecture
6
Arts & Culture
4
Buzz
7
Food & Drink
4
Quality of Life
5
World Status
2
Total
28/60
Rank
58

Left: La Canebière. Top: L'Epuisette seafood restaurant. Right: jazz, blues and rock venue L'Intermédiaire. Far right: Le Corbusier's Cité Radieuse

linger over freshly caught tuna or sardines. The more culinarily ambitious will select at least six varieties required for that most famous of southern dishes: bouillabaisse. Originally a humble meal boiled up by fishermen and their families, this spicy fish soup has grown in sophistication to the point where it is deconstructed by the three-starred Michelin chef Gérald Passédat, or sipped as a milkshake through Lionel Levy's parmesan-coated straw.

Clinging tightly to its other traditions – siesta and soap – the Phocean city is also super-modern, criss-crossed by a gleaming tramway and home to Zaha Hadid's stunning 28-storey glass tower for CMA CGM which has altered the skyline forever. Everywhere, streets are being torn up by the state-financed

Euroméditerrannée project which has renovated the wonderful Haussmann-era apartments on the Rue de la République and successfully tempted film director Luc Besson whose company has built a 14-cinema multiplex next door.

Breathtaking in ambition, the 20-year revamp has yet to reach the Noailles quartier, a fantastic melting pot whose souk-like feel is from a far-away land. Senegalese shop keepers sell the world out of cardboard boxes on doorsteps overflowing with yams from Brazil, peppers from the West Indies and green mangoes from Madagascar. Streets teem with shoppers, the din is deafening, and the easy-going vibe irresistible.

Adrienne Bourgeon

Instant Passport

Population
1,350,000

Area
1,204sq km

Where is it?
Southern France, on the Mediterranean coast between Montpellier and Cannes

Climate
Chilly in winter, scorching in summer and pleasant in between. Hit by the Mistral, the cold wind that blows down the Rhone valley from Northern Europe

Ethnic mix
European, Mediterranean (Greek, Russian, Armenian, Italian, Spanish, Corsican), North African, West African, the Comoros Islands; 25% of the population is Muslim

Major sights
Le Panier and the Vieille Charité cultural centre, Le Corbusier's Cité Radieuse, Notre-Dame-de-la-Garde cathedral, Palais Longchamp, Château d'If and Frioul Islands, the Calanques

Insiders' tips
Quartier Belsunce, Musée de la Mode, Alcazar public library, Cours Julien, Cantini Museum, Velodrome stadium, La Vallon des Auffes

Where's the buzz?
Bars and clubs at La Plaine; pubs, cafés and restaurants along the Vieux Port quays – the Quai de Rive Neuve and Quai du Port

Days per year when the mistral blows
Around 100

Days of sunshine per year
Around 300

Painful past episodes
Great plague in 1720, the bombing of Le Panier by the Germans in 1943

Famous footballer
Zinedine Zidane, who grew up in the northern housing estates, *les quartiers chauds*

Chant of Olympique de Marseille football fans
On craint dégun ('scared of no-one')

Number of *quartiers*
110

Oldest church
Fifth-century St Victor Abbey

Immortalised in
Robert Guédiguian's *Marius et Jeanette* and *La Vie est Tranquille*, the *Taxi* films by Luc Besson, clean-cut soap opera *Plus Belle la Vie,* Alexandre Dumas's *The Count of Monte Cristo*, Jean-Claude Izzo's *Total Kheops*

'When Parisians came here, they were a bit afraid. Now it's the TGV, the second city and all that'
Anonymous hotelkeeper

Architecture	5
Arts & Culture	7
Buzz	7
Food & Drink	7
Quality of Life	9
World Status	3
Total	38/60
Rank	18

Melbourne

AUSTRALIA

Sun, sea and, yes, sophistication

Despite being located on the opposite side of the globe, Melbourne has a wide-eyed hunger for art, culture, food and fashion that is often compared to that of New York City. The capital of the state of Victoria may only be Australia's second largest city (after Sydney), but Melbourne does pack a surprisingly heavy cultural punch.

The city is characterised by its hidden laneways, stencil graffiti sprayed on alley walls, leafy tramlines, obscure bars tucked in unassuming corners and alluring eateries dotted throughout the centre of town. Shopping is key. There's couture clothing at the 'Paris end', independent fashions in Flinders Lane and Little Collins, plus world-class restaurants that make Melbourne one shake European and two shakes original. Food is taken very seriously. The Flower Drum was declared by *New York Times* restaurant critic Patricia Wells to be the best Chinese restaurant in the world for its sensational Peking duck, while other icons such as Vue De Monde wear their Michelin stars with aplomb. The fussiest coffee drinkers down-under live in Melbourne and pride themselves on all that is fashionable and stylishly noir.

Melbourne has long been a breeding ground for creative talent, birthplace of Nick Cave, Cate Blanchett, Germaine Greer, Barry Humphries and Kylie. The arts are nurtured wholeheartedly. The music scene is underground and eclectic, but the city also has highly visible cultural landmarks: the National Art Gallery of Victoria on St Kilda Road, the neo-Gothic buildings of Collins Street and Victorian Gothic churches such as St Paul's Cathedral.

With a long history of immigration, Melbourne is Australia's most ethnically diverse city. It is famed for having the largest Greek community outside Greece, concentrated around Lonsdale Street,

Instant Passport

Population
3,162,000

Area
2,080sq m

Where is it?
On the banks of the Yarra river, close to Port Phillip Bay in Victoria

Climate
Moderate, but famous for its temperamental weather. Melbourne's 'four seasons in one day' supplied the inspiration for a Crowded House song

Ethnic mix
More than a third of the population were born overseas, primarily in Britain, Italy, Greece, China, Vietnam, India and Sri Lanka

Major sights
National Gallery of Victoria, Yarra River, Melbourne Zoo, Melbourne Cricket Ground (the 'G'), Royal Exhibition Buildings and Carlton Gardens

Where's the buzz?
Lygon Street cafés, Collins Street 'Paris end', Carlisle Street in St Kilda East, Fitzroy's Brunswick Street for bohemian and rock scenes, Northcote's High Street

Insiders' tips
Free nightclubs such as Mother's Milk on the Windsor end of Chapel Street, rooftop drinks at Madame Brussels, alfresco cinema at Cookie

Tallest skyscraper
At 253m, the Rialto Towers are the Southern Hemisphere's tallest office, with a 360° observation deck

Number of tram stops
1,813. The longest tramway system outside Europe, with 244km of track

Home to Australian Rules Football
Invented in 1858 by HCA Harrison and Thomas W Wills, supposedly to keep cricketers fit during winter

World's first eight-hour day
Right won by stonemasons in 1856. Now celebrated as a public holiday

World's first full-length feature film
The Story of the Kelly Gang, screened at the Athenaeum Theatre on 26 December 1906. Ned Kelly was from Melbourne

Vegemite invented
1922, by Fred Walker and Cyril Callister. Every jar of Vegemite since has come from the Melbourne factory at Fisherman Bend

Bushfire season
November-April. Hot, dry, windy days are often declared days of Total Fire Ban (TFB). Victoria's worst bushfire, in February 2009, killed 210 people

Immortalised in
Chopper, *Romper Stomper*, *Dogs in Space*, *Love & Other Catastrophes*, *Neighbours*, *Kath & Kim*, *The Secret Life of Us*, *Prisoner Cell Block H*

as well as strong Italian, Chinese and Jewish connections forged in the 1950s after World War II. Consequently, there's a wild mix of cuisines on offer. At Queen Victoria Market, fishmongers shout the daily specials in one corner, while crusty French breads and creamy cheeses tempt your tastebuds in the food hall at the other.

The city centre is laid out in a grid pattern, drawn up in 1837 by Robert Hoddle and giving an orderly feel to the otherwise brooding city. But it was during the 1850s gold rush that Melbourne boomed from a provincial town into a world city of fine colonial architecture. Its main station, Flinders Street, is a grand Edwardian building that became a symbol of the city, its clocks the default meeting place for Melbourners. Modern additions to the cityscape range from the 36-storey Republic Tower to kooky Federation Square.

Melbourne's much-envied, laid-back lifestyle is found in suburbs such as St Kilda Beach – a south-side favourite for those of the glamour set who need to live near water. The bohemian core is on the north side – Brunswick East, Carlton North, Northcote and Fitzroy, oozing a pre-2003 Williamsburg, Brooklyn, kind of cool for artists, musicians and poets.

Melbourne isn't about being fast-paced; the people who flock here tend to come to embrace its tolerant nature, to lap up its art, fashion and food, or to seek inspiration. It always has something interesting tucked up its sleeve.

Jane Rocca

Mexico City

MEXICO

Beyond a bad reputation

A persistent reputation for crime and pollution has kept Mexico City's charms under wraps for all but the most intrepid city lovers. Though the problems this immense, high-altitude metropolis faces are real, the impression with which many first-time visitors arrive – of a dirty, dystopian, unmanageable megacity – gives way, by the time they leave, to memories of a charming, hospitable and historic city that's steeped in tradition.

That sense of the past permeates the old-town city centre, where pre-Columbian archaeological treasures nestle in situ beside architectural jewels from colonial times and classic *cantinas*. It reaches along the grand avenue that runs through the city, the Paseo de la Reforma, under the gaze of statues that include Christopher Columbus and Cuauhtémoc, the last Aztec emperor, Diana the huntress, and the Angel of Independence – the latter a focal point for Mexico City's incessant, varied demonstrations and celebrations, and for the bats that whirl around the winged golden statue at night as the ceaseless traffic circles below.

Away from the downtown statuary and architectural grandstanding, children in pedal cars squeak along shady forest paths in lush, damp Parque México in the heart of Condesa, one of the city's most atmospheric neighbourhoods. In nearby Roma, grand, crumbling houses line picturesque streets that are at once elegant and seedy, studded with art galleries and dotted with hip restaurants, inviting cafés and buzzing street food stands. It can be hard to feel you are in a city of almost 18 million here, where there is space to breathe and circulate and where, in springtime, green parks and plazas meet riotous purple jacaranda blossom.

The sprawling, crowded, working-class Tepito neighbourhood gives a better sense of the scale and density of Mexico City, as

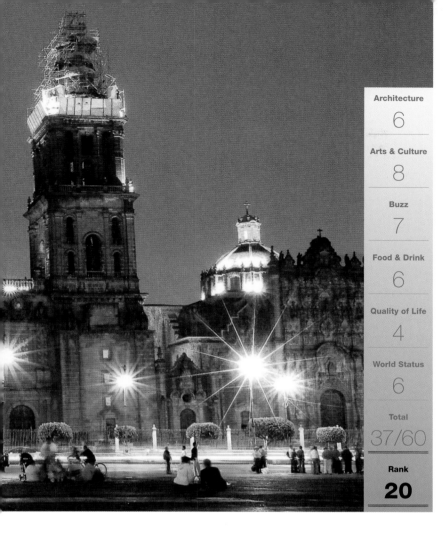

Architecture	6
Arts & Culture	8
Buzz	7
Food & Drink	6
Quality of Life	4
World Status	6
Total	37/60
Rank	20

'The Centro is the most diverse wasps' nest I know beside Kolkata. It's full of surprises and always open to rediscovery. For me, Fermín Revueltas's Virgin of the Guadalupe mural at the Antiguo Colegio de San Ildefonso says it all: an atheist artist painting a symbolic virgin linked to the fight for independence is totally Mexico City'

Paco Taibo crime writer

Top: Catedral Metropolitana. Above: Campo Marte

does the busy Centro Histórico, its old-fashioned streets rather reminiscent of Quito and perhaps even of Cusco. From a vantage point high above the Zócalo, the imposing main square, you can trace the long urban horizon into the distance towards shining Popocatépetl, the snow-capped volcano that still belches occasional bulges of grey smoke and ash. The volcano – along with its twin, Ixtaccíhuatl – was once visible from downtown, but is now masked by the dense smog that still plagues the city. Pollution has improved since its nadir in the 1980s, but there are still days on which the smoky amber air hangs heavy and low, and when taking vigorous exercise is discouraged by the authorities for health reasons.

With crime, heavy traffic and water shortages just a few of the other problems still facing this, one of the world's largest metropolitan areas, Mexico City is an unapologetically complicated place, neither all good nor all bad; it's just a city, but one with a dozen assets to offset every drawback, and a mass of modest, friendly, delightfully hospitable inhabitants to offset every rogue and crook.
Claire Rigby

Instant Passport

Population
17,400,000 (core city 8,235,000)

Area
2,072sq km

Where is it?
Dominated by the volcanic peaks of Popocatépetl and Ixtaccíhuatl, Mexico City is in the Valley of Mexico in central Mexico

Climate
Colder than the rest of the country, due to the altitude (2,240m), with rain often starting mid-afternoon during coastal hurricanes (May to October)

Major sights
Templo Mayor, Museo de Antropología, Museo Nacional de Arte, Bosque de Chapultepec, Alameda, Palacio Nacional, San Ángel, Coyoacán, Catedral Metropolitano, Palacio de Bellas Artes, Xochimilco Ecological Park, Basílica de Guadalupe

Where's the buzz?
Restaurants, bars and boutiques in fashionable Condesa and Roma; the bustle and colour of the Centro Histórico and the magnificent Zócalo; the colonial streets of Coyoacán

Insiders' tips
Lucha libre (Mexican masked wrestling); old-school cantinas like Salón Cantina La Mascota; a michelada (cold beer with salt and lime); sprawling, lush Chapultepec Park to escape the stress of the city

Where to watch *lucha libre*
Arena Naucalpan, Arena México, Arena Coliseo

Estimated number of metres the city has sunk in the last 100 years
Nine; it is sinking more rapidly than Venice

Year the Spanish conquistador, Hernán Cortés, set eyes on Tenochtitlán (Aztec name for what is now Mexico City)
1519

Number of *pre-contingencia* ('pollution crisis' days) in 2007
Four; between 1990 and 1994, ozone levels on four out of every five days triggered a *pre-contingencia*

Litres of tequila exported in 2008
150 million

Best for ice-cream
Nevería Roxy (founded in 1946)

Host of the football World Cup Finals
1970 and 1986

Number killed in 1985 earthquake
10,000; another 30,000 were injured and 6,000 buildings destroyed

Immortalised in
Carlos Fuentes' *Where the Air is Clear*, *Amores Perros*, *Los Olvidados*, *Nosotros los Pobres*, Kerouac's *Tristessa*, *Y Tu Mamá También*

Opposite: Paseo de la Reforma.
Top: left, Auditorio Nacional;
right, Xochimilco. Centre left:
Parque México. Bottom left:
Los Portales de Tlalpan

Miami

USA

A flashy, splashy adult sandbox

As much as Miami is a place full of hip, hype, pomp and circumstance, as much as Miami is sat on the verge of an urban explosion – or, as some sceptics would have it, an implosion – it just isn't a city in the way that New York, Paris or London are cities. Miami is a sprawling expanse of sand, palm trees, highways, urban and suburban enclaves. It is a benchmark for the 21st-century incarnation of the city known as the high-rise condo. Add to that a small-town atmosphere and you've got what could well be the single most oxymoronic place in America.

And delightfully so. It wasn't until the late 1980s and early '90s that Miami finally emerged, as it had previously for a brief time back in the fabulous '50s, as something other than a beachy retirement community. Thanks to TV show *Miami Vice*, the city was seen as a sexier version of *Scarface*, where drug runners and dealers ruled – along with corrupt politicians – in pastel blazers and shoes without socks.

Eventually the pastel blazers gave way to a splashier, flashier fashion explosion by the name of Gianni Versace, who saw an opportunity during Miami's nascent, not-yet-hip stage to use the city's backdrop of sex and sun for selling his flashy threads. With Versace came the models and Madonna, and that was the beginning of what was once known as the American Riviera, Miami's first, fabulous moniker of over two decades ago, a time locals like to refer to as the city's halcyon days.

Rents were cheap and creative arty loafers contributed to an explosion of hedonism, fuelled by a party-all-the-time mentality in which 'society' was a term loosely left to be defined by the so-called 'velvet mafia' – the dapper gang of VIPs who had the

Architecture	6
Arts & Culture	4
Buzz	4
Food & Drink	6
Quality of Life	6
World Status	4
Total	30/60
Rank	51

'Miami loves to party. We party to celebrate when something good happens, such as winning the World Series, which we do, like clockwork, every six years. When something bad happens, we party to cheer ourselves up. When nothing is happening, we party because we are bored. If Fidel ever dies, Miami will not regain consciousness for decades'

Dave Barry **humorist and writer**

power to part the red ropes and live out their very own Studio 54 fantasies in a haze of dry ice, Absolut and, of course, Versace.

After the designer's untimely death – shot on his own doorstep by Andrew Cunanan on 15 July 1997 – the city was left with a void that was eventually filled by a bountiful crop of boutique and luxury hotels, swanky restaurants and the swarm of a new crop of celebrities in the form of hip hoppers, rappers and Paris Hilton. The American Riviera adopted its new nickname of Bling Beach and continued to evolve into a city where style and money, lots of it, ruled over substance.

But that was then. Miami today is a very different city. Hedonism is still an affliction suffered gladly by many, but the city has also suffered through several identity and economic crises, trying to keep its Riviera reputation fresh and fabulous. What was once a place devoid of culture beyond its obvious Latin roots had become a city with a burgeoning arts scene – showcased annually in the prestigious Miami version of Switzerland's swankier-than-thou Art Basel. Miami has finally become a place where you can party with tabloid stars and starlets until the wee hours of the morning and then shake off your hangover, shower off the vapidity and catch a renowned author waxing intellectual on something or other. And then do it all over again the next night. Or take in a show at the multimillion-dollar Adrienne Arsht Center for the Performing Arts, the Cesar Pelli designed white elephant in downtown Miami that cost a fortune but forgot to build a car park. Only in Miami. At least we now have a cultural centre.

Previous page: Ocean Drive, heart of Miami's Deco District. Top right: Emmanuel Perrotin Gallery. Above and bottom right: Lummus Park Beach. Far right: Roberto Behar and Rosario Marquardt's Living Room in the Design District

As much as South Beach has been evolving, the rest of the city – Coconut Grove, Coral Gables and the domino-playing old Cuban men in Little Havana – remains steeped in old Florida tradition, architecture and history. The vast wasteland known as downtown is still waiting for the much-discussed moment when developers and planners transform it into a bustling city centre. Real-estate developers jumped on the Miami bandwagon like a pack of ravenous wolves, scrambling to change Miami's majestic but meagre skyline with sleek and chic high-rise condos aimed at the international jet-set crowd. Such optimism has been defeated by the economic bust to the point where TV news programme *60 Minutes* dubbed Miami the 'Repo Riviera' in late 2008. The skyline has been left full of empty apartment buildings, much like the city's unspoken mantra: if you build the style, eventually the substance will come.

If it doesn't, at least it all looks pretty on the outside.

Lesley Abravanel

Instant Passport

Population
4,919,000

Area
2,891sq km

Where is it?
On the southern coast of Florida

Climate
Hot, humid. Winter air is warm, dry and pleasant, but summer gets very hot and unpleasantly humid during the day, remaining sultry at night. Hurricanes can be expected between June and November

Ethnic mix
Latin American, South American, European, Russian, New Yorkers, Midwesterners

Major sights
South Beach, Art Deco District, Vizcaya Museum and Gardens, Coconut Grove, Coral Gables, Venetian Pool, Freedom Tower, Little Havana, Miami Design District, Museum of Contemporary Art, Jungle Island, Miami Seaquarium

Insiders' tips
Jimbo's on Key Biscayne, the El Credito Cigar Factory in Little Havana, city tours led by Dr Paul George, a fascinating human encyclopaedia of the history and assorted vices of Miami

Where's the buzz?
Until downtown Miami emerges as a hotbed of hipster activity, the boho galleries, furniture showrooms and – increasingly – restaurants, lounges and cafés of the Design District and Wynwood Arts District

Exports
Gloria Estefan, freestyle and rap, nightlife, bottle service and tan lines

Historical milestones
Granted city status (July 1896), draining of the Everglades, Fidel Castro takes power in Cuba and 100,000 Cubans take refuge in Miami, the Mariel Boat Lift, Elián González, *Cocaine Cowboys*, *Scarface*, *Miami Vice*, Hurricane Andrew

Tallest building
Four Seasons Hotel

Number of art deco buildings on Miami Beach
960

Place not to take your mother
World Erotic Art Museum

Percentage of the population South Beach that claim they are models
65%

Immortalised in
Eco-thrillers by Carl Hiaasen, *Scarface*, *Miami Vice*, *CSI: Miami*, *Nip/Tuck*, *Miami Rhapsody*, *Cocaine Cowboys*, *The Birdcage*, Will Smith's *Miami*, Jerry Lewis in *The Bellboy*, *Get Shorty*

Architecture	4
Arts & Culture	5
Buzz	5
Food & Drink	4
Quality of Life	5
World Status	5
Total	28/60
Rank	**58**

Milan

ITALY

Fashion, furniture and football

Very few people come to Milan by choice. The city makes no effort to compete with Rome, Florence or Venice for the title of most beautiful or well-loved city in Italy. It doesn't even go out of its way to be likeable.

And yet, despite the gruff exterior, the city offers much that is unique, and most people leave before they are ready. Business people who come to work regret having booked themselves on the first flight back. The mini-break couple who came for a weekend, far from running out of things to do as they expected, instead run out of time. 'If only we'd known,' they all say. Bereft at the airport, they promise to come back. And they do.

The city grows on you. Part of the country's industrious North, there's a lively business community, manufacturing expertise, creative zeal, an enthusiastic approach to innovation, and a cosmopolitan atmosphere that helps people feel at home in a way that other Italian cities don't.

Milan is small. Compared to Rome, very small; compared to London, tiny. Most of the landmarks are within walking distance of the centre. The public transport system is efficient. Compared to Rome, very efficient indeed.

There isn't the architectural unity of Florence, but once you leave behind the wide modern roads you find a world of narrow streets, 17th-century palaces, pretty piazzas and delicate terracotta churches. Take a stroll in the Galleria Vittorio Emanuele, visit the Castello Sforzesco, admire the mosaics in the beautiful Basilica Sant'Ambrogio, or window shop in luxury goods stores in the Quadrilatero della Moda ('fashion rectangle').

In the past, the city has been influential enough to attract Leonardo da Vinci to paint his *Last Supper* for the church of

Galleria Vittorio Emanuele II

The magnificent, glass-roofed Galleria Vittorio Emanuele II isn't known as *il salotto di Milano* ('Milan's living room') for nothing: the upper echelons of Milan society all pass through here at some point. The Galleria's designer, Giuseppe Mengoni, pioneered its complex marriage of iron and glass two decades before the Eiffel Tower was built. However, when it was officially opened in 1867 by Vittorio Emanuele II, king of a newly united Italy, a sour twist of fate meant that Mengoni wasn't present. He had fallen to his death from his own creation just a few days earlier.

The ceiling vaults are decorated with mosaics representing Asia, Africa, Europe and America, while at ground level are further mosaics of more local concerns: the coats of arms of Vittorio Emanuele's Savoia family, and the symbols of Milan (red cross on white), Rome (she-wolf), Florence (iris) and Turin (bull). If you can't see Turin's symbol, look out for the tourists spinning on their heels on the bull's privates – it's said to bring good luck.

Fashion flagships radiate out from Prada and Louis Vuitton in the centre, statuesque shop assistants operate the tills, suited businessmen happily pay €10 for a cappuccino on Zucca's terrace, elegant grandmothers carry their chihuahuas in Fendi bags, and a volley of new designer cafés are on hand to serve the Prosecco pick-me-up that pre-lunch shoppers need.

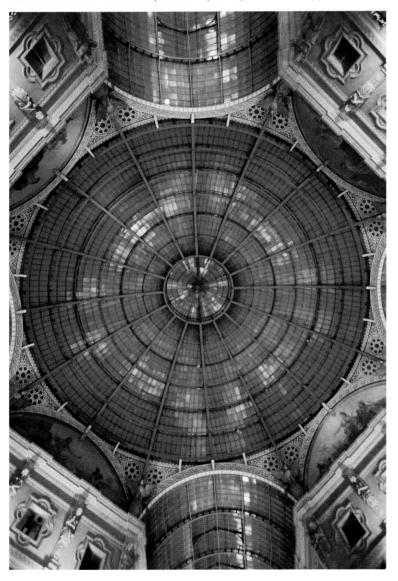

Instant Passport

Population
4,250,000 (core city 1,305,000)

Area
1554sq km

Where is it?
In the Po valley of northern Italy, with the Alps to the north and the Appenines to the south-west

Climate
Hot humid summers, but bitter winter winds blow from the Alps. Plagued by thick fog due to its valley location

Ethnic mix
98.5% white European, 1% Asian, 1% African, 0.5% American. It's hard to find a native-born Milanese in Milan, however: as Italy's business capital, it's a magnet for young professionals from all over the country

Major sights
Duomo, Galleria Vittorio Emanuele, La Scala, Pinacoteca di Brera, Leonardo da Vinci's *Last Supper* in Santa Maria delle Grazie, Castello Sforzesco, Basilica Sant'Ambrogio, Basilica San Lorenzo, Portinari chapel, Santa Maria presso San Satiro for the Bramante trompe l'oeil

Insiders' tips
Corso di Porta Ticinese for up-and-coming fashion designers, Achille Castiglioni's studio, happy hour at the Bulgari hotel, summer bars at public swimming pools, a Roman bath at Acquae Calidae spa, family mansions donated to the city (Bagatti-Valsecchi Museum, Poldi Pezzoli Museum, Casa-Museo Boschi di Stefano)

Where's the buzz?
Via Montenapoleone, via della Spiga, via Sant'Andrea, via Verri, corso di Porta Venezia, Galleria Vittorio Emanuele

Number of boutiques in the fashion rectangle
Via Montenapoleone, 85; via della Spiga, 77

Number of exhibitors at the annual Milan Furniture Fair
More than 1,650, plus 200 off-site exhibitions

Tallest building
Pirelli Tower, designed by Gio Ponti and Pier Luigi Nervi

Capacity of the San Siro stadium
85,700. The second largest football stadium in Europe, it is also known locally as Stadio Giuseppe Meazza

Historical milestones
Edict of Milan, Ambrosian liturgy, foundation of the *Corriere della Sera* newspaper, La Scala, Thomas Edison, Liberty (Italian art nouveau), the Futurist art movement, Triennale di Milano

Named after Milan
Millinery

When in San Francisco
See the Milan trams (1928 vintage) on the Market Street line

Previous page: the Duomo. Above: top, Corinthian columns outside San Lorenzo Maggiore church. Bottom: left, high fashion in the *Quadrilatero d'Oro*; right, Central Station

Santa Maria delle Grazie, and for Thomas Edison to choose it as the location for the first electric street lighting and first electric tram.

The city has maintained its global reach: in the 20th century, architect Gio Ponti helped shape European modernism through his magazine *Domus*; fashion houses such as Prada, Gucci and Versace have become bywords for contemporary glamour; the annual Salone Internazionale del Mobile ('furniture fair') is the acknowledged highlight of the design world calendar. In addition, the city boasts one of the world's most revered opera houses – La Scala – and one of its legendary football stadia, the San Siro, home to both Inter and AC Milan.

The lack of obvious sights fails to attract guide-clutching tourists but, especially for its residents, life in Milan is very rewarding.
Roberta Kedzierski

Moscow

RUSSIA

Hard times where smiles are rare

A born Muscovite is a rare bird in our growing, cosmopolitan city, and a *moskovskaya propiska* (the passport mark used in Soviet times to control population movement) still a prized possession. Though natives are often snobbish towards 'first-generation Muscovites', they are also less prone to the bouts of shameless breast-beating consumerism that is often characteristic of ambitious provincials who came to the capital to seek success and found some. The latter are responsible for the fact that in the centre of town, it's easier to buy a pair of Prada shoes than a sandwich, and the 3am traffic jams of pimp-style Hummers and Lamborghinis that clog Tverskaya, the city's main street and shopping artery.

It is duly noted that, in general, the people of Moscow are rude and unfriendly. Indeed, the sea of grey and black clothes and unsmiling faces on a cold winter day can be quite depressing, and a single encounter with the dreaded Sphinx of every official institution, from a museum to a Metro ticket desk or a local council, an elderly woman with microscopic power which she likes to abuse at every little opportunity, can turn an unprepared visitor from our city forever.

This is a very fast, tough and demanding city, and in order to cope it is necessary to shut oneself in an emotional shell. In fairness to Muscovites, the lack of smiles on the street is understandable. But inside these shells are some of the nicest people you'll ever meet.

Likewise, the city itself can seem inhospitable: insane traffic, bad air, architectural styles that range from boring to kitsch. But again, behind its official façade, the city reveals its true charm and beauty. Everyone knows the tourist favourites such as Red Square,

Architecture	4
Arts & Culture	7
Buzz	7
Food & Drink	4
Quality of Life	4
World Status	8
Total	34/60
Rank	**34**

Left and above: utilitarian residential architecture in suburban Moscow. Above: centre, Easter celebrations at St George's church in Koptevo

Left: Indus restaurant. Above: UK Style. Right: a new Light Metro line in the southern suburb of Butovo. Opposite: Shanti – restaurant by day, techno bar at night

St Basil's Church and the Kremlin, but what about the things that really inspire affection for the city? From the Sparrow Hills (Vorobyovi Gori) viewpoint you can play a game of 'spot all seven of Stalin's wedding cakes' – the nickname given to seven skyscrapers commissioned by Stalin and built in a very recognisable style of totalitarian Gothic/Baroque. You may, however, miss the most dramatic, as it is right behind you – the majestic Moscow State University's main building, one of the tallest academic buildings in the world. From here, the maze of footpaths that run down the steep slope provide immediate relief from the intimidating grandeur of Moscow's landmarks, offering the friendship of landscape on a more human scale.

In spite of its reputation for drabness, Moscow does offer the odd splash of colour and ornamentation. The Central Palace of Young Pioneers, now a youth centre, is adorned with giant mosaics intended to inspire younger Soviet generations. You'll find them even in the most unpromising places, like artist Alexander Deyneka's 34 mosaics on the ceiling of Mayakovskaya metro station A sign of the city granting a reluctant smile. **Alexey Kovalev**

'Moscow is extremely noisy and busy. Every day something changes. One day you're walking past a typical Old Town street with small cosy houses, tomorrow there's a construction site. Maybe it's too rough, but I still like it'

Alexey Chadov **actor**

Instant Passport

Population
10,500,000 (core city 8,297,000)

Area
2,150sq km

Where is it?
On the banks of the Moskva River in the Central Federal District of Russia

Climate
Continental: Moscow is on the same latitude with Edinburgh and Toronto. Winters are long, with February the coldest month, but temperatures rarely drop below -15°C. The best months are May and September

Ethnic mix
Russians, Ukrainians, Belarussians, Azeris, Armenians, peoples of Northern Caucasus and Middle Asia (Chechens, Tadjiks, Uzbeks, etc), Jews, Gypsies and many others

Major sights
St Basil's Cathedral, Tretyakov Gallery, Red Square, Kremlin, Moscow State University

Insiders' tips
The central Moscow Metro stations are universally recognised as architectural masterpieces; vodka drunk the traditional way, with a hot rich soup like borsch or Caucasian hartscho, at U Nikitskikh Vorot, a cult Soviet-style boozer; a sweaty *banya* at the Krasnopresnenskie

Where's the buzz?
Tverskaya Street, Tretyakovsky Proyezd, Volts, Tons, Jazztown

A brief history of communist Russia
1848 publication of the *Communist Manifesto* (in London, in German), Bolshevik Revolution, named capital of Soviet Russia in 1918, Battle of Moscow (1941-42), *perestroika* (political and economic restructuring) 1986; final collapse of Soviet Union 1991

Coldest recorded temperature
-42.2°C in January 1940

Heaviest snowfall
January 2005, precipitation of 9.4mm

Earliest reference
1147 in the *Ipatievskaya Chronicle*

Tallest building
Naberezhnaya Tower C, 268m (59 floors)

Vodka consumption
70% of the total alcohol consumed in Russia

Famous writers
Alexander Pushkin, Leo Tolstoy, Fyodor Dostoevsky

Immortalised in
War and Peace, Andrei Bely's Moscow trilogy, *The Master and Margarita*, *Gorky Park*, *Red Heat*, Boris Akunin's Erast Fandorin novels

Main picture: a train colourfully
decorated for the Hindu festival
of Dasara. Top left: Marine Drive

Architecture	4
Arts & Culture	6
Buzz	10
Food & Drink	6
Quality of Life	3
World Status	7
Total	36/60
Rank	25

Mumbai

INDIA

No room left, but still they come

This city has some nerve – holding on to 15 million people; squeezing them all into small apartments, small cars and even smaller cubicles; letting them stand head-to-armpit every day in crowded railway compartments; making them work round the clock; and still getting them to think they're the luckiest people on earth.

Mumbai is that kind of city. Every street corner offers an opportunity for profit. Entrepreneurs support families of six on their pavement snack-stall business. Swish hotels like the Four Seasons rise out of slums, reserving lower floors for service areas and letting guests look out to better views on the floors above. Stylish boutiques operate out of former garages, and little boys make big bucks from minding people's shoes outside temples. If you elbow hard enough, Mumbai will let you get to the top.

Of course there are too many people. Of course they're all going in the direction you're going, no matter where you're headed, and at what hour of the day or night. Of course someone will be in your way. Mumbai is tiny, a little tongue sticking out of the west side of the Indian peninsula. More than 800 people come to the city every day, and every day there's a little less room for you.

But everybody makes do, and there's fun to be had while doing it. Plump housewives have shopped their way through the economic slowdown, buying everything they didn't need from new malls and hypermarkets. 'Fine dine' is the phrase of the moment, with cocktail bars and multi-cuisine restaurants opening every other week. Multiplexes play out young urban stories made by young urban crews for a young urban audience. Mumbaikars are starting to understand just what it feels like to be home to

'Mumbai now, Bombay then, had always been a fascinating city and it still is. It wakes you up in the morning, pushes you out of the bed and demands that you get going'

Amitabh Bachchan actor

cutting-edge art, cinema, design, theatre and music. They're buying up city-inspired kitsch, originally intended for tourists, and learning to laugh at themselves. They're even starting to look beyond themselves, rallying after November 2008's terror attacks and forming civic groups to reclaim public space, deal with religious fundamentalists and outwit bureaucrats.

They're also standing on nothing more than a reclaimed archipelago of seven islands. Mumbai – ruled by Ashoka in 300 BC, Raja Bhimdev in the 13th century, ceded to the Portuguese by Bahadur Shah in 1534 and disposed of to Britain as part of Catherine of Braganza's dowry to Charles II in 1661 – didn't

become a city until the British reclaimed lands and erected a township in the century that followed. And it didn't become a manic, fast-paced metropolis that sets the pace for India until after Independence in 1947. Rivers have been choked, mangroves cleared and forests denuded to accommodate its shiny new office complexes, apartment buildings and department stores. The city floods every monsoon, reminding everyone just who's boss. But eventually the rain clouds part, and Mumbai's millions roll up their trousers, hike up their saris and wade through the waters to work. After all, what good is a city of dreams if you spend the day in bed?
Rachel Lopez

Instant Passport

Population
14,350,000 (core city 9,925,000)

Area
484sq km

Where is it?
Capital of the state of Maharashtra, built across seven islands on the west coast of India, jutting into the Arabian Sea. Official name changed from Bombay to Mumbai in 1995

Climate
Tropical. Short, comparatively cool winter, otherwise hot all year. Severe monsoons from mid June to October

Ethnic mix
Maharashtrians, Gujaratis, Tamils, Punjabis, Parsis

Major sights
Gateway of India, CST Railway Station, Dhobhi Ghat, Elephanta Caves, Rajabai Tower, Amitabh Bachchan's bungalow, Dharavi, Marine Drive

Insiders' tips
International bands at Blue Frog, thalis at Thakers, south Indian meals at Mani's Lunch Home, Iranian-style berry pulao (fragrant rice with chicken or mutton) at Britannia Café, Mughlai menus at Kebabs and Curries, seafood at Trishna, chaat (sweet-sour crispy snacks) at Juhu Beach, pav bhaji (spiced puréed vegetables with bread) at Sardar, vada pav (potato patties in a bun) from the nearest street vendor

Where's the buzz?
Railway stations, cinemas on the first day of a big release, Chowpatty and Juhu beaches, Bandra's hip little restaurants and bars, Leopold's bar and restaurant in Colaba, the Marine Drive and Carter Road Promenade seafronts after sunset, strolling through Oval Maiden on a Sunday

Record annual rainfall
3,452mm (1954). Mumbai has the most monsoon rain in India

Percentage of the population living in slums
55% (including 44% of Mumbai's police officers)

Tiffins carried a day
Up to 200,000 of these ubiquitous metal boxes, containing a hot lunch, taken by tiffinwalas from workers' homes in the suburbs to their offices

Films produced annually by Bollywood's film industry
Approximately 900

Bollywood stars
Amitabh Bachchan, Aishwarya Rai, Shah Rukh Khan, Aamir Khan, Hrithik Roshan, Kareena Kapoor, Priyanka Chopra, Saif Ali Khan

Solutions most likely to change Mumbai, least likely to be ready on time
Bandra-Worli Sea Link, Ghatkopar-Versova Metro

Immortalised in
Midnight's Children, *Satanic Verses*, *Salaam Bombay*, *Lage Raho Munna Bhai*, *Deewar*, *Satya*, *Bombay Talkie*, *Slumdog Millionaire*

Opposite: top left, Dome rooftop bar-restaurant; top right, an idol of Ganesh; bottom left, Mirchi market at Dadar station. Above: celebrations of the Hindu festival of Krishna Janmashtami

Architecture
5

Arts & Culture
4

Buzz
7

Food & Drink
8

Quality of Life
5

World Status
1

Total
30/60

Rank
51

Naples

ITALY

Seeking sanity amid the madness

Few cities in the world have a location as picture-perfect as Naples. The islands of Capri, Ischia and Procida float in the bay, the Sorrento peninsula shimmers in the distance, and Mount Vesuvius, Europe's only active mainland volcano, towers above it all. Yet the expansive panoramas are counterbalanced by claustrophobic dark alleyways, silent cloisters by chaotically noisy streets, spaciously elegant royal palaces by overcrowded slums, extremes that have co-existed so long, they've entered the character of the inhabitants. Neopolitans are at once heart-burningly proud of and soul-crushingly ashamed of their city, a duality that comes out in a daily oscillation between optimism and pessimism about the current state of affairs.

In the heart of the Centro Storico, you walk just a few metres above the old Greco-Roman theatre where Emperor Nero fiddled for his bored subjects two millennia ago. The surrounding streets once formed the corridors of this same theatre, leading down to the *decumani* and *Spaccanapoli* ('split Naples'), the main east-west thoroughfares of the old city. This is where Naples' 2,500-year history is most evident – an open museum and an essential stop on the 17th-century Grand Tour, the one-time capital of the Kingdom of Two Sicilies is now a UNESCO World Heritage site. Unlike most other such sites, however, a living community thrives here, mostly uncompromised by tourism.

For lunch, you pop into one of your favourite restaurants, to chat to the friendly owner over a plate of spaghetti alle vongole or a steaming hot pizza margherita, staples of the local diet and unsurpassed elsewhere. After a glass of limoncello you wander to a local bar, avoiding the omnipresent *motorinos* buzzing past, at times carrying whole families, pets included, and not a helmet in

sight. Here you grab an espresso, and maybe discuss the football results with the barman, if you can decipher his thick local dialect. Most people are fiercely passionate about *calcio* here, and Napoli are in top form after a prolonged period in the lower leagues.

Maybe in the evening you stroll down to Piazza Bellini for a glass of wine and a crostone (sandwich), perhaps catch an impromptu concert in another piazza, or maybe head along the seafront to the more chic Chiaia area, where slick clubs, restaurants and designer stores punctuate narrow streets and the beautiful people hang out to see and be seen. The *lungomare* (sea front) is also here, with Castel dell'Ovo sitting on a tiny island, and the *villa comunale*, a public park, stretching along to the small port of Mergellina.

The original Greek name Neapolis ('New City') may now seem inappropriate, but the city's metropolitan museum (which was declared the world's most beautiful by *The Times*) and other innovative collections display contemporary art, demonstrating that Naples has its cultural eye firmly on the present day.
Fergal Kavanagh

'The people here are the best in the world – Neapolitans think with their hearts, and will always help someone in need. The city administrators are responsible for giving the city a bad name, but Naples is the most beautiful city in the world'

Ernesto Cacialli award-winning *pizzaiolo* (pizza-maker)

Previous page: the view across the Bay of Naples. Far left: the 13th-century church of Sant'Eligio Maggiore. Bottom right: Pozzuoli's *macellum* (market), west of the city

Instant Passport

Population
2,400,000 (core city 1,046,987)

Area
583sq km

Where is it?
Bay of Naples, on the Amalfi Coast of southern Italy

Climate
Mediterranean. Hot and humid in July and August, made bearable by refreshing sea breezes on the islands and by the coast

Ethnic mix
Italians, Polish, Ukrainians, Sri Lankans

Major sights
Castel Nuovo, Naples National Archaeological Museum, Museo di Capodimonte, Piazzo Reale, Parco della Floridiana, Il Duomo

Where's the buzz?
Mappatella Beach; for nightlife, the busy Superfly on via Cisterna dell'Ollio, Intra Moenia on piazza Bellini or S'move, the smartest club in town; beautifully flouncy art deco café Gambrinus

Insiders' tips
Live music in Bourbon Street, a centrally located venue that is dedicated to local jazz

Typical Neapolitan names
Gennaro, Ciro, Pasquale, Concetta, Annunziata

Famous imports
Argentinian footballer Diego Maradona, who joined Napoli from Barcelona in the mid 1980s

Earliest evidence of civilisation
Founded by the Ancient Greeks as Neapolis ('New City'). The city's history can be traced back to the 7th century BC

Proudest inventions
The mandolin, by the Vinaccia family; pizza, with the 'margherita' having been named after Margherita of Savoy when she visited the city

Typical dishes
Alici marinate (sardines marinated in garlic, chilli and parsley), funghi trifolati (cooked diced mushrooms with garlic, chilli and parsley), gattò di patate (a shepherd's pie-like dish with mozzarella and ham), parmigiana di melanzane (baked aubergines), pasta alla barese (pasta with broccoli), pasta e ceci (pasta with chickpeas), pasta e fagilio (pasta with beans), spaghetti alle vongole (spaghetti with shellfish)

Famous ingredients
Olive oil, tomatoes, lemons

Customs
Capuzzelle, a Neopolitan version of the cult of the dead that involves caring for skulls. People adopt a skull in one of the city's hypogea and shower it with gifts

Architecture	
9	
Arts & Culture	
10	
Buzz	
10	
Food & Drink	
9	
Quality of Life	
6	
World Status	
9	
Total	
53/70	
Rank	
1	

New York

USA

The ultimate North American metropolis

New York is a place of limitless possibility. Deeply embedded in the civic psyche, this notion is embodied by the 19th-century immigrants who were welcomed into the harbour by the Statue of Liberty and the myth of the chorus girl who becomes an overnight Broadway star. Yet, the 'anything can happen' buzz is palpable on an everyday level: you might stumble upon a fashion shoot on a cobbled corner of the luxed-up Meatpacking District, or sit next to someone starrier than the performers onstage at a cabaret show. Then there's the constant sense of being on location as almost every street scene recalls a celluloid equivalent, and even a routine Midtown walk is elevated to cinematic excitement when the Chrysler Building or the Empire State Building winks above the cityscape. The observant are rewarded by countless less-obvious architectural gems: a gargoyle crouching on an early 20th-century apartment block; a frieze of classical heads wrapping around an industrial building. Nowhere else will you see a more compellingly lurid parade of humanity. Here, the local eccentrics become self-made celebrities, like the Naked Cowboy, who struts around Times Square wearing little more than a ten-gallon hat.

Not so much a Big Apple as an overstuffed deli sandwich, the slender island of Manhattan – just 2.3 miles (3.7km) across at its widest point – packs an incredibly varied cross-cultural mix into a relatively small geographical area. Chinatown's frenetic food markets rub up against the (diminishing) red-sauce joints and mafia landmarks of Little Italy. The genteel, brownstone-lined streets of the Village give way to Soho's cast-iron industrial façades; while, uptown, priceless art collections housed in opulent, Upper East Side mansions are mere blocks from the bodegas and salsa bars

'In what we condescendingly call the outer boroughs, you see little theatre companies and restaurants that remind me of what the Village used to be like. And though Manhattan's changed, all the changes aren't bad… I have an office on Union Square that I've been in for years. Union Square used to be a police holding-pen. It was surrounded with a fence and they would grab a criminal and throw him in there overnight. Now it's a lovely park'
Tony Kushner playwright

PS1 Gallery

This is one of the oldest, and largest, not-for-profit contemporary art institutions in the USA. Housed in a former public school, PS1 exhibits cutting-edge work by contemporary international artists and emerging talent, as well as commissioning some intriguing site-specific installations. It was founded back in 1971 by Alanna Heiss and has thrived since becoming affiliated to MoMA in 2000, which brought in more money, publicity and artistic clout, and so allowed the gallery to expand its artistic programme. Artwork can be found in every corner of the building, from the classrooms and stairwells to the roof. In the summer months, the courtyard hosts some of the most anticipated underground clubbing events in the city, under the banner of the 'Warm Up' series.

Across the road on Jackson Avenue is a rougher display of urban art: the graffiti-covered 5 Pointz. The façade of this block-long converted warehouse offers an ever-evolving tableau of different tagging styles in brilliant hues.

Previous page: Empire-Fulton Ferry State Park. Opposite: top left to right, 59th Street subway, Yankees fan, Lenox Avenue; centre left to right, Statue of Liberty, Koreatown, Gay Pride; bottom left, Element; bottom right, Nublu. Right: Lower East Side. Following page: Times Square

Instant Passport

Population
17,800,000 (core city 8,008,000)

Area
8,683sq km

Where is it?
On the east coast of North America, where the Hudson River opens into the Atlantic Ocean

Climate
Temperate: cold winters; mild springs and autumns; hot, humid summers

Ethnic mix
Caucasian, African American, Hispanic, Latino, Asian

Major sights
Statue of Liberty, Times Square, Empire State Building, Chrysler Building, Museum of Modern Art, Metropolitan Museum of Art, Macy's, Solomon R Guggenheim Museum, Grand Central Terminal and the Oyster Bar, Katz's Deli, Central Park, Brooklyn Bridge

Insiders' tips
PS1 Contemporary Art Center and 5 Pointz in Long Island City, Queens; idiosyncratic boutiques on Orchard, Ludlow and Rivington Streets in the Lower East Side; Green-Wood Cemetery, Brooklyn

Where's the buzz?
Williamsburg, Brooklyn, for indie music; the Bowery and Bushwick, Brooklyn, for boundary-pushing art; clandestine bars in the East Village and the Lower East Side; Chinatown

Number of yellow taxis
12,778

Annual feature-film shoots
More than 250

Number killed in the 9/11 attacks on the World Trade Center
2,752, estimated to be from 90 different countries

World's largest department store
Macy's (at 151 W 34th Street) claims to be the world's joint largest department store, with 198,500sq m of retail space. It is rivalled by GUM in Moscow and Harrods in London

Total length of shelving at Strand Book Store, Broadway
Famously '18 miles of books'

Best burger
Corner Bistro in the West Village

Sports teams
Yankees, Mets (both baseball); Giants, Jets (both American football)

Immortalised in
Annie Hall, *Manhattan*, *Angels in America*, *Mean Streets*, *Breakfast at Tiffany's*, *Midnight Cowboy*, *Sex and the City*, *Ugly Betty*, *On the Town*, *The French Connection*... plus photographs by Weegee and Diane Arbus

of 'El Barrio'. At Manhattan's heart, the artfully landscaped Central Park breaks up the concrete jungle, drawing joggers, cyclists, dog walkers and sun-worshippers from right across the city to create a verdant microcosm.

Whatever you want, whenever you want it – a haircut at 2am, a tub of ice cream delivered to your door – it's yours. It's impossible to keep up with the relentless influx of new restaurants, bars, shows, shops... yet although New Yorkers are constantly clamouring for the Next Big Thing, we're protective of our past, which keeps a fair number of chrome-covered diners and tin-ceilinged dives (and some new ersatz ones, too) in business. In many ways, New York is surprisingly retro. It contains some of the world's most cutting-edge architecture, yet 10,000 wooden water towers – more 19th-century agrarian than 21st-century urban – perch atop many highrises. And while the loss of downtown bohemia to 'mallification' is universally mourned, it hasn't really died; the experimental art spaces, bare-bones rock clubs and underground warehouse parties have simply migrated to Brooklyn or the Bronx, reflecting the ever-changing scenes of this city.
Lisa Ritchie

WHAT KIND OF PROPERTY DOES $350K BUY ON YOUR LATITUDE?

Garage, Chelsea, London

1 bedroom apartment, Manhattan, N

Paris

FRANCE

A city of constant discovery

Morning. 8.25 am, the great dome of the Panthéon, a fragmented glimpse of the two towers of Notre-Dame amid the wintery, still blue-grey, misty half-light as kids hurry their parents in a last minute dash for school; the city awakening. One of the paradoxes of Paris is this duality between the city that everyone thinks they know, with its monuments and vistas, and the private, living city going on behind.

Few cities are as public and ostensibly urban – and urbane – as Paris, whose image has been controlled by centuries of architects and planners, monarchs and powerful civil servants, putting up royal statues, the place Vendôme, Arc de Triomphe, the wilfully unfunctional Eiffel Tower, the riotous marble of Palais Garnier, the vast sweep of the Louvre. But just as there's a *décalage* between the image France likes to project of itself as *cocorico* purveyor of fashion, gastronomy, literature, art and intellectuals, and an equally vital France of industry, scientific research and high-speed trains, so there's a gap between the elegant Paris of myth and monuments and the intensity of the densely populated working hub this hides, where each street can resemble an entire village or town.

Paris likes to mislead, to present a demeanour of indolence, the much vaunted *art de vivre*. This is not just about place but about lifestyle. Parisians have perfected the art of *flânerie* and people-watching from café terraces. Parisians don't do the New Yorkers' power-walking (although you might now catch them hopping nonchalantly on a bike). Parisians don't do Londoners' afterwork pub throng. Every city has its secret places, but Paris seems to cultivate one image to hide another. There's a discrepancy between what the city projects and what exists within: a Parisian shrug of the shoulders that says take us or

Architecture	9
Arts & Culture	9
Buzz	6
Food & Drink	9
Quality of Life	7
World Status	8
Total	48/60
Rank	3

'Paris is a city on a very human scale. The distances are short which makes journeys simple. You can cross it in less than 30 minutes by bike. Small, but of a richness of culture and a diversity that means you must choose your district carefully. I prefer the districts that are still changing to the historically frozen parts of Paris. I live in Belleville, which is wonderful yet not a cocoon. I like to cross my quartier and say to myself that there are still plenty of things to do'

Matali Crasset designer

Top: left, Point Ephémère; right, Cité de la Mode et du Design. Centre: left, Musée du Quai Branly; middle, Fondation Cartier; right, Louvre Pyramid. Bottom: left, Printemps; right, Café Charbon

leave us, that welcomes you to the most visited city in the world with the gorgeous grandiose panoramas everyone knows but challenges you to go a bit further, that keeps itself to itself yet rewards curiosity.

Even long-term residents still stumble on the unexpected. The ancient Roman pottery kilns on the rue St-Jacques, or unlikely courtyards and ateliers through open doorways. An alleyway containing a cluster of publishers and radio stations. The view from Le Corbusier's Salvation Army hostel. A garden with palm trees. Industrial premises behind Haussmann façades, a statue of a pharoah and the triangular house of a silent movie star. Perhaps the Chinatown of today, with its Buddhist temple in an underground car park, and video stores lurking among concrete malls. The strange layerings, dead ends and changes of street level that reflect centuries of history. You could spend the rest of your life in Paris; there will always be something to discover.

Natasha Edwards

Instant Passport

Population
9,645,000 (core city 2,152,000)

Area
2,723sq km

Where is it?
Built up around two islands in the River Seine in northern France

Climate
Temperate: chilly winters and warm summers

Ethnic mix
White European with North African, West African and Asian minorities

Major sights
Eiffel Tower, the Louvre, Centre Pompidou, Musée d'Orsay, Notre-Dame Cathedral, Sainte Chapelle, Montmartre, the Arc de Triomphe, Cimetière Père Lachaise, the Champs-Elysées, the Catacombes

Insiders' tips
Food markets everywhere, Musée Marmottan-Claude Monet, Palais de Tokyo, Canal du Nord, Parc André Citroën, Cité de l'Architecture, Jardin des Plantes, Bois de Vincennes

Where's the buzz?
The narrow streets and boutiques of the Marais, multicultural Belleville, the regenerating 13th arrondissement

Number of prisoners in the Bastille Prison when it was stormed on 14 July 1789
Seven. A symbolic victory, it precipitated the French Revolution and is celebrated every year

Year Napoleon commissioned the Arc de Triomphe
1806 (it was completed in 1836)

Number of restaurants and cafés
10,000

Number of art objects in the Louvre museum
35,000

Interred at Cimetière Père-Lachaise
Molière, Oscar Wilde, Honoré Balzac, Marcel Proust, Frédéric Chopin, Guillaume Apollinaire, Georges Bizet, Edith Piaf, Jim Morrison

Tons of sand used to create the Paris Plage
2,000. Inititated in 2002 this popular public beach springs up along the Seine and around the Basin La Villette every summer

City centre vineyards
Rue de Saules, Monmartre. It produces 500 bottles of red wine a year, all are sold for charity

Immortalised in
A Bout du Souffle, Les 400 Coups, Subway, The Hunchback of Notre-Dame, Tropic of Cancer, Baudelaire's *Le Spleen de Paris,* the paintings of Manet and Toulouse Lautrec

Prague

CZECH REPUBLIC

Sad and soulful

Only a world-class cynic wouldn't be captivated by Prague's flourishes and dark secrets. Its architecture, true to the jaw-dropping accounts it earns in every guide, really does stun and confound. It's an effect not fully explained by the simple juxtapositioning of the highest forms of Baroque with the grimmest Gothic and the full-tilt modernism of Cubism (a form that only Czechs, giddy with newfound independence in the early 20th century, could have thought to apply to buildings).

But even as you sip an espresso at the café in Staré Město's House of the Black Madonna, it's clear that something else is at work. Some say it's the ghosts. In the district's Josefov quarter, a small tangle of streets that once made up the Jewish ghetto, there's a palpable sense of melancholy and loss. Even Prague Castle, despite the soaring Sonder Gothic spires of St Vitus's Cathedral and the hordes of tour groups by day, feels strangely empty otherwise. Try to listen for the echoes of the alchemists, seers, cosmologists and astronomers collected by the brooding Rudolf II and you'll find them all too faint.

Modern-day Praguers are a stressed-out lot, dark circles visible beneath their eyes, generally unresponsive to smiles unless you're in their immediate social circle, and seemingly obsessed by complicated rules – and the fear they'll be caught breaking one. They're dogged by consumer debt (they proved as eager as Americans to spend what they could never hope to earn) and seem to get little joy from their new Audi when not using it to chase pedestrians off crossings.

So where's the energy gone? The revolutionary thinking that drove Johannes Kepler to divine the laws of planetary motion? The wondrously impractical, impudent embrace of not just Cubism but Picasso, Tolstoy, Stravinsky and Dadaism – at least until the

Architecture
8
Arts & Culture
6
Buzz
5
Food & Drink
4
Quality of Life
6
World Status
3
Total
32/60
Rank
45

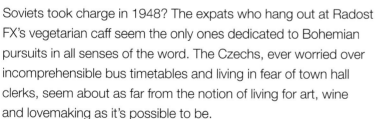

Previous page: main picture, Old Town Square. Left: top to bottom, Charles Bridge, Astronomical Clock, Cross Club. Clockwise from left: Charles Bridge, Pils, Smíchov, Kampa Museum, St Vitus's Cathedral. Far right: Lucerna Passage

Soviets took charge in 1948? The expats who hang out at Radost FX's vegetarian caff seem the only ones dedicated to Bohemian pursuits in all senses of the word. The Czechs, ever worried over incomprehensible bus timetables and living in fear of town hall clerks, seem about as far from the notion of living for art, wine and lovemaking as it's possible to be.

Shouldn't residents of the flushest capital of the former Eastern bloc show signs of dash and whimsy? Admittedly, it's a high bar for any 21st-century city, but signs of enjoyment are particularly elusive. Evidence of cashing in, acquisition and ostentation are far easier to mark. Bars and clubs such as Duplex fill up with monied patrons in designer clothes but there's a predatory feel to these places. There's more funding for Czech film than ever before, yet the multiplexes are supplied with only tired situation comedies and teen movies. A couple hoping for a romantic dinner out had better have at least 1,000 Kč in hand and be prepared for theatrically

unconcerned waiters. And on Wenceslas Square, it's impossible to walk 20 yards without being assaulted by the neon of *herny* (gambling rooms) or a tout for a strip club.

Any population undergoing titanic societal shifts, especially in an emerging economy where people were too long denied access to the vice and toys of capitalism, is bound to produce searching and scrambling as people try hard to make up for lost time. But already there's a backlash, with the thousands of perhaps less visible residents pursuing science, medicine, engineering and, yes, even the arts. Enough to fill the photo gallery at Café Velryba and to keep the Czech Republic in the headlines of professional journals.

Slowly, the courage to pursue worthwhile ambitions is emerging. Credit the ghosts, who still speak to some people, especially around twilight on quiet, traffic-free squares in the Old Town, or from a blackened Gothic façade.

Will Tizard

Instant Passport

Population
1,200,000

Area
496sq km

Where is it?
On the Vltava river in the Bohemia region of central Czech Republic

Climate
Long, cold winters and warm (rarely hot) summers; autumn is crisp and cool with blue skies

Ethnic mix
94.4% Czech and 1.9% Slovak, with the remainder made up of Poles, Germans, Romanies and Hungarians

Major sights
Old Town Square, the Astronomical Clock, Old Jewish Cemetery, Jewish Museum, Municipal House, Prague Castle, St Vitus's Cathedral, National Gallery Collection of 19th-, 20th- and 21st-Century Art, Rudolfinum, Žižkov Tower, U Černého vola pub, U Medvídků pub

Insiders' tips
Soviet hangover at the National Memorial, Olsany Cemetery, the new Dox arts centre in Holešovice, eating jelení guláš (stew made from venison and served with fluffy dumplings), trying every Pilsner beer

Where's the buzz?
The Žižkov district, home of run-down, busy bars and dozens of pubs

Communist party assumes power
1948

Václav Havel elected president of Czechoslovakia
1990

Czechoslovakia separated
1993. It formed two states – Czech Republic and Slovakia

Stalin's statue in Letná park briefly replaced by one of Michael Jackson
1996 – as part of his History tour

Beer consumption
Czechs drink 156 litres of beer per person per year and are very proud of having invented the pils style of lager which tends to be highly carbonated with a floral aroma and crisp taste. Famous Czech beers include Pilsner Urquell, Radegast, Staropramen, Gambrinus, Budvar, Velvet, Kelt, Branik

Estimated number of street prostitutes
Between 3,000 and 6,000

Number of homeless people
4,600

Famous writers
Franz Kafka, Václav Havel, Milan Kundera, Jan Neruda, Karel Čapek, Bohumil Hrabal, Jáchym Topol

Rio de Janeiro

BRAZIL

Alive to the sound of samba

ocals, those ever-proud carioca, have long called Rio 'the Marvellous City'. It's not just the sun-soaked city beaches, which stretch for kilometres along the Atlantic coast. It isn't just the headline-grabbing carnival – the four days of excess that attract half a million foreign visitors a year – or the scantily clad carnival queens who take to the Sambódromo each year, flanked by deafening percussion sections and nimble-footed flag bearers.

Every carioca has their own reasons, but for many, it's music. Rio lost its status as Brazil's political capital in 1960 when the futuristic city of Brasilia was erected, but it remains the undisputed cultural capital. The birthplace of samba, bossa nova and, more recently, Brazilian funk, Rio remains a place of pilgrimage for music lovers and musicians. More than 2.5 million tourists flock here each year to immerse themselves in the local rhythms: *forró* and *frevo* from the north-east, *carimbo* from the north, and myriad others. It is impossible to escape music here. It is there in the twang of guitar strings from the samba clubs in the bohemian district of Lapa; in the rattle of percussion that chases you down the cobbled beachfront of Copacabana; in the contagious boom of Rio funk that rattles your bones up steep alleys and into the hilltop favelas.

Music is not just in the way the people sing and dance, but in the way they talk and walk. You can hear it in the south zone, the north zone, the slums and suburbs, in Copacabana's tiny Bip-Bip bossa nova club or Botafogo's vast Canecão concert hall. You can buy it at the downtown LP markets and learn to dance to it at any number of classes. Rio may be dangerous in parts, it is certainly beautiful, but it is also one of the most musical cities in the world. As locals say, 'In Rio everything ends up in samba.'

Tom Phillips

Architecture
8
Arts & Culture
6
Buzz
8
Food & Drink
4
Quality of Life
5
World Status
4
Total
35/60
Rank
28

'You're going to see men with guns if you go to the favelas, sure, but if you want to see the real Rio, you have to go'

Jose Padilha **film director**

Instant Passport

Population
10,800,000 (core city 5,613,000)

Area
1,580sq km

Where is it?
The south-east coast of Brazil, on Guanabara Bay, opening on to the Atlantic Ocean

Climate
Hot nearly all year round, Rio doesn't really experience seasons. It's generally wetter from June to August, but there's always the chance of a huge downpour

Ethnic mix
Descendents of (Portuguese) Europeans, Africans and indigenous Brazilians

Major sights
Christ the Redeemer statue, Sugar Loaf Mountain, the Botanical Gardens, the beaches of Copacabana and Ipanema

Insiders' tips
Centro Cultural Carioca music club, Rua do Lavradio antiques fair

Where's the buzz?
The dance clubs of Lapa

Percentage of the population living in the favelas
20%. There are nearly 1,000 favelas in Rio

Litres of cachaça produced in Brazil each year
1.3 billion litres. The average Brazilian consumes 11 litres of this sugar-cane spirit each year

Number of condoms distributed free by the government during the annual Carnival
More than 3 million

Breakthrough for funk Carioca
1989, with the first official hit by MC Batata

Record number of people who have been in the Maracanã stadium at any one time
199,854, in 1950 for the World Cup final between Uruguay and Brazil. Uruguay won 2-1. Brazil is the only national football team to have qualified for every World Cup tournament, and has won it five times – more than any other country

Height of Christ the Redeemer
38m. Created by French sculptor Paul Landowski in 1931 on top of Corcovado Mountain, it became a globally recognised symbol of the city

Immortalised in
Fred Astaire and Ginger Rogers in *Flying Down to Rio*, Jorge Amado's *Dona Flor and Her Two Husbands*, Astrud Gilberto's 'The Girl from Ipanema' and Tom Jobim's *Wave*, *Blame It on Rio*, *Central Station*, *City of God*, *Elite Squad*

Previous page: Sugar Loaf Mountain cable car. Opposite: top, Ipanema; centre middle, Carnival; centre right, 00 club-bar-restaurant; bottom left, Santa Teresita; bottom right, Rocinha favela. Above: Escadaria Selarón

Rome

ITALY

Playing up to an august history

Architecture	9
Arts & Culture	7
Buzz	7
Food & Drink	6
Quality of Life	6
World Status	7
Total	42/60
Rank	9

It seems clichéd to say that Rome is all about history. But it *is* all about history. That's not to deny that the city has a vibrant present and a future full of promise – it very definitely does – but it's a city where everything is filtered through past glories. And why not? It has a heritage well worth basking in.

Fitting a 21st-century city into an urban fabric woven over several millennia is always going to be a challenge, and Rome works best when it works with its past: when it accepts that cobbled medieval alleyways don't chime with the combustion engine and pedestrianises them (alas, too infrequently); when it recognises the sound-proofing potential of grottoes dug over centuries into the flanks of an artificial hill made solely of discarded amphorae – Monte Testaccio – and allows that archaeological site to become the city's main nightlife hub. It works worst when it kicks against what time has bequeathed it.

There's a blasé acceptance among Roman residents that the jumble of masonry in the fenced-off area across from their front door has been there for 2,000 years, that motorised traffic jostles chariot-like around an ancient Roman gate or through holes hacked into mighty second-century walls, or that the church down the road displays, with no fanfare, a couple of Caravaggio masterpieces. As befits the descendents of a people who once ran the Western world, grandeur is commonplace, artistic and architectural excellence is everyday.

In fact, for Romans, this dramatic backdrop is the only possible one for the spectacle of their everyday lives. From fur-coated matrons deftly negotiating sampietrini cobbles in their high heels, to suavely perma-tanned youths enhancing façades of Baroque churches while blocking pavements with their carelessly parked

Left: the Colosseum. Above: top, mosaic at Santa Prassede church; middle, view from the Forum; bottom, the Constantine Colossus outside the Capitoline Museums

'I could say that Rome is beautiful because of its ancient remains, its museums, its squares, its monuments. I could cite the Colosseum or the Vatican, write about the charm of piazza di Spagna or the buzz of campo de' Fiori. But Rome's true beauty lies in its soul, which makes everyone feel at home, whether you live here or you're just visiting – for a day or for a lifetime'

Walter Veltroni novelist, journalist, jazz lover, film critic, politician and mayor of Rome (2001-2008)

Above: top, Guiseppe Momo's staircase in the Vatican Museums. Far right: top, the Ara Pacis; bottom, Bernini's curved colonnade at the Vatican

motorini; from leather-aproned craftsmen repairing antiques in the sunny street outside their dark medieval worshops, to gaggles of shrieking girls looking immaculately emo-chic as they pile out of Renaissance *palazzi* tranformed into graffitied places of learning: they all play up to their surroundings, while simultaneously redefining them. The archetypal Roman may be pushy and arrogant, and given to moaning about anything that impedes his or her smooth progress through this hopelessly obstacle-strewn metropolis, but they have a stylishness that is unique, determined by their unique habitat.

To the visitor, Rome offers up its iconic side with a hint of irony. You want piazza Navona? Here it is, complete with Bernini fountains, tacky souvenir sellers and rip-off cafés. You want the Colosseum? Part the waves of kitsch 'centurions', determined to relieve you of your holiday euros in exchange for a cheesy snapshot. We Romans will be the ones skirting round or hurrying through, probably so intent on our cellphone conversation that our surroundings barely register. If you want to find the real Rome, just follow us into the Eternal City's backstreets. For it's here, in the humbler bits of history, that the soul of the city lies.
Anne Hanley

Instant Passport

Population
2,500,000

Area
842sq km

Where is it?
Famously built on seven hills, on the banks of the Tiber, 30km inland
from Italy's west coast

Climate
Balmy in spring and autumn, with raking yellow light; searing heat and
energy-sapping humidity in July and August

Ethnic mix
95% Italian

Major sights
Pantheon, Colosseum, Vatican (technically part of its own city state),
Trevi Fountain, Spanish Steps, Roman Forum, Santa Maria in Trastevere,
Theatre of Marcellus, Capitoline Museums, Galleria Borghese, Palatine
Hill, Ponte Fabricio

Where's the buzz?
Testaccio-Ostiense for nightlife, Pigneto for boho-chic and eating

Most famous work of art
Michelangelo's *Creation of Adam* in the Sistine Chapel

Earliest evidence of civilisation
Huts on the Palatine dating to the 9th century BC

Seating capacity of the Colosseum
50,000

Number of obelisks
13

Inauguration of the Vatican State
11 February 1929

Population of the Vatican State
800, only 450 of whom have Vatican citizenship

Rival football teams
AS Roma, SS Lazio

Traffic accidents in 2007
40,000, with 180 fatalities

Local flavours
Baccalà (fried salt cod), carciofi alla Romana (artichokes with lemon,
parsley, mint and garlic), fiori di zucca (deep-fried courgette flowers
stuffed with mozzarella and anchovies), pecorino con fave (salad of
fava beans and pecorino romano, a sheep's milk cheese)

Immortalised in
Juvenal, Virgil, *Ben-Hur*, *Roman Holiday*, *La Dolce Vita*, *Three Coins
in the Fountain*, *Caro Diario, Gladiator*

Architecture

9

Arts & Culture

10

Buzz

6

Food & Drink

3

Quality of Life

5

World Status

3

Total

36/60

Rank

25

Saint Petersburg

RUSSIA

Regimented splendour

Built in 1703 by Peter the Great, the first Zsar to travel in Europe, Saint Petersburg is the physical manifestation of a personal obsession. Peter had first raised a European army and navy, then waged war with a European country (challenging Sweden for supremacy of the Baltic Sea), so what he really needed next was a European-style capital for the new-born empire.

The original architects of the city wanted it to look like Venice, with numerous channels crossing the islands and mainland of the Neva delta. Unfortunately, regular flooding made the plan too dangerous, though the alias of 'Venice of the North' is still popular with guidebook writers. 'New York of the North' would be a more fitting description; both being cities created by immigrants. Thousands of Europeans came to Saint Petersburg chasing the Russian Dream (or fleeing persecution, or the law, in their own countries) and from 1703 till 1918, when the government returned to Moscow, the city was full of foreigners, mostly English, German, French and Dutch, settling as communities that became the ghettos of the 18th century. Right up until the end of the 19th century, English clubs were at least as popular as English pubs are today. An ordinary barber in France could call himself a professor in Russia and start to teach the children of nobles, or trade some suspicious 'French' medicines. And many made their fortunes. Even in 1812, when French soldiers had set Moscow on fire, French architects continued to build palaces in Saint Petersburg.

The French influence remained even after 1917, with the ideas of Le Corbusier inspiring the constructivist masterpieces of the 1930s, though many, sadly, were lost during World War II and contemporary 'reconstructions'. Even so, the total number of major historical monuments in Saint Petersburg has still proved

'Saint Petersburg is a harsh, cold city. It cannot really be a comfortable place to live, but it is a perfect one for a writer. Literature, unlike other fine arts, is supposed to prepare you for death, not life. Going to Saint Petersburg is like reading a book, touching the Art which is an art of death'

Maroussia Klimova writer

Instant Passport

Population
5,300,000 (core city 4,678,000)

Area
622sq km

Where is it?
In the Neva river delta spread over many islands at the edge of the Baltic Sea. There were originally 101 islands, but redevelopment has reduced this to 44, connected by 620 bridges

Climate
Winters are very cold with freezing winds and snow. Summers are warm but temperatures remain low. On average it rains 126 days a year

Ethnic mix
Russians, Tatars, Ukrainians, Bashkir, Chuvash, Chechens, Armenians

Major sights
Hermitage Museum, Mariinsky Opera and Ballet Theatre, Imperial Palace and park ensemble at Peterhof, Palace Bridge at night

Insiders' tips
Swimming in the Gulf of Finland from June till August, coffee at Sever or Blinnaya, the decor and food at Yeliseyev's art nouveau delicatessen, hidden splendour of the metro stations (particularly Awtowo, red line number one), a round-trip on tram line number five

Where's the buzz?
Dumskaya Street for grungy bars such as Fidel, Konyshennaya Street for chi-chi club Arena-3

Also known as
The Venice of the North, the City of 101 Islands, the Palmyra of the North

Latitude
59 degrees 57' north – the most northerly city (of more than 1million inhabitants) in the world

Number of deaths during the 900-day siege of Leningrad by the Nazis
800,000. 750,000 of them from starvation

Football team
FC Zenit

Beers brewed in St Petersburg
Baltika, Tinkoff, Nevskoye

White nights
From June 11 to July 2 the sun barely dips below the horizon

Number of students at the Vaganova Ballet Academy
300. On average, just under half graduate

Number of objects in Saint Petersburg State Hermitage Museum
More than 3 million

Main brand
Hermitage (museum, radio, restaurants and cafés, chocolate)

Previous page: Divo Ostrov.
Opposite: Smolny Institute.
Right: Neva River embankment.
Below, left: Winter Palace

too big for UNESCO to count – instead it has put the entire historic centre on the World Heritage list.

St Petersburg is probably the most unnatural and regimented city in the world. Though it was supposed to be Russia's first European city, full of ornamental splendour, its street plan makes it look like a chess board. Such flamboyance was out of step with the spirit of stringency at the heart of the capital of the Russian Empire, not to mention the latterday enthusiasm for bureaucracy displayed by many Russian officials. It is like it has been built in Lego by da Vinci – a beautiful but modular construction set, very much of its time, and one of the few cities that looks better without any inhabitants.

Saint Petersburg has changed its name three times, including Petrograd (patriotic and anti German kitsch of 1914-1924) and Leningrad (1924–1991, in glorification of the deceased communist leader Vladimir Ilyich Lenin). It has also originated three revolutions (failed in 1824, successful in February 1917, and glorious in October of the same year), as well as numerous coups d'etat.

In the 1980s, St Petersburg became the rock-capital of the USSR; even today the spirit of underground is present in the numerous marginal groups of angry boys and girls. But it is the city's literary history that dominates. You can still find editorial offices where young and tough artillery officer Leo Tolstoy ruined sofas with his foppish spurs, visit Raskolnikov's house or repeat Dostoevsky's alco-tour in Colomna's bars. You can even try to enter the court where Brodsky was accused of sponging. In many ways, a classical Russian novel will tell you far more about the real spirit of this rich city than any guidebook ever can.
Dmitry Shestakov

Sana'a

YEMEN

An architectural marvel of ancient skyscrapers

Laced towering buildings stand side by side, ancient high-rises built from baked bricks, decorated with white fringes and traceries. Alabaster sheets shade the windows while coloured glass fanlights, set in gypsum and excecuted in perfected geometric and floral patterns, penetrate the thick walls. The city so infatuated Italian film director Pier Paolo Pasolini when he visited in the 1970s that he filmed a documentary on Sana'a's city wall, bringing this architectural marvel to the attention of UNESCO, winning Sana'a a place on the World Heritage List.

This is a taste of a medieval Arabia no longer found in the Middle East. Historians boast that Sana'a is one of the oldest cities, said to have been founded by Sam, son of Noah. Time has not stopped here though, and the hustle and bustle of modern life is ever present. There is only one cinema in old Sana'a but entertainment is not in short supply. Men dressed in robes, sporting ceremonial daggers and different types of headdress, and women covered in colourful Indian printed sheets – or more recently shrouded in black – add to the atmosphere. Ancient mosques, gardens, wells and beasts of burden still operate. Traditional *samsarah* (caravansaries) with large courtyards, still stand in hidden alleys, behind heavy wooden doorways and brass gates, reached by meandering paths. Tribal men and women from all over the country continue to drift in, shopping or selling merchandise in stores or on the pavement stalls.

At the street markets, traders sell silver jewellery, glass or brass bracelets from Maarib, archaeological fakes, and authentic smuggled artefacts. Natural produce such as henna, almonds, pistachios, raisins and spices are piled high; in more serious markets staple foods are richly displayed in the same way they

Architecture
10
Arts & Culture
2
Buzz
7
Food & Drink
1
Quality of Life
1
World Status
1
Total
22/60
Rank
71

مبروك يافارس
الأمة العربية
السمك للعطور

have been for hundreds of years. There are specialist markets for hot food, *qat* (a narcotic leaf), silver and gold, cows, fabrics, carpets and antiques, and markets where local craftsmen – potters, carpenters and ironmongers – ply their trade. Merchants sit on raised platforms behind their wares, sipping tea and chewing qat.

The street markets are undoubtedly where the buzz is, but most people live around the Suq civil and commercial zone, in proud, protected houses, their privacy carefully designed and cleverly maintained, behind thick walls, whitewashed on the interior. In these traditional homes, the main living rooms are at the top, next to the roof terraces and away from the streets and public life below, commanding panoramic views of the cityscape,

Sadly, modern building and concrete structures have failed to emulate the original elegant architecture, with some hideous interventions. Restoration of the Ottoman entrance to the old city, Bab al-Yaman (Yemen Gate), now looks foreign, its architectural style out of keeping with its surroundings.

Despite widely-reported kidnappings of foreigners outside Sana'a (mainly in Shabwa and Maarib provinces) to settle tribal grievances,

and more recent attacks targeting tourists in Hadramut, or Western Embassy buildings in the capital, one feels safe amid people who are, on the whole, generous, hospitable, warm and friendly.

Many stories remain untold behind the mud coloured walls of old Sana'a, but so rich a city is it that whatever is written remains a scant portrait of other levels and layers that continue to unfold.

Salma Samar Damluji

Instant Passport

Population
1,200,000

Area
247sq km

Where is it?
In a mountain valley in the heart of the Yemen highlands, at an altitude of 2,200m

Climate
Dry mountain climate with warm summers and chilly winters

Ethnic mix
In Sana'a most Yemenis belong to the Zaydi sect; there are also communities of Sunni Muslims and Shi'a Muslims

Major sights
Suq al-Milh (Salt Market); al-Jami'al-Kabir (Great Mosque); Dar al-Hajar; Wadi Dhahr, 14 km northwest of Sana'a

Insiders' tips
Historic districts of Bir Al Azab, Rawdah and Al Qa'a. Traditional *hammamat* (steam baths)

Where's the buzz?
The markets, the square behind Bab al-Yaman

Inhabited for
2,500 years

Religious and political heritage
103 mosques, 14 hammamat, over 6,000 houses: all built before the 11th century

Oldest known copy of the Qur'an
Found in Sana'a in the Great Mosque in 1972, dated to 645-690 AD

Age of the Liberty Gate, formerly known as Bab al-Yaman (Yemen Gate)
More than 700 years old

Declared a World Heritage City
1986

Traditional buildings
Pisé: multi-storeyed tower-houses built of rammed earth. The space between them is just wide enough for pedestrians and mule-drawn carts

Percentage of Yemenis that chew qat (a plant with stimulant properties)
72% of men and 32% of women chew qat for between two and six hours a day

Qat's contribution to the Yemeni economy
6% GDP growth, 12% total employment

Local flavours
Mikhbazah (charcoal grilled fish cooked in clay ovens) served with khubz (freshly baked flabread), salta (hot lamb, pepper and coriander stew), Yemeni coffee flavoured with cardamom

Previous page: main square by Bab al-Yaman. Above, left: mud-brick high-rises. Above: tribal merchants set up makeshift pavement stalls

San Francisco

USA

A smalltown place with big city pride

Architecture
7

Arts & Culture
7

Buzz
7

Food & Drink
7

Quality of Life
8

World Status
5

Total
41/60

Rank
11

For better or for worse, San Francisco is the Miss America of cities, blessed with natural beauty, a congenial temperament, a competitive spirit, and more than its fair share of charm, poise, grace and talent. It uses picture-postcard good looks – the dazzling white-capped smile, the leggy span of the Golden Gate Bridge, those adorable toddling cable cars – to full advantage, attracting 16 million tourists who come to ogle every year. But, like most pretty girls, San Francisco suffers from being perceived as a bit of an airhead – a ditzy flower child who you want to get into bed with, but don't take very seriously.

For the most part, San Franciscans don't really care what people think. One can afford to be gracious in a town where you can play Frisbee on the beach in the middle of February, and where, when you ask how fresh the crab is, the waiter looks at his watch. San Franciscans also understand that, compared to the rest of the world, their problems – traffic jams, lack of parking, expensive housing, an ever-growing homeless population – seem pretty trivial. Besides which, they're usually too obsessed with more pressing matters, such as how to score that prized bag of organic microgreens at the Ferry Plaza Farmers Market, or whether the latest political protest is going to make their drive home a living hell.

In truth, San Francisco's physical beauty masks a conflicted soul. It is a small town with a big city heart; a place that grew up overnight in the mercurial heat of the Gold Rush, only to turn around a century later and launch the decade of 'Free Love'; a city where neighbourhoods sport not only unique personalities, ethnicities, and sexual preferences, but often their own weather systems; a chameleon that can, in the course of only seven

Left: Golden Gate Bridge and the city. Above: top, the Berkeley campus; middle, Yerba Buena Center for the Arts; bottom, Lombard Street

'San Francisco is something of a Californian Amsterdam, its liberal politics and social views coupled with a fierce resistance to change. Our city's footprint may be small, but the impact of its politics and innovation is indisputably global'

Matt Markovich writer and computer programmer

square miles, metamorphose from the Paris of the Pacific into Baghdad by the Bay, the Athens of the West, Barbary Coast, Little Italy and Disneyland.

In San Francisco, it's possible to nibble Hong Kong dim sum in the largest Chinatown outside Asia, and then ten minutes later find yourself listening to 'O Sole Mio' performed by opera-singing barristas at one of the beatnik cafés in Little Italy. You can veer wildly from places of excess and eccentricity, such as Supperclub, where guests lounge on beds in an all-white room while being served dinner by feather-clad satyrs (or, if you prefer, Opaque, where your meal is brought to you in pitch-black darkness by an entirely blind team of waiters), to places where every single thing on your plate – including the plate itself – is organic, sustainable and recyclable.

In this town, earthquakes are the mother of reinvention; fog comes straight from a Dashiell Hammett mystery novel; and no niche is too narrow that it can't have an entire film festival devoted to it. It may not be everyone's cup of monkey-picked chai, but you'd be hard-pressed to find any San Franciscan who'd want to live anywhere else.

Bonnie Wach

Above: the 'Painted Ladies', typical San Franciscan Victorian terraced houses. Right: Ocean Beach. Far right: Powell Street cable car line

Instant Passport

Population
3,229,000 (core city 824,525)

Area
1,365sq km (core city 123sq km)

Where is it?
Peninsula on America's west coast, joined to mainland by eight bridges

Climate
Mediterranean. Summer days can be chilly and summer nights mild.
September and October are warmest; December and January wettest

Ethnic mix
White American, Chinese American, Hispanic, African American

Major sights
Golden Gate Bridge and Park, Chinatown, the Haight, San Francisco
Museum of Modern Art, Palace of the Legion of Honour, Palace of Fine
Arts, California Academy of Sciences, Alcatraz, Cable Car Museum

Insiders' tips
Ocean Beach, De Young Museum, brewpubs, Mission burritos

Where's the buzz?
Milk, DNA Lounge, SoMa, the Castro Theatre

Historical milestones
Golden Gate Bridge is completed, 1964 student sit-ins and mass
protests, Human Be-In rally and music festival of 1967, Harvey Milk
elected to the city's Board of Supervisors, first same-sex marriage
licences to be granted in the US (4,000 gay and lesbian couples wed)

Length of Golden Gate Bridge
2.737km (1.7 miles)

Percentage of the population who identify themselves as gay,
lesbian or bisexual
15.4%

Number of hills
43 official hills (50 unofficial) within city limits

Steepest streets
Filbert Street, between Hyde and Leavenworth, and 22nd Street, between
Church and Vicksburg; both with a gradient of 31.5°

Number of cyclists
40,000 commuting regularly, with over 100km of bicycle lanes and paths

Eco credentials
69% of the city's waste was recycled in 2007, more than double the
national average; first US city to ban plastic bags in large supermarkets

Immortalised in
The Maltese Falcon, *Vertigo*, *Bullitt*, *Escape from Alcatraz*, *Harold and
Maude*, *X Men: The Last Stand*, *Pursuit of Happyness*, *Milk*, *Streets of
San Francisco*, *Charmed*, *Tales of the City*, Jefferson Airplane's *Surrealistic
Pillow*, *The Bridge* trilogy, *The Dharma Bums*, *The Golden Gate*

São Paulo

BRAZIL

Infuriating and ravenously inventive

Architecture	6
Arts & Culture	7
Buzz	7
Food & Drink	6
Quality of Life	2
World Status	7
Total	35/60
Rank	**28**

São Paulo is a city that creates by consuming. Whether it is immigrants, artistic movements or even ecosystems, the city is ravenous in its exhilarating self-renewal. The Paulistano's hunger to be at the forefront of global culture, creativity and innovation has been consummated in a city that surpasses the familiar clichés about a booming economy's maddening metropolis.

Present-day São Paulo incorporates several hundred years of precious colonial architecture. Remnants of luscious jungle canopy that dominated the hilly landscape prior to the arrival of the Jesuits now breathe oxygen into leafy middle-class retreats. Matchless baroque and Victorian structures in the city centre compete with the façades of financial powerhouses like South America's largest stock exchange, the Bovespa.

Not everything in the 'Hallucinated City' is seamlessly integrated. Modest dwellings and slums are levelled to make way for glittering multimillion-dollar high-rises, palatial hotels and outrageous malls. And if the proud favela can't be moved or the rage-inducing traffic lightened, the second-largest private helicopter fleet in the world is on hand to ferry the upper crust from meeting to meeting and from penthouse to high-end shopping excursion. This, then, is the meaning of the Brazilian national motto: 'Order and Progress'.

The Paulistano establishment is not alone in co-opting the rhetoric of reinvention: outstanding works of graffiti, vibrant as rainforest flowers, devour each day a little more of the seemingly endless stretches of concrete box and bypass that were poured in the energetic, albeit hasty building frenzy of the 20th century. São Paulo is a city almost five centuries old that never rests in its quest to be an urban reference point for the 21st century.

Main picture: Bar Mangueira. Above: top left, Teatro Municipal; top right, food courts at Mercado Municipal; bottom left, Parque do Iburapuera; bottom right, a cocktail at Bar Exquisito

São Paulo contains multitudes, multitudes that live beyond the millionaire driving his bullet-proof BMW along Avenida Paulista, the club-kid championing the new food craze (high-end hamburger restaurants) and the art snob extolling a new sculpture at the second-largest art festival in the world (the São Paulo Biennial). Walk outside the leisure-loving, excess-craving upper-crust enclaves, and you'll find a middle-class city filled with workers and immigrants. The nightlife hotspot Villa Madalena is home to both the beer-drinking hipsters and the old-school sambistas strumming their repertoire of songs about *saudade* on four-stringed *cavaquinhos*. Tempura stands and Japanese grocery stores abound in the neighbourhood of Liberdade, the largest Japanese community outside Japan. In Bexiga, Brazil's Little Italy, the scents and flavours of garlic and tomatoes give way to baking pizza. Further away, kosher groceries from a Jewish neighbourhood's heyday fight a losing battle next door to Korean restaurants advertising pork ribs.

> '*São Paulo is a crowded town, it has so many buildings, so much traffic and so many people in one small place. I miss the energy of being there*'

Alice Braga actress

In the 1920s, Paulistano artists discovered the essence of São Paulo when they reinvented European modernism for Brazil, mounting legendary Old World meets New World artistic shows. Their theme: cannibalism. The result: the notion of ingesting the old to create the new exploded not only for modern artists, but for São Paulo itself. This city, hungry for stature on the world scene, has been four-and-a-half centuries in the making and is far from sated.

Anna Katsnelson

Instant Passport

Population
17,700,000 (core city 10,009,000)

Area
1,968sq km

Where is it?
On a plateau in the Serra do Mar, part of the Brazilian highlands in the south of the country

Climate
Subtropical. Humid with plenty of rain, hence its nickname 'city of drizzle'

Ethnic mix
Italian, Portuguese, African, Arab, German, Japanese, Chinese, Jewish, Bolivian, Greek, Korean

Major sights
São Paolo Museum of Modern Art, Parque Estadual do Jaraguá, Catedra da Sé and Praça da Sé, Ibirapuera Park

Insiders' tips
Oscar Niemeyer's Edificio Copan; the neighbourhoods of Jardim Paulista, Vila Madalena, Pinheiros, Itaim Bibi, Vila Olimpia, Liberdade and Higienopolis

Where's the buzz?
Avenida Paulista, Rua Oscar Freire, Rua Alameda Lorena and the bars and cafés of Jardim Paulista Pinheiros, Higienopolis 'dining triangle' on Rua Armando Penteado

Population in 1940
1.3 million. Since then, it has grown by an average of more than a million each decade

Murder rate
In 2006, 15.1 per 100,000, down from 35.7 per 100,000 in 1999

Number of favelas
400

Largest favela
Heliopolis. 120,000 residents live within about half a square mile

Number of people of Japanese extraction
700,000

Tallest building
Mirante do Vale tower (170m)

Highest mountain
Pico do Jaraguá (1,135m above sea level)

Number of works in the São Paulo Museum of Art
8,000. It is regarded as the largest and most comprehensive collection of Western art in the southern hemisphere

Visitors to the São Paulo Biennial art fair
1 million

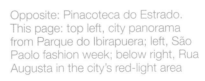

Opposite: Pinacoteca do Estrado.
This page: top left, city panorama
from Parque do Ibirapuera; left, São
Paolo fashion week; below right, Rua
Augusta in the city's red-light area

Architecture
3

Arts & Culture
7

Buzz
5

Food & Drink
4

Quality of Life
7

World Status
5

Total
31/60

Rank
48

Seoul

SOUTH KOREA

Truly ancient, aggressively new

Picture the scene: you're a bustling, fiercely ambitious city with at least 2,000 years of history and, by some measures, the second-largest population of any metropolitan area in the world. You are the headquarters for a string of globe-straddling electronics giants, with a feisty and diverse arts scene that has rippled across much of the region. You have achieved one of the most astonishing economic successes of the 20th century, transforming from post-war rubble to riches in scarcely four decades. And yet, outside of East Asia, most people would struggle to find you on a map, never mind name one of your famous areas or landmarks.

And what a shame that is. Because while the South Korean capital, Seoul, may never win any gongs for urban beauty, there can be few cities in the world that combine the fantastic and the familiar, the rough and the refined, the traditional and the ultra-modern to such giddy, restless effect. Everywhere you go in Seoul, the collision between a long, dilatory history and the crashing, sharp-elbowed arrival of modernity shapes the city and its people. In the enchanting city-centre palaces whose vast, serene grounds are encircled by 16-lane roads; in bustling Jongno and Gangnam districts, where vendors hawk dizzyingly high-tech mobile phones right next to tents housing goateed fortune tellers; and in the modern, ultra-reliable subway system, whose most fearsome passengers are pensioners for whom etiquette means not trampling on your feet after they've barged you out of the way.

To most visitors, the overwhelming first impression of Seoul may be of a city where any semblance of tradition has been hastily concreted over in a mad rush to functional, if visually unappealing,

Previous page: Gyeongbukgung Palace. Top: left, Gwanaksan mountain; right, Cheonggyecheon, downtown Seoul. Centre left: Angel Festival. Centre right & below right: Bongeunsa temple

'*Seoul does not need special angles –
every sight is a panorama to me*'

Anuchai Secharunptong **photographer**

modernity. Yet even among the neon-drenched streets of shopping havens like Myeongdong, you are never more than a block away from a poky side street where every restaurant sells old-style omelettes, or from a gloriously down-at-heel watering hole serving up rice wine in metal pots. Amid all the comforts of the ubiquitous Starbucks and US restaurant chains, it is the familiar pleasures of street-side food vendors that will often draw the biggest queues of Koreans.

Do a bit more searching, and Seoul yields plenty more. Tucked away in improbably quiet spots around the city, ancient Buddhist temples offer rare moments of quiescence amid truly beautiful forested mountains. In Hongdae and Daehangno, Seoul's ever more boho youth unleash their creativity in a blizzard of theatres, music venues and nightclubs. Look hard enough, and you'll even discover islands of urban allure in the sea of soulless high-rises: in artsy Samcheong-dong, concrete towers are replaced by charming, eaved-roof structures housing boutiques, galleries and delightful old teahouses.

Seoul's long past and rollercoaster present have passed many people by. They shouldn't any more.

Niels Footman

Instant Passport

Population
17,500,000 (core city 10,231,000)

Area
1,049sq km

Where is it?
On the Han River, about 40km inland of South Korea's north-west coast

Climate
Cold winters, hot, humid summers, and temperate springs and autumns

Ethnic mix
Overwhelmingly ethnic Korean, some Chinese

Major sights
The 'Five Grand Palaces' (of which Gyeongbukgung is the grandest), Cheonggyecheon Stream, War Memorial, Jogyesa Temple, National Museum of Korea, Jongmyo Shrine, N Seoul Tower, Insa-dong, the historic Dongdaemun Gate and surrounding fashion market, 63 Building

Insiders' tips
Samcheong-dong, Garosugil, Heyri Art Village, Namhansanseong Mountain Fortress in Gyeonggi Province, Songbuk-dong, Bukchon Hanok Village

Where's the buzz?
Hongdae, Itaewon, Myeong-dong, Daehangno

Historical milestones
Designation of Seoul as Joseon Dynasty capital in 1394, March 1st Independence Movement, Korean War, Park Chung-hee's military coup in 1960, 1987 pro-democracy movement, 1988 Summer Olympics, 2002 World Cup

Number of *noraebang* (karaoke rooms)
6,733

Most famous foods
Kimchi (spicy fermented cabbage), bibimbap (steamed rice, vegetables and red pepper paste), bulgogi (marinated barbecued beef), naengmyeon (cold noodles served in ice with radish, slices of Korean pear, bits of beef and a boiled egg), samgyetang (chicken broth made with ginseng)

Cost of a 375ml bottle of soju (Korea's national spirit, around 20% alcohol by volume)
£1

National sport
Taekwondo

Main sporting arenas
Olympic Stadium, World Cup Stadium

Exports
Electronics (Samsung), cars, films, pop singers

Amount of Canada you could buy if you sold Seoul
75%, exorbitant real-estate prices being a common complaint

Seville

SPAIN

The guardian of Andalucían tradition

The heat reflecting off cobbled pavements, the castanet chatter of old women gossiping on street corners, the cacophony of bells ringing out from church belfries in tiny squares and patios… Seville might be home to the big Spanish stereotypes – flamenco, bullfighting and guitar – but it is the rhythms of daily life that define it.

Unlike so many historic towns, Seville has not sold its soul to the tourist trade. Of course there are miniature matador statues and polyester flamenco frocks for sale in shops around the Giralda, but the rest of the old town, with its labyrinthine lanes and Moorish courtyards, remains a hotbed of Andalucían activity – a place where children play, families eat and drink, and grandmas ritually throw buckets of bleach over their front doorsteps every morning.

Weekend visitors adore the authentic tapas bars, the experience of eating juicy olives and slices of jamón among tables of laughing, chattering locals, but it takes time to do more than scratch the surface of this city. Sevillanos – a fiercely proud people – prefer to keep their traditions and culture to themselves. Even attempts by visitors at the local lingo can be met with levels of indifference not even seen on the streets of Paris. This exclusivity might seem isolating and parochial, a sentiment collaborated by Seville's geographical location at the extreme South of Europe, but it has preserved the city's traditions and ensurerd its way of life remains pure and unadulterated.

That Sevillano families still congregate at local *peñas* to see the sweat flung from the brow of an impassioned flamenco dancer is proof the *gitano* heritage lives on. That the afternoon siesta is still rigidly adhered to, while other Spanish cities have extended their working day, is a marvel (even if it does mean occasionally missing

Architecture	7
Arts & Culture	5
Buzz	9
Food & Drink	5
Quality of Life	7
World Status	1
Total	34/60
Rank	**34**

Left: Casa de Pilatos. Above: top right, flamenco at Los Gallos; bottom left, feeling the heat in Plaza d'España

lunch). That even the most minor feast days continue to attract, on a weekly basis, the fanfare and fervour of religion in centuries past, is testament to a city basking in its traditions.

Seville's future, however, is less certain. Citizens might think a spanking new tramline through the heart of town heralds a coming of age, but this is no Madrid or Barcelona. There are but a handful of five-star hotels, even fewer world-class restaurants. There may be an H&M and a Topshop, but the retail units designed for high-end boutiques are still waiting to attract tenants.

Herein, of course, lies its beauty. As long as Seville keeps its hold on the past, its future as the guardian of the Spanish tradition is assured.

Penny Watson

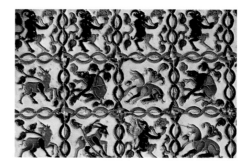

Top: bullfighting at Plaza de Toros de la Real Maestranza. Middle: left, Los Gallos; centre: tiles in the Alcazar and famous Seville oranges. Centre right: Casa Placido fino bar. Bottom: left, Puente de Isabel II; right, Casa de Pilatos

Instant Passport

Population
1,450,214 (core city 704,414)

Area
140sq km

Where is it?
On the Guadalquivir river plain in south-east Spain

Climate
Mild winters, but hot, hot summers. Seville is known as *la sarten de Europa* – 'the frying pan of Europe' – because it holds the record for the highest recorded temperature in a European city: 50°C

Ethnic mix
Spanish and other Europeans, Moroccan, Ecuadorian, Colombian

Major sights
Alcázar, Casa de Pilates, Palacio Arzobispal, Barrio de Santa Cruz, Catedral, La Giralda, Ayuntamiento, Museo de Bellas Artes, Palacio de Lebrija, Torre del Oro, Archivo de Las Indias

Insiders' tips
Salty prawns outside Cerveceria La Grande, on Calle San Jacinto in Triana

Where's the buzz?
Calle Betis, on the waterfront in Triana; the bars around Alameda de Hercules in the Macarena district

Roman name
Hispalis

Arabic name
Isbilya

Period of Moorish rule
711 to 1492

Symbol of the city
The *madeja*. Found all over the city, it looks like NO-8-DO (the '8' is to represent a looped skein of wool) and means 'she never abandoned me'

Artists born in Seville
Diego Velázquez, Bartolomé Murillo, Juan de Valdés Leal, Juan Martínez Montañés

Host of international expos
Ibero-American Exhibition of 1929, Expo 1992

Second-largest building in Spain
Royal Tobacco Factory. It had stables for 400 mules, 24 patios and a jail

Number of bullrings in Andalucía
150

Operas set in Seville
Bizet's *Carmen*, Rossini's *The Barber of Seville*, Verdi's *La Forza del Destino*, Beethoven's *Fidelio*, Mozart's *Don Giovanni* and *The Marriage of Figaro*, Prokofiev's *Betrothal in a Monastery*

Tapas

The original *tapa* was a small dish the *camarero* (barman) placed over your drink – hence the name: lid. The reason for him doing so is unclear, most likely simply to keep flies off, while the small size of the portions thus served was probably due to a combination of poverty and heat, neither of which made eating a large meal desirable. Such snacks were originally always served free, but nowadays in Seville, where tapas have evolved into something of an art form, you can expect to pay a couple of euros a dish.

They are not all always on offer, but tapas come in four basic sizes: a *pincho* (more or less a mouthful), a *tapa* (a saucerful or so – though, traditionally, the same size as a *pincho*), a *media-ración* (half a plateful) and a *ración* (a plateful). Typically, customers choose what they want from trays under a glass counter, but the tapas list is sometimes displayed on a bar menu or a board. The bill is always settled after you've eaten.

The enormous variety of dishes runs from some olives or a few slices of cheese to concoctions such as calamares rellenos (stuffed baby squid) or riñones al jerez (kidneys in sherry). Classics include chorizo al vino (spicy sausage in red wine), boquerones en vinagre (anchovies in vinegar), jamón serrano (cured ham) and patatas bravas (potatoes in spicy tomato sauce).

Shanghai

CHINA

Life lived out on the streets

Although much has been written about Shanghai chic – its aspirational skyscrapers, molecular gastronomy, Philippe Starck-designed interiors and luxury boutiques lining the Bund – the city is really more at home when it's sitting out in the street in its pyjamas, chewing on a plate of duck tongues, swigging a bottle of Qingdao and shouting crass jokes to its friends.

Take a wander down Yunnan Lu and you'll find people gathered around miniature tables, mowing through piles of crayfish; or head to the old city on Xuegong Jie where crowds of people crouch at miniature plastic tables, shrouded in smoke from the Dongbei barbeque so thick that you could part it with your hands. Shanghai has a strong tradition of *paidang*, or eating out on the street, and it's common to see shopkeepers set up their fold-out card table on the pavement where they'll spoon pieces of golden-fried yellow fish and warty-looking bitter melon into the mouths of restless youngsters.

The streets are also home to armies of itinerant food vendors: from the Science and Technology Museum, where fleets of Uighur minorities drive bicycle carts laden with mountains of apricot and walnut nougat, to the Jiangsu Lu Bridge, where phalanxes of sweet potato sellers wheel mobile barrel carts, trailing wafts of carmelised pumpkin behind them.

It's a city that attracts starry-eyed migrants from the Yangtze River Delta and beyond, a stepping stone for those on the make. Anyone with a bit of entrepreneurial zeal and access to some tourist tat is free to bring a tarpaulin and try their luck on the street (free, that is, until the police come and the whole makeshift souvenir store is hastily tossed into a carry-all). Along the

Architecture
7
Arts & Culture
4
Buzz
8
Food & Drink
6
Quality of Life
7
World Status
7
Total
39/60
Rank
16

Previous page: morning t'ai chi on the Bund, in front of misty Pudong. Opposite, clockwise from main picture: Nanjing Dong Lu, 'China's number one shopping street'; desserts and cocktail bar Sugar; Shanghai Gallery of Art; Crystal Jade dim sum restaurant; the Fabric Market; Yin Jianxia's boutique Estune. Above: *yuefenpai* calendars and posters

Instant Passport

Population
10,000,000 (core city 8,214,000)

Area
746sq km

Where is it?
In the middle of China's eastern coastline, at the gateway to the Yangtze River Valley

Climate
Extremely hot and humid in summer; autumns are often windy; winters are cold with sub-zero temperatures at night

Ethnic mix
44 ethnic groups make up Shanghai's permanent population. The Han ethnicity accounts for 99.53% of the population, the rest are Hui, Man, Mongolian and Zhuang

Major sights
The Bund, Nanjing Lu, Shanghai Museum, Fuxing Park, Xintiandi, Dongtai Antiques Market, Yu Gardens and Bazaar, Huangpu Park, People's Square, Jade Buddha Temple, Jingan Temple

Insiders' tips
Shanghai dumplings at Ding Tai Fung, the Fabric Market for tailor-made clothes, cup of tea at Shanghai Dabutong Tianshan Tea City

Religious mix
Buddhism and Taoism 98%, Islam 1%, Christianity 1%

Percentage contribution to China's economy
11% (although just 2% of China's population live in Shanghai)

World's busiest port
In 2007, Shanghai Port handled 560 million tons of cargo, ranking it first in the world for a third consecutive year

Top speed (with passengers) of the Shanghai Maglev
450kph (280mph)

Proportion of the world's cranes
In the mid-1990s, one quarter

China's only carbon-neutral hotel
URBN was built with recycled and locally sourced products, and offset using carbon credits

Typical Shanghainese dish
Xiaolongbao (literally 'little basket bun'; dumplings filled with a fragrant, rich soup and juicy pork or crab)

City emblem
A triangle consisting of a white magnolia flower, a junk and a propeller

Immortalised in
Shanghai Express; André Malraux's *Man's Fate*; JG Ballard's *Empire of the Sun*; *Suzhou River*; *Shanghai Story*; *The White Countess*; *Mission: Impossible III*; *Lust, Caution*

waterfront promenade of the Bund you can buy illuminated wheelie skates; flashing crystal replicas of the pearl tower are for sale outside boutiques such as Armani and Zegna. Walk down towards People's Square and you might see a cricket vendor, his bicycle laden with tiny bamboo latticed baskets, surrounded by a deafening cloud of chirping, like a biblical plague on wheels.

In a city so cramped, where communal living is common, the pavement becomes an extension of the home. People take advantage of the cool evening air to lie outside on slatted bamboo beds; old women hunch over basins cleaning bok choi; men stand in buckets taking a bath in the street, their red briefs bright against the grey, Stalinist architecture.

There's a wonderfully carnivalesque atmosphere created by Shanghai's street life; it even comes with such sights as men wheeling carts of overstuffed giant teddybears, Chinese opera performers and troupes of grey-haired grannies in tracksuits doing choreographed dances with swords. It's a perfect example of what urbanist Jane Jacobs calls the 'sidewalk ballet' – the pungent mix of food, commerce and human interaction that is the defining element of any truly vibrant city.

Rebecca Catching

Singapore

REPUBLIC OF SINGAPORE

The city with a Napoleon complex

The Little Red Dot, the Lion City, Disneyland with the Death Penalty… whatever you want to call it, there is only one Singapore. A young nation, in less than 50 years Singapore has transformed itself from a rustic fishing village into an Asian metropolis. Its Napoleonic ambitions have seen the city-state turn out one of the world's top airlines, a bustling port, and host the world's first Formula One night race; all the while keeping the city clean, green and ultimately very safe. Here, people leave their iPhone on a chair to reserve a seat in a café – only in Singapore.

Likewise only here will you find *all* of the following: a commercial ban on chewing gum, a zero-tolerance drug policy, zoned but perfectly legal prostitution, and a law that outlaws homosexuality, even though a drag queen is one of the national icons.

And the paradoxes continue. In the streets, rag-and-bone men ply their trade as designer-clad yuppies rush by clutching their Starbucks takeaway. Glass-and-steel skyscrapers sit alongside charming 19th-century shops and houses, and on the trains of the MRT (Singapore's metro system) at rush hour it is not unusual to see an old dhoti-clad man standing shoulder to chin with a blonde Swedish exchange student.

Criticised for its lack of soul, Singapore's urban landscape is slowly evolving. The nightlife scene is expanding, getting bigger, brighter and louder – clubs now open till 6am and burlesque shows are on the rise. Local creative talent is celebrated, when once it would have been ignored. The advent of two 'Integrated Resorts' (aka casinos) will undoubtedly boost tourist numbers, and the ethnic quarters – Little India, Chinatown, Arab Street – are increasingly becoming *the* places to live, eat and breathe.

Previous page: Loof rooftop bar.
Top: left, Haw Par Villa; centre,
Jurong BirdPark; right, Chinatown.
Below: Chomp Chomp hawker
centre. Opposite: Anderson Bridge

'Singapore is a paradox of success and insecurity amid a constant search for achievement – in the most positive and loving way possible. It wants to be New York, Paris, London, Switzerland, Shanghai, Hong Kong… but thankfully ends up being only Singapore'

Jing Quek photographer

The true spirit of Singapore lies in the hawker centres. While many locals are not as sophisticated as those of London, New York or Paris, their palate for good food is certainly refined. Eating is the national pastime and the great social equaliser. Wealthy Chinese businessmen sit beside minimum wage construction workers, each tucking eagerly into bowls of noodles, making small talk about what they'll have for supper, even if it is only seven in the morning.

Singapore may be a country full of quirks and idiosyncrasies, but it is proving itself to be a city of the third millennium.
Charlene Fang

Instant Passport

Population
4,000,000 (core city 3,894,000)

Area
479sq km

Where is it?
In south-east Asia, at the southern tip of the Malay Peninsula

Climate
Equatorial. Singapore is located one degree (85 miles) north of the equator and has a tropical rainforest climate that is hot and humid

Ethnic mix
76% Chinese, 15% Malay, 6% Indian

Major sights
Singapore Zoo, Night Safari, Sentosa, Singapore Flyer, Asian Civilisations Museum, Peranakan Museum, National Museum

Insiders' tips
Manchester United café, Little India, Chinatown, Arab Street

Where's the buzz?
Shopping on Orchard Road, lunching on pan-fried radish cakes at the Maxwell Food Centre, nightlife on Robertson Quay

Religions
Buddhism, Islam, Christianity, Taoism, Hinduism

Key religious buildings
Thian Hock Keng Temple, Sultan Mosque, Sri Mariamman Temple

Highest peak
Bukit Timah Hill (163.63m)

Number of eateries
Over 4,000

Local flavours
Chicken rice, fish-head curry, char kway teow (wok-fried flat noodles with dark soy sauce, cockles, beansprouts and possibly Chinese sausage), chilli crab, rojak (raw fruit and vegetables in an addictive sweet spicy sauce), roti prata (unleavened bread with curry sauce)

First Singapore Sling
1915, served in the Long Bar at Raffles Hotel

Fine for first littering offence in Singapore dollars
1,000

Number of buildings with more than 25 storeys
700

Percentage of Singaporeans living in public housing flats
Almost 90%

Linguistic confusion
In Singlish, 'keep your clothes' means 'put your clothes away'

Stockholm

SWEDEN

Self-conscious purveyors of Scandinavian style

Tucked midway up the east coast of Sweden, along the Baltic Sea, Stockholm comes portioned out in islands. These islands and their watery views supply much of the city's charm, from the fishermen reeling catches of salmon and sea trout in front of the parliament building, to the ferries transporting tourists to the amusement park and museums on the green island of Djurgården.

At Stockholm's centre lies Gamla Stan, the 'Old Town', founded in the 13th century and now one of the best preserved medieval cities in northern Europe. The foreign invasions, fires and plagues that once swept through the island's narrow cobblestone streets have given way to souvenir shops, restaurants, and cafés smelling of cinnamon buns and waffle cones. To the west is Riddarholmen, which provides a spectacular view of Lake Mälaren and the brick Stadshuset in the distance, site of the annual Nobel Prize awards banquet. To the east lies Skeppsholmen, a former naval base where the Modern Art Museum looks down on the sailboats lining its shores.

So far, so picture-postcard. During the 1950s and '60s, Stockholm was desperate to modernise itself, and much of the historic districts to the north of the islands were bulldozed to make way for a rebuilt downtown. This controversial regeneration took the form of widened roads, boxy concrete buildings, and five 'skyscrapers' at Hötorget that fall a good deal short of scraping the sky. The heart of this project – or its soulless pit, depending on your point of view – is at Sergels torg, where the Kulturhuset (cultural centre) stands, a giant glass wall dominating the square and busy roundabout beneath. Although the rebuilding was aesthetically questionable, it resulted in a clean, well-organised

Above: top, Engelbert Monument; centre, Café Blå Porten. Overleaf: centre, colourful flags along Drottninggatan; top right, Millesgården statues. Last page: Gamla Stan

Architecture
7
Arts & Culture
6
Buzz
5
Food & Drink
6
Quality of Life
9
World Status
5
Total
38/60
Rank
18

city that can be crossed just as easily on foot as by bus or underground. Stockholm is not large by international standards, but it is now undoubtedly the economic centre of the region, with many of the country's key businesses located here.

Stockholmers have a reputation in Sweden for being snobbish and overly trend-conscious. Though this opinion probably results from a provincial inferiority complex, there is something decidedly un-laidback about Stockholmers hurrying along in their black clothing and designer eyeglasses, texting and talking as they go. Ever the efficient Swedes, meeting up for coffee with a friend is

often planned weeks in advance. Relaxation – or an alcohol-fuelled form of it – comes at the weekend, when Stockholmers do their best to win the ongoing Scandinavian Binge-Drinking Contest. In their defence, the long cold winters and grey slushy streets of the city do tend to darken even the most illuminated minds: Strindberg was certainly scowling about something. Summertime, thankfully, is a different story. Clean water means beaches and swimming right downtown. And if you're lucky, a beaming, strolling, ice-cream-licking Stockholmer might even say hello to you.
Chad Henderson

'Visitors tell us that in Stockholm we are never more than 15 minutes from beautiful forests or the archipelago. As residents we work or party hard, depriving ourselves of time to actually leave the centre to find out. Are we dreaming of the Big City? Please don't wake us up, we're quite enjoying it'

Mårten Claesson **architect and partner in Claesson Koivisto Rune designers**

Instant Passport

Population
1,400,000

Area
518sq km

Where is it?
On Sweden's south-east coast, where Lake Mälaren meets the Baltic Sea

Climate
Mild summers and cold winters, with snow falling December to March

Ethnic mix
Predominantly Swedish; the largest minority is Finnish, with smaller Iraqi, Iranian, Turkish and Somali communities

Major sights
Skansen open-air museum, Vasamuseet, the Royal Palace, Gröna Lund amusement park, Stadshuset tower, Södermalm cliffs, ABBA the Museum

Insiders' tips
The orchard café at Rosendals trädgård on Djurgården, swimming from the beach on Långholmen island, free art exhibitions at Kulturhuset and Östermalms Saluhall

Where's the buzz?
For clubbing, Stureplan; the trendy shops and lively bars of Götgatan and SoFo (south of Folkungagatan, east of Götgatan) on Södermalm

Number of islands
14, connected by 57 bridges. The whole archipelago has 24,000 islands

Stockholm subway
68 miles long. Although described as the world's longest art gallery, the subway's Kungsträdgården is one of the few stations worth seeing

Number of hours of daylight
An hour in December; up to 18.5 hours in June

Number of days of snow a year
95

Exports
Design (IKEA and H&M are famous success stories), music (the world's third largest exporter of music)

Richest Swede
Ingvar Kamprad, IKEA founder and the world's fourth-richest person

Most successful band
ABBA, the world's second-most successful group after the Beatles. Having sold 380 million records, they still sell two or three million a year

Average Stockholmer
39 years old, earns SEK20,500 per month, has 1.36 children

Famous Stockholmers
Greta Garbo, Ingmar Bergman, Björn Borg, August Strindberg, Alfred Nobel, Lasse Hallström, Annika Sörenstam

Architecture
7
Arts & Culture
6
Buzz
7
Food & Drink
7
Quality of Life
10
World Status
5
Total
42/60
Rank
9

Sydney

AUSTRALIA

A city of sun and self

Melbourne might have got the brains, but boy-oh-boy, Sydney got both the looks and the outgoing personality – and it sure knows how to work it. If you want be shown a good time, then Sydney is the kind of place that will put out on the first night and it'll be love at first sight. It's famed for its irresistible physical charms: the Harbour Bridge, the Opera House, the world-class surfing beaches on its doorstep, the New Year's Eve fireworks, the alfresco restaurants, the weather… Easy to get to know, its brazen style and sunny hedonism have caught the roving eye of the world.

In contrast to the founding European culture, there is a classless egalitarianism to Sydney where traders and 'tradies' (labourers) drink their flat whites and their schooners of Coopers in the same places, where 'Tall Poppy Syndrome' soon sees the bigheads cut down to size, where the Prime Minister can put his arm around the Queen if he so pleases. There is also an obsessively healthy, body-beautiful, outdoors feel to the city – all early morning surfs and banana smoothies – although this is often just the hangover cure for the big night before.

Sun-drenched with colour by day, Sydney is arguably even more colourful after dark. Along the city's pink strip – the 'bottom end' of Oxford Street in Darlinghurst – every night is Mardi Gras. Seven-foot drag queens with names like Tora Hymen and Carmen Geddit totter down the same stretch as rugby boys on bar crawls without batting a fake eyelash. Over in Kings Cross, the neon-streaked nightlife finds a harder edge as high-end cocktail bars and strip clubs hawk for trade in the glare and blare alongside the unbalanced freakosystem of ghoulish prostitutes, crack addicts and 24-hour deep-fried-pizza stalls.

'Everyone in Sydney has a place to be, a place they're going, which can frustrate people that come from Melbourne or Queensland. It's an amazing lifestyle. It's very headstrong and you've got everything going for you. There's not really anything about it that's slacking, messy. It's a sexy place where people can achieve their goals and live their dreams'

Ruby Rose VJ on MTV Australia

Instant Passport

Population
3,502,000

Area
1,687sq km

Where is it?
On Australia's south-east coast, in New South Wales, around a collection of bays where the Parramatta River opens into the Tasman Sea

Climate
Moderate with hot and sunny summers (but with more rain than you might expect) and mild in winter

Ethnic mix
European, south-east Asian, Lebanese, Aboriginal; 40% of the population were born overseas

Major sights
The Opera House, Harbour Bridge, Bondi Beach, the 'pink strip' of Oxford Street, Sydney Cricket Ground, ferry to Manly, the world-class Sydney Aquarium, Palm Beach

Insiders' tips
Museum of Contemporary Art, Belvoir Street Theatre, Bronte Beach, Harry's Café de Wheels, Hotel Hollywood, Quay restaurant, Ivy Pool Club, Bondi to Coogee cliff walk, seaplane to Jonah's, Harbourview Park, Paddington Maze

Where's the buzz?
The urban grittiness of Newtown; the bars, restaurants and vintage shops of Surry Hills; the café society and independent boutiques of fashionable Paddington; the beach culture of Bondi and Manly; for village atmosphere, Balmain

Exports
Lamb, beer, wine, bar staff, sports stars, soap starlets, A-list actresses, surfers, shark-attack news stories, media moguls

Imports
Convicts were transported to New South Wales from 1788 and 1840

Percentage of workforce with a university degree
20%

Length of foreshore around Sydney Harbour
More than 240km

Number of tiles in the Sydney Opera House
1,056,006

Number of people who died during construction of the Harbour Bridge
16. It was completed in 1932

Tallest building
Sydney Tower, 304m

Record amount spent on Sydney's New Year's Eve fireworks
A$5 million (£2.3 million)

Gorgeous as Sydney is from a distance, a closer inspection reveals dirt under the nail polish. Founded in 1788, but dreamed as Aboriginal tribal land many moons before, this city was once the world's largest open prison. To this day, Sydney neither forgives nor disowns its criminal past; like a scar, it's worn defiantly, almost proudly. Scratch Sydney's gloss and all that bad blood bubbles back up. But even in the gutter of the Cross and Oxford Street, the city is still gazing at the stars.

Dan Rookwood

Previous page: Harbour Bridge. Opposite: top left to right, Opera House, Botanical Gardens, Harbour Bridge; centre left, Luna Park; bottom left to right, Slip Inn's Garden Bar, Paddington, Bather's Pavilion at Balmoral Beach. Above: walking the cliffs from Bondi to Coogee

Architecture	6
Arts & Culture	6
Buzz	9
Food & Drink	4
Quality of Life	5
World Status	5
Total	35/60
Rank	**28**

Tel Aviv

ISRAEL

A relative youngster high on hedonism

It's hard to believe that a city so intense and dynamic has stood for only 100 years – a fleeting moment compared to the history of other great cities around the world. Israel's 'bubble' is so full of life, surely it's always been here?

Tel Aviv's youth explains much about its character, temperament and neuroses. In a region so steeped in history, a land where under every stone you can find fruit pips tossed by Jesus's pals, Muhammad's friends, Richard the Lionheart's soldiers or Napoleon's warriors, 100 years is a heartbeat. And so Tel Aviv is the Middle East's recalcitrant teenager, rebelling against its conservative parents, experimenting with drugs and alcohol, and up for anything. Party nights are longer, experiences are more extreme, the pace is faster and the search for excitement more intense. That's why Tel Aviv's nightlife is legendary. Bars are open every night untill dawn and throb with the beautiful people. But if you want to check any out, you'll need the freshest inside information; last summer's hot bar is often closed for renovations (to be replaced by a fashion store), and the abandoned wreck of a loft from last autumn is now the coolest club in town, though who knows if it'll make it through winter.

Tel Aviv is a vibrant city. Zealous. Passionate. At 3am the streets are bustling, cars zipping from one place to the next, shaken by the bass beats of their powerful stereos. People on their nights out swallow pills of Hagigat (a popular designer drug sold in kiosks at NIS 50), frantically look for a parking spot in the winding alleys and debating the smörgåsbord of bars and clubs on offer.

During the afternoons and at weekends, the cafés along the beach promenade are packed. The annual love and gay parades continuously expand, their crowds increasing and

Previous page: Whiskey A Gogo. Above: Tel Aviv Port.
Right: top, Florentine neighbourhood; centre, Shenkin Street;
bottom, banks of the Yarkon River

Instant Passport

Population
2,300,000

Area
453sq km

Where is it?
On Israel's Mediterranean coast, on the outskirts of the ancient port of Jaffa

Climate
Mild winters; hot, humid summers

Ethnic mix
Jewish majority, the rest Arabs (Muslims, Christians) and non-Arab (Christians, Buddhists)

Major sights
The beach, old Jaffa, Rothschild Boulevard, Neve Tzedek, Hassan Bek Mosque

Insiders' tips
Tel Aviv's White City, in north Tel Aviv, contains more than 5,000 modernist buildings inspired by the Bauhaus and Le Corbusier

Where's the buzz?
The Cantina, the Brasserie, Barzilay Club, Levontin 7

City founded
1909

Meaning of Tel Aviv
Spring Hill. The name was taken from the Hebrew title of a novel by Zionist leader Theodor Herzi

Israel's capital
1948, when the state of Israel was proclaimed. In 1949 the government was transferred to Jerusalem but it is not internationally recognised as Israel's capital

First time Tel Aviv was hit in the history of the Arab-Israeli conflict
January 1991. An Iraqi Scud missile attack during the first Gulf War caused damage but few casualties

Israel's defense against guerrilla attack
500 warplanes and what is assumed to be the Middle East's only arsenal of nuclear missiles

Major economic institutions
Tel Aviv Stock Exchange, Diamond Exchange

Football teams
Hapoel Tel-Aviv FC, Maccabi Tel Aviv

Also known as
The White City, The Big Orange

Proclaimed a UNESCO World Cultural Heritage site
July 2003

become synonymous with the good life. The answer is its people. A surge of high energy and fervent entrepreneurship has passed along the boulevards, shaking the city. Long abandoned streets and neighbourhoods have undergone a total transformation. Dozens of entertainment venues have opened in the old port, on Ha'araba'a Street, Lilenblum Street and Yad Harutzim Street, each one bigger and more glamorous than the next. This is why it's called 'The Bubble'. Tel Aviv has turned its back on the hardships of existence in favour of the clichéd triangle of sex, drugs and rock 'n' roll. One thing is for sure though: there's never a dull moment. **Amir Ben-David**

becoming more uninhibited from one year to the next. The youth sport of-the-moment looks, complete with tanned hips and six-packs religiously cultivated in the gyms that pop up on every corner. Even astute foreign onlookers have noticed there's something going on here – the *New York Times* dubbed Tel Aviv the coolest city in the Middle East.

What remains a mystery, though, is how a city that has seen economic depression, a wave of terror attacks, two wars (one in Lebanon, the other in Gaza) and political instability caused by the ongoing struggle between Israeli and Palestinian aspirations, has

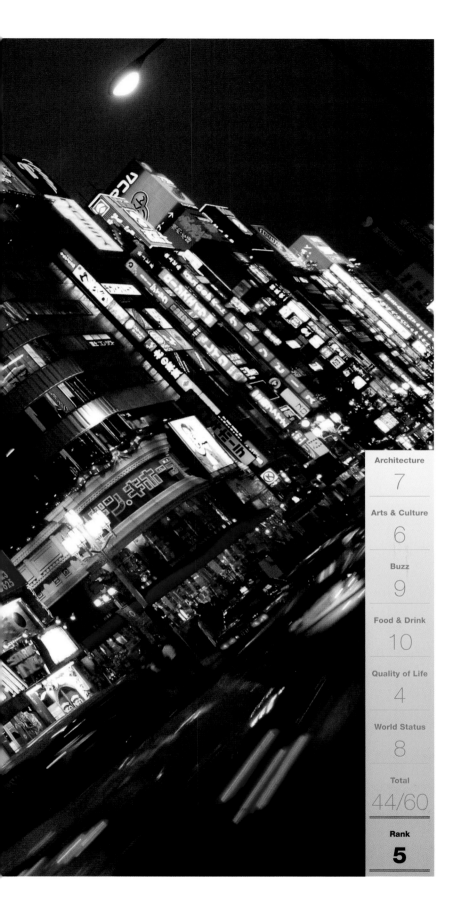

Architecture	7
Arts & Culture	6
Buzz	9
Food & Drink	10
Quality of Life	4
World Status	8
Total	44/60
Rank	5

Tokyo

JAPAN

The world's biggest metropolis

Shibuya Crossing assaults the senses. The gateway to Tokyo's youth-fashion hub, it is one of the most overwhelming locations in a city full of insane energy. Every three minutes a flood of people gushes out across the intersection, heading to department stores, mega-clubs, love hotels and karaoke joints. Sounds from giant video screens bleed into one another, saccharine J-pop topped off with computer-game gun blasts.

Few places in the world can match Shibuya's buzz – maybe Times Square in New York, perhaps London's Piccadilly Circus. But Tokyo also has Shinjuku, the station of which sees 3.6 million people pass through daily; not to mention Ikebukuro, Ginza and Roppongi, all shopping and nightlife districts with energy to burn.

This relentless pace is at the heart of Tokyo's appeal. It is the most populous metropolitan area in the world: nearly 35 million people live in Greater Tokyo, including Kanagawa, Saitama and Chiba. Despite more than a decade of stagnant economic growth, the city still has the world's second-largest stock exchange, and its residents have turned conspicuous consumption into an art form.

Tokyo can look ugly. From up high, a strange geography opens up – a jumble of shoddy buildings, power lines, expressways and concreted rivers. The Great Kanto Earthquake of 1923 and the firebombing of the city during World War II destroyed most of the Edo-era wooden buildings, and many newer structures seem designed to last a decade at most.

Pick through this mess, however, and you'll find pockets of beauty: shrines, temples and parks dot even the busiest neighbourhoods. Hipper areas are accentuated by cutting-edge architecture. At night, when thousands of kanji-covered neon signs

come alive, the mess itself becomes beautiful, although it's a dystopian beauty that's not to everyone's taste.

And then there's the food. There are more than 80,000 restaurants in Tokyo – more than you could try in a lifetime – ranging from greasy yakitori joints to world-class establishments. The city has more Michelin-starred restaurants than any other in the world, but even at cheap places the grub is mostly great.

Tokyo's subcultures are fascinating. Harajuku's street fashions are world famous; US pop star Gwen Stefani was so enamoured of the area's gothic lolitas and *kogals* that she named her backup dancers the Harajuku Girls. The *otaku* (geek) subculture produces an astounding variety of animé and manga. Maid cafés (where

Previous page: Shinjuku's Yasukuni Dori. Opposite: top centre and right, Harajuku street style, Omotesanto Hills mall; middle centre and right, Kabuki-za theatre, Camelot club; bottom left to right, yakitori at Sensoji, Prada in Omotesando, Inokashira Park. Next facing page: Tokyo Tower

Shibuya Crossing

Hachiko is the world's busiest pedestrian crossing, with crowds pouring out of Shibuya station and across its broad stripes every three minutes. Traffic is simultaneously stopped in all directions, allowing pedestrians to cross the junction diagonally as well as one street at a time. The crossing takes its name – Hachiko – from the nearby statue of a loyal dog, who sat waiting for his dead master at the station every day; the statue is now one of the city's most popular meeting points.

Shibuya is one of Tokyo's most youth-oriented districts, the epicentre of its teen culture and street style. To a backdrop of blaring video screens and neon-clad buildings, this is the Tokyo of popular imagination, the first choice of foreign TV crews looking for an instant symbol of the manic city. You can watch it all from the second floor of Starbucks.

Instant Passport

Population
33,200,000 (core city 8,130,000)

Area
6,993sq km

Where is it?
On the east of Japan's main island, Honshu

Climate
Spring and autumn are mild, winters are cold, and summers are hot and humid. The rainy season begins in June

Ethnic mix
248,363 foreigners were living in Tokyo during the last census – just 2% of the total population

Major sights
Tokyo Tower, Shibuya's Hachiko Crossing, Takeshita Dori in Harajuku, Sensoji Temple in Asakusa, Tsukiji fish market, Odaiba

Insiders' tips
Shimokitazawa and Naka Meguro for indie cool, yakitori (grilled chicken) under the train tracks at Yurakucho, Kichijoji's Inokashira Park for a lazy Sunday, authentic Korean food in Shin-Okubo

Where's the buzz?
Shinjuku, Shibuya, Harajuku

Former name
Edo

Number of restaurants
More than 80,000

Number of Michelin-starred restaurants
173

Tons of fish and seafood handled at Tsukiji fish market each day
2,000

Number of train lines
121

Number of days Mount Fuji is visible per year
79

Number of mobile phones
13,351,000

Worst earthquake
The Great Kanto earthquake of 1923 – over 142,000 people were killed

Number killed by the 1945 bombings
Around 100,000

Immortalised in
Tokyo Story; *Godzilla, King of the Monsters*; Tanizaki's *Diary of a Mad Old Man*; *Akira*; Haruki Murakami's novels; *The Ring*; *Lost in Translation*

pretty girls dressed in stylised maid's uniforms serve tea and cakes, treating customers like masters), fan-drawn erotic comics and figurines of naked pre-pubescent girls are standard fare.

This kind of thing gives Tokyo a reputation for being 'weird' that is only partially deserved. Most locals find them unusual too, but non-Japanese really struggle to understand. Meaning is only glimpsed through the cracks in the cultural barrier. Perhaps it's impossible to comprehend such a complex place, and perhaps it doesn't matter – Tokyo fascinates just as much as it confounds.
Shaun Davies

Architecture	5
Arts & Culture	7
Buzz	5
Food & Drink	4
Quality of Life	8
World Status	4
Total	33/60
Rank	**39**

Main picture: CN Tower. Above: middle, Grano; bottom, Nathan Phillips Square

Toronto

CANADA

Excelling – on its own terms

Let's ease you into the idea of Toronto, because it's not a city that jumps up and proclaims itself. It's not that it's a modest place – you don't hold for three decades the (recently eclipsed) title of having the world's tallest freestanding structure by being a wallflower. But in seeking to emulate other cities' attributes and graft them on in an ungainly fashion ('world-class!', 'Little New York!', 'Hollywood North!') to fit a local mould, civic boosters miss the point. Quietly, organically, and in any of the hundred-plus commonly heard languages that abide in relative harmony along its clean and orderly streets, Toronto shapes itself as a compelling place on its own terms.

As Canada's English-language business and culture centre, this sprawling metropolis gets to strut and swagger in a classic big-fish, small-pond style. It's a young city (incorporated in 1834) and draws on its extensive international pedigree to give it shape and definition – the polyglot Toronto is the Toronto story.

Stroll through Kensington Market, an inner-city enclave – part Third World bazaar, part breeding ground for audio installationists and sundry other artistic groups – to get a feel for its lifeblood. Or venture further afield, to its sylvan streets and ravines, and consider them as tentacles reaching into the vast expanse of wilderness that lies somewhere in the Canadian imagination, starting Up North and stretching for thousands of miles.

Toronto is on the same latitude as Florence, so it doesn't share the bold clichés of Canadian iconography – of moose, mountains and men in lumberjack shirts. Being urbane and literate (its public library system is one of the most used anywhere in the world), homegrown voices address themes of communicating across great distances, both physical and cultural, from Marshall McLuhan

NEED OR WANT
A BUTTON?
Go Ahead —
Take ONE!

Left and above right: Kensington
Market. Above: Gooderham
Building. Opposite: top, Kensington
Market; bottom, Power Plant
contemporary art gallery

to Mike Myers and Margaret Atwood, and filmmakers David Cronenberg, Atom Egoyan and Deepa Mehta.

With much of its past shamefully demolished in the name of progress, Toronto is reinventing itself, growing at a clip, compelling locals to document this transformation on any number of wildly popular Internet-based streams and in publications such as spacing.ca. Bold, new architecture offers some dazzle to what has traditionally been a visually underwhelming destination: Mies van der Rohe now stands in good company with Toronto-born Frank Gehry and has some dialogue-inducing competition in Daniel Libeskind's reworking of the Royal Ontario Museum. The city is making itself green, too: it harnesses cold lake water to cool skyscrapers in the summer swelter and imagines a redeveloped docklands, but to date lacks the willpower to make it happen. Reconnecting with the waterfront – an essential character from the city's past, hidden behind a forest of condos – is what will make this Great Lakes city truly great for the many who choose Toronto, not as a nice place to visit, but as somewhere they love to live.
Paul French

Instant Passport

Population
4,367,000 (core city 2,500,000)

Area
1,655sq km

Where is it?
On the north-western shore of Lake Ontario

Climate
One of the mildest in Canada. Winter temperatures hover slightly below freezing (colder in January) and summers are warm

Ethnic mix
European, Chinese, Black, Filipino, South-east Asian, Korean, Arab, Japanese, South Asian, Latin American

Major sights
CN Tower, Harbourfront, Chinatown, Royal Ontario Museum, the Beach, Art Gallery of Toronto, Distillery District, Toronto Islands, Rogers Centre, Casa Loma

Insiders' tips
Queen Street West, the Danforth, College Street

Where's the buzz?
Kensington Market, Chinatown, Greektown, the Beach, Cabbagetown, Yorkville

Combined length of rivers and creeks running through the city
307km, all flowing into Lake Ontario

Percentage of the city's area that is parkland
18.1%

Number of households powered by Exhibition Place's wind turbine
250

Years as site of the world's tallest free-standing structure
34; CN tower (553.33m) finally beaten in 2009 by Burj Dubai (818m)

World's longest street
Yonge Street (1,896km)

Biggest annual parades
Gay Pride, Caribana, Santa Claus Parade

Film and television stars
Mary Pickford, Jim Carrey, Mike Myers, Dan Ackroyd, Eugene Levy, Catherine O'Hara, Rick Moranis, Eric McCormack, John Candy, Keanu Reeves, Christopher Plummer

Sports teams
Toronto Argonauts (American football), Toronto Blue Jays (baseball), Toronto Maple Leafs (ice hockey), Toronto Raptors (basketball), Toronto Rock (lacrosse)

Vancouver

CANADA

Pretty but provincial, and a great place to live

Architecture	4
Arts & Culture	4
Buzz	4
Food & Drink	7
Quality of Life	9
World Status	3
Total	31/60
Rank	**48**

Look down on Vancouver from the Olympian heights of Cypress Mountain, some 4,000 feet above the Strait of Georgia. The city is a sparkly pin-cushion of concrete and glass spires. North by north-west, the firs and pine of densely wooded Stanley Park present an early morning shadow to the downtown peninsula. At 1,000 acres, the park is fully two-thirds the size of the downtown core, larger than Manhattan's Central Park, and maybe the best reason Vancouverites feel so good about their vaunted 'most livable' city.

Now cut to the reverse angle, looking up at the Coastal Mountains from the southern beaches of Kitsilano and Point Grey, sundered from the downtown by the calm waters of English Bay. Yachts, kayaks, canoes and windsurfers share the inlet with passenger ferries, motorboats, and tankers. Cruise ships and float planes dock on the far side of the city, near the photogenic (and Sydney-esque) white sails of Canada Place.

Whichever way you look at it, Vancouver is as pretty as a picture, just so long as your gaze doesn't stray to the shameful squalor of the 'downtown eastside', several blocks bordering the tourist districts Chinatown and Gastown that are notorious for their homeless population, drug problems and high rate of HIV infection.

Such big city blight seems out of proportion with Vancouver's residual small town feel – you can easily traverse the downtown area on foot, or cycle the full extent of the seawall that traces the perimeter of the downtown peninsula in a couple of hours. While it's cosmopolitan in its ethnic mix and fusion cuisine, and basks in its fresh reputation as a 'world class destination' and 2010 Winter Olympic host, the city hasn't shaken its provincial roots just yet.

Left: Capilano Suspension Bridge, swinging on steel cables 70 metres above the river. Above: a totem pole in Stanley Park

Opposite: top left, Hunt & Gather boutique, in reclaimed Blood Alley Square; top centre, the exterior of Arthur Erickson's Museum of Anthropology at UBC; top right, flying kites in Vanier Park; bottom left, Lions Gate Bridge, built in the 1930s. Above: Chinatown

We're a long way – more than 2,000 miles – from the government in Ottawa and the financial powerbrokers of Bay Street. Immigrants from the Asian Pacific may see Vancouver as a gateway to better things, but ambitious young British Columbians head elsewhere in search of fame and fortune. There are pockets of creativity and enterprise, to be sure; but in terms of major cultural institutions, civic infrastructure and architectural accomplishment, Vancouver isn't really there yet.

And yet… 'excitement' is too strong a word, but there is palpable promise and potential here. For all its rapid growth, unlike so many bigger, greater, older towns, it isn't choking on the fumes of over-population and its arteries haven't hardened into permanent gridlock (a 1960s plan to run a highway through the oldest part of town was mercifully quashed by resident protests).

There are less mercenary ambitions that Vancouver is able to accommodate very well: the ideal of an urban existence that's still in touch with nature is the reality here. The ocean and the mountains aren't just a backdrop or a playground, they're a situation, a climate and an atmosphere, and they permeate Vancouverites' attitudes toward body, mind and spirit. Yoga and physical exercise are de rigueur. Greenpeace was born here. It's a peculiarly West Coast phenomenon, perhaps, but as we well know, this eco-consciousness will be central to 21st-century development across the globe.

Tom Charity

Instant Passport

Population
1,830,000

Area
1,120sq km

Climate
Moderate oceanic. Sheltered by Vancouver Island and the mountains, and warmed by the Japan Current, it is notoriously rainy

Where is it?
In the south-west corner of Canada, on the Strait of Georgia, surrounded by the ocean and bordered by mountains. It is Canada's gateway to the Pacific Rim

Major sights
Stanley Park, Capilano Suspension Bridge, Grouse Mountain, Granville Island, Vancouver Island, Museum of Anthropology at the University of British Columbia

Insiders' tips
Hot chocolate infusions at Yaletown's Chocoatl, Havana restaurant-cum-gallery-cum-independent theatre, cycling everywhere, skipping the expensive Capilano Suspension Bridge to visit the Lynn Canyon Park bridge for nothing

Where's the buzz?
Gastown – while Robson Street is all about the brands, the oldest neighbourhood in the city is attracting eclectic, upmarket designer stores

Sports teams
British Columbia Lions (American football), Vancouver Canadians (baseball), Vancouver Canucks (ice hockey), Vancouver Whitecaps (football)

Exports
Seth Rogen, New Pornographers, Black Mountain, Hayden Christensen, Diana Krall, Greenpeace

Distance from Toronto
4,800km

Distance from Tokyo
4,706km

Festivals
International Film Festival every autumn

Number of ice rinks
8

Types of indigenous wild salmon
Coho, spring (also known as king, chinook or tyee), chum (silver bright), sockeye (red, kokanee), pink

Immortalised in
Douglas Coupland's *Girlfriend in a Coma* and *City of Glass*, William Gibson's *Spook Country,* Wayson Choy's *Jade Peony*, Nancy Lee *Dead Girls*, Timothy Taylor's *Stanley Park*

Venice

Beauty, beauty everywhere

Architecture	10
Arts & Culture	8
Buzz	4
Food & Drink	2
Quality of Life	5
World Status	5
Total	34/60
Rank	**34**

The protagonist of Antal Szerb's *Journey by Moonlight* notes that 'by stretching his arms out wide he could have simultaneously touched the opposing rows of houses… The sense of intimacy made it feel almost an intrusion to have entered these streets.' Of all the metropolises described in this book, Venice is probably the smallest and most intimate. Its claustrophobic alleys and maze of streets and squares act as a backdrop to many short stories and novels, often a metaphor for loss or disorientation.

The reality is that Venice, while cheerfully disorientating many a visitor, is less melancholic and disturbing than writers would have us imagine. After the initial shock of the bewildering warren of streets, the newcomer soon feels safe and relaxed enough to abandon their map and take their chances down the city's *calli* and *campi*. Wherever one ends up, there is a guarantee of architectural gems, such as Renaissance churches or Venetian-Byzantine palaces – and water, water everywhere.

Each of the six *sestieri* (neighbourhoods) offers something fabulous to see, to visit, to taste, and there's a cornucopia of bars serving excellent local wines – though the spritz is this city's quintessential pre-dinner tipple. And Venetians do like a drink. In fact, it is in the bars and on the streets that one gets the real feel of the place. The dearth of traffic (at least the four-wheeled variety) creates a unique environment in which children are allowed to run wild and friends exchange gossip as they pass on the bridges.

This is not to detract from Venice's many problems, including a dwindling and ageing population, a lack of jobs, rocketing house prices and the huge influx of visitors, putting a strain on the city's

Previous page: St Mark's canal, with the Basilica and Campanile to the left, San Giorgio Maggiore island to the right. Above and below: St Mark's Square

struggling infrastructure. 'Nothing works, everything's expensive, the tourists are a pain,' Venetians grumble. And how Venetians like to grumble! But if modern Venice has a host of problems, having lost her superiority and independence many centuries ago, she retains a sense of magnificence and extravagance.

Despite no longer enjoying political clout, Venice is putting great effort into becoming a cultural and artistic centre, both in Italy and across Europe. The Biennales and film festival already bring in flocks of artists, filmmakers and architects; the new international university on the island of San Servolo promotes global research and development; and millionaire businessman François-Henri Pinault has single-handedly breathed new life into the city's contemporary art scene with two important projects: Palazzo Grassi and the Centre of Contemporary Arts.

Venice is a problematic and complex little city, but there is a glimmer of hope that it will not sink to become a Disneyland of the Renaissance, instead rising to fresh prominence as an exciting hub of new culture.

Jo-Ann Titmarsh

Burano

The island immediately to the north of the elongated Mazzorbo (and to which it is joined by a long wooden bridge), Burano might have inspired the adjective 'picturesque'. Social life here still centres around the *fondamente*, where the fishermen repair nets or tend to boats moored in the canal below, while their wives – at least in theory – make lace. Of Burano's two major industries, fishing and lace-making, the latter is in a major decline, despite the efforts of the Scuola di Merletti ('Lace School') to pass on the old skills to the younger generation. According to local lore, the fishermen – who have been recorded on the island since the seventh century – first painted their homes in bright colours so they could recognise them when fishing out on the lagoon; in fact, only a tiny proportion of the houses are visible from the lagoon. Whatever the reason, the buranelli still make great efforts in the decoration of their homes. Facing Burano from Mazzorbo, architect Giancarlo De Carlo's attractive, modern, low-cost housing, in shades of lilac, grey and green, makes an interesting counterpoint.

Instant Passport

Population
297,743, of whom only a fifth live in central areas of the city

Area
7.8sq km

Where is it?
In the Venetian Lagoon, on the Adriatic Sea in north-east Italy

Climate
Cold and damp in winter, hot and humid in summer

Ethnic mix
Predominantly white European

Major sights
St Mark's Basilica; the Doge's Palace; Rialto Bridge; the island of San Giorgio Maggiore; the Peggy Guggenheim Collection; the Church of San Zaccaria; the cemetery island of San Michele; Murano, Burano and Torcello islands; the Fondazione Querini Stampalia; Museo Correr; the Jewish Ghetto

Insiders' tips
The restaurants down Calle Lunga San Barnaba in Dorsoduro, the contemporary arts centre at Punta della Dogana, get away from the hordes and into the real city in the neighbourhood of eastern Dorsoduro

Where's the buzz?
The bars around Campo Santa Margherita and the Rialto market; St Mark's Square

Historical milestones
First Doge of Venice elected, theft of St Mark's body from Alexandria to Venice, 14th-century Venetian expansion, Venetian victory against the Ottoman Empire in the Battle of Lepanto, the early 17th-century demise of Venetian power and wealth

Most famous cocktail
The bellini (white peach purée and prosecco), invented in Harry's Bar

Most famous architect
Andrea Palladio (1508-1580), whose late Renaissance style and perfect proportioning swept through Europe and is still admired today

Tallest building
The bell tower in St Mark's Square (just under 99m)

Sports teams
Venezia (football)

Number of islands making up Venice
118

Number of bridges
About 400

Immortalised in
Death in Venice, *Don't Look Now*, *The Comfort of Strangers*, the paintings of Canaletto

Vienna

Facing the future from a retro interior

The post-1989 euphoria bestowed considerable excitement on Prague, Budapest and the other capitals of Vienna's newly liberated eastern neighbours, so why did it take so long for Vienna itself to be recognised? The city was the last stop on the eastern branch line of Western capitalism and for a thousand years was the cosmopolitan centre of European history, its residents hailing from all the Habsburg outposts. However, the events of the 20th century, culminating in Austria's fateful pact with the Nazis in 1938, put paid to this tapestry of nationalities and Vienna became the capital of a stunted Alpine republic of eight million souls. After the war, Vienna was sold to the world as a litany of chocolate-cake clichés of bewhiskered emperors, irascible composers and liveried lackeys. It was natural, then, that outsiders thought it too boring, too authoritarian, too schmaltzy, too expensive even. To make matters worse, Austria's more recent flirtations with extreme-right parties and the international echo of the Natascha Kampusch and Josef Fritzl cases, in 2006 and 2008 respectively, have done little to dispel the common perception of Vienna as a city with a gloomy, navel-gazing disposition, the cradle of investigation into humanity's darkest, most inexplicable motives.

While few residents would dispute the Viennese reputation for melancholy, short tempers and a pathological culture of complaint, there are signs this magnificently appointed city is becoming more open, communicative and happier. After all, it is commended year after year in surveys by Mercer Consulting and the Economist Intelligence Unit as one of the world's top-three most liveable cities. Like neighbours Zürich and Geneva, it has enviably high standards in education, healthcare, public transport and safety; unlike them, it has a vibrant cultural scene, hands-on political activism, and great

Architecture	8
Arts & Culture	7
Buzz	7
Food & Drink	4
Quality of Life	9
World Status	5
Total	40/60
Rank	12

Main picture: Stephansdom. Above: top left, Artner; top right, Strauss memorial Stadt park; bottom left, Danube Island; bottom right, Song

eating and drinking. The Viennese are also intensely attached to their leisure – don't try calling an office after 2pm on Friday.

Although Vienna has done very nicely out of flogging Mozart, the Habsburgs, Klimt and sailor-suited choirboys to tourists, outside its historic centre the city has moved on. The dynamism of the Naschmarkt, MuseumsQuartier, Gürtel bars and streets of the 7th district is largely powered by the city's more recent arrivals. About 30 per cent of Vienna's inhabitants are first- to third-generation immigrants; 18.8 per cent of them are not Austrian citizens; an increasing number come from bordering EU states such as mighty Germany, and Austrians can barely disguise their glee when served by a waiter from what used to be their all-powerful neighbour.

Still, Vienna is hardly a multicultural paradise. Austria has Europe's toughest laws on asylum and Amnesty International constantly chides the authorities for flagrant cases of police brutality involving foreigners. Immigrants make their way in the city via the trades and the restaurant business, and the sight of the first headscarf-wearing tram driver in 2008 was enough to make the

'In many ways, Vienna is a little known capital with many, many secrets that would take lifetimes to appreciate. Sitting at the right table in the right café is as important as a good accessory – something immaterial that makes all the difference!'

Francesca von Habsburg **gallery owner**

Instant Passport

Population
1,550,000

Area
453sq km

Where is it?
On the Danube at the eastwards extent of the Alps, in the north-east corner of Austria

Climate
Mild continental. Hot in summer and cold in winter, with the wind often making the temperature seem lower than it is. Rain is frequent in summer

Ethnic mix
68% German-speaking Austrian, with increasing numbers of immigrants: former Yugoslavians, Germans, Turks, Hungarians, Poles and Czechs

Major sights
Belvedere, Heeresgeschichtliches Museum, Hofburg, Karlskirche, Kunsthistorisches Museum, Prater, Ringstrasse, Schönbrunn, Secession, Staatsoper, Stephansdom, Zentralfriedhof

Insiders' tips
Classic Polish sandwich bar Trzesniewski, Karl-Marx-Hof Socialist housing complex, classic Viennese eating at Gasthaus Ubl off the Naschmarkt, the art nouveau Café Rüdigerhof on Hamburger Strasse, Otto Wagner's Kirche am Steinhof, contemporary art galleries on Schleifmühlgasse, bucolic wine tavern Heurigen Zawodsky in Grinzing

Where's the buzz?
MuseumsQuartier, 7th district streetlife, Kettenbrückengasse flea market, open-air foodstalls at the Naschmarket, Gürtel and Danube canal bars

Famous emigrants
Sigmund Freud, Ludwig Wittgenstein, Fritz Lang, Billy Wilder, Josef von Sternberg, Romy Schneider, Peter Lorre, Joe Zawinul

Revolutionary artists and musicians
Gustav Klimt, Egon Schiele, Schönberg, Hermann Nitsch and the Viennese Actionists, Fennesz

Vineyards
7sq km, making Vienna the world's largest wine-growing city

Local flavours
Beuschl (offal stew), Kaiserschmarrn (chopped-up, fluffy pancake, with plum compôte), Käsekrainer (aka Eitriger, 'pus-stick'; sausage filled with melted cheese), Leberkäs ('liver-cheese'; meatloaf made from horse flesh), Leberknödelsuppe (clear beef broth with liver-flavoured dumplings), Sachertorte (heavy chocolate cake with apricot jam filling), Tafelspitz (tender boiled beef with spinach and apple-horseradish sauce), Wiener Schnitzel (veal or pork escalope fried in breadcrumbs)

Immortalised in
The Magic Flute, Haydn's *Creation*, Beethoven's Ninth, Schubert's *Lieder*, Mahler's Eighth, *Blue Danube*, Freud's *The Interpretation of Dreams*, *A Man Without Qualities*, Schönberg's *Pierrot Lunaire*, Joseph Roth's novels, *The Third Man*, *Before Sunrise*, *Kruder & Dorfmeister Sessions*

more retrograde locals choke on their schnitzel. Whether they like
it or not, Polish grocers, Russian restaurants and Balkan turbo-folk
clubs are all firmly part of Vienna today. You can exit a deliriously
decorated Baroque church and enter an avant-garde gallery; drink
locally made wine at a traditional tavern before settling in at one
of many DJ bars; switch from Mozart to Goth-metal as the mood
takes you. The musty air of retrospection that still pervades the
city – particularly in its coffee houses, art nouveau shop façades,
statuary and stiff handshakes – creates a unique feel that gives
Vienna its special character, but now that the city's inhabitants
hail from so many more diverse backgrounds, these trappings
of Old Vienna form a backdrop that inspires rather than stifles.
Geraint Williams

Architecture	6
Arts & Culture	6
Buzz	5
Food & Drink	5
Quality of Life	6
World Status	9
Total	37/60
Rank	**20**

Washington, DC

USA

Watched by the world

It's a bit much to ask everyone to suspend what they know about Washington, DC. Most of the world sees Washington through a news camera of limited scope, focused on a correspondent who is paid to read yet another dull report on war or trade or jobs, inevitably with the White House, the Washington Monument or the US Capitol behind them. This is the boilerplate image, as metonymic as a dateline. It shows only the city's foreground, its large, imposing, and austere front yard. In the flesh, this setting is actually rather picturesque, especially for those who love gleaming marble and neoclassical architecture, but it is also entirely out of scale with the fine, rich grain of the complex and intimate city that surrounds it.

Step one degree away from Washington's monumental core and it is apparent that entire worlds cycle in and out of its streets daily, all drawn in some way by its soberly costumed circus of influence. There are global bureaucrats and bankers, busloads of eighth-grade kids, conventioneers sharing taxicabs, proud sommeliers, expert witnesses, day labourers, protestors with big puppets, retired couples from Ohio or Texas, defence attachés, partying salary gals considering grad school, cross-looking film crews, disgruntled farmers, congressmen washed up after one term, and the occasional sheik, sultan or queen.

And then, just two or three degrees away, there is Washington's very own world, inhabited by hundreds of thousands of lifers settled on intimate rowhouse blocks, to whom politics is a necessary sideshow, one best not observed too closely lest it spoil the scenery, which is gorgeous. Washington is a small, green city. The long, low axes of its shady streets are studded with heroic statuary, but when it's warm, there are flowers everywhere. The

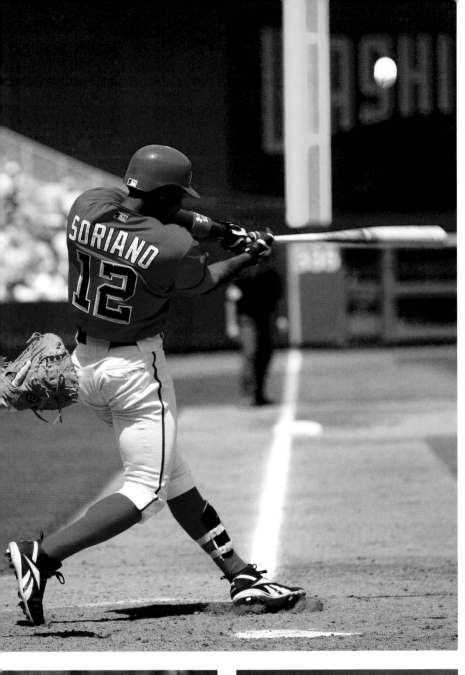

Previous page: ceiling of the Capitol rotunda. Opposite: top right, National Museum of the American Indian; bottom centre, Iwo Jima Memorial; bottom right, Washington Monument. Above: the Washington Metro

neighbourhoods are like villages, each with their own points of pride, some celebrated with block parties and others enforced informally with guns.

In no other American city – except for, perhaps, New York – do the rich, middle-class and poor live so closely together, living with a mixture of pleasure and alarm, since their city has changed in unimaginable ways thanks to a surge of investment and construction in the late '90s. But any progress in the city is hampered by the fact that everything the city's elected leaders want to do must first be scruitinised by Congress, which holds the local taxpayers' purse, though it does not grant them a vote in the House of Representatives – a source of constant chagrin among Washingtonians.

But when Barack Obama arrived as the new president, it gave the city's confidence a boost. Besides acting as analgesic for a wounded nation, Obama has signalled that he, too, believes that the District of Columbia ought to join the 50 states in Congress. The move would wipe the last American colony from the continent, but it will never erase the city's essential character as a stronghold of rationalist hopes, long ago carved out and self-consciously designed as the capital of a virgin nation.

Brad McKee

Instant Passport

Population
3,934,000 (core city 581,530)

Area
2,996sq km

Where is it?
On the Potomac river between Maryland and Virginia

Climate
Hot, humid summers and cold winters, with heavy snowfall and icy winds

Number of visitors a year
In 2007, Washington received 16.2 million visitors – of these, 15 million were domestic visitors and 1.2 million from outside the United States

Ethnic mix
Black, white, Hispanic, Native American, Alaskan, Hawaiian, Pacific Islanders and Asian

Major sights
White House, Smithsonian, Tidal Basin, Lincoln Memorial

Insiders' tips
Old-style political bars, the Hawk & Dove and Bullfeathers; the Tabard Inn

Where's the buzz?
Ben's Chilli Bowl; U Street, around 14th Street

Speeches
Martin Luther King's 'I have a dream' speech was given at the Lincoln Memorial in 1963. In 1957, Senator Strom Thurmond spoke for more than 24 hours straight in delivering the longest ever US Congress speech

Popular museum
National Air and Space Museum. With 219 million visitors in its first 25 years, it is the world's most popular museum

Skyscraper-free
According to the District code, a new building can be no taller than the width of the street it fronts on to plus 20 feet

Taxi drivers
Most of Washington's cab drivers come from Ethiopia

Famous dish
The 'half-smoke' – a pork and beef sausage that is slightly larger and spicier than a standard hot-dog

Wine consumption
The inhabitants of Washington DC consume more wine per capita than residents of any other state

State bird
American goldfinch, aka the wild canary

Immortalised in
All the President's Men, *Mr Smith Goes to Washington*, *Independence Day*, *The West Wing*

Metropolists

THE WORLD'S CITIES COMPARED

The 40 fastest growing

Rank	City/urban area	Country	Average annual population growth 2006 to 2020 (%)
1	Beihai	China	10.58
2	Ghaziabad	India	5.20
3	Sana'a	Yemen	5.00
4	Surat	India	4.99
5	Kabul	Afghanistan	4.74
6	Bamako	Mali	4.45
7=	Faridabad	India	4.44
7=	Lagos	Nigeria	4.44
9	Dar es Salaam	Tanzania	4.39
10	Chittagong	Bangladesh	4.29
11	Toluca	Mexico	4.25
12	Lubumbashi	Congo	4.10
13	Kampala	Uganda	4.03
14	Santa Cruz	Bolivia	3.98
15	Luanda	Angola	3.96
16	Nashik	India	3.90
17	Kinshasa	Congo	3.89
18	Nairobi	Kenya	3.87
19	Dhaka	Bangladesh	3.79
20	Antananarivo	Madagascar	3.73
21	Patna	India	3.72
22	Rajkot	India	3.63
23	Conakry	Guinea	3.61
24	Jaipur	India	3.60
25	Maputo	Mozambique	3.54
26	Mogadishu	Somalia	3.52
27	Gujranwala	Pakistan	3.49
28	Delhi	India	3.48
29	Pune	India	3.46
30	Las Vegas	USA	3.45
31	Addis Ababa	Ethiopia	3.40
32	Indore	India	3.35
33	Faisalabad	Pakistan	3.32
34	Rawalpindi	Pakistan	3.31
35=	Brazzaville	Congo	3.29
35=	Peshawar	Pakistan	3.29
37	Khulna	Bangladesh	3.24
38	Suwon	Republic of Korea	3.23
39	Karachi	Pakistan	3.19
40	Asunción	Paraguay	3.17

Source: www.citymayors.com (2008)

The 50 most visited

Rank	City	Country	Tourist arrivals per year
1	London	UK	15,340,000
2	Hong Kong	China	12,057,000
3	Bangkok	Thailand	10,844,000
4	Singapore	Singapore	10,284,000
5	Paris	France	8,762,000
6	New York City	USA	7,646,000
7	Toronto	Canada	6,627,000
8	Dubai	UAE	6,535,000
9	Istanbul	Turkey	6,454,000
10	Rome	Italy	6,123,000
11	Barcelona	Spain	5,044,000
12	Seoul	South Korea	4,994,000
13	Shanghai	China	4,800,000
14	Dublin	Ireland	4,627,000
15	Kuala Lumpur	Malaysia	4,403,000
16	Pattaya	Thailand	4,387,000
17	Mecca	Saudi Arabia	4,200,000
18	Moscow	Russia	4,050,000
19	Macau	China	3,953,000
20	Amsterdam	The Netherlands	3,909,000
21	Beijing	China	3,900,000
22	Cairo	Egypt	3,896,000
23	Prague	Czech Republic	3,696,000
24	Vienna	Austria	3,637,000
25	Madrid	Spain	3,404,000
26	Guangzhou	China	3,300,000
27	Phuket	Thailand	3,160,000
28	Vancouver	Canada	3,127,000
29	Montreal	Canada	2,736,000
30=	Ho Chi Minh	Vietnam	2,700,000
30=	Shenzhen	China	2,700,000
32	Los Angeles	USA	2,652,000
33	Rio de Janeiro	Brazil	2,627,000
34	Mexico City	Mexico	2,560,000
35	Berlin	Germany	2,552,000
36	Mumbai	India	2,436,000
37	Tokyo	Japan	2,422,000
38	Miami	USA	2,341,000
39	Brussels	Belgium	2,328,000
40	Athens	Greece	2,300,000
41	Buenos Aires	Argentina	2,286,000
42	San Francisco	USA	2,270,000
43	Warsaw	Poland	2,210,000
44	Budapest	Hungary	2,119,000
45	St Petersburg	Russia	2,100,000
46	Munich	Germany	2,098,000
47	Orlando	USA	2,055,000
48	Cancún	Mexico	2,022,000
49	Delhi	India	1,920,000
50	Milan	Italy	1,914,000

Source: Euromonitor International Top City Destinations Ranking, www.euromonitor.com (2008)

The 20 oldest continuously inhabited

Rank	City	Location	Earliest habitation
1	Jericho	Palestinian Territories	9,000 BC
2	Byblos	Lebanon	5,000 BC
3=	Aleppo	Syria	4,300 BC
3=	Damascus	Syria	4,300 BC
5	Susa	Iran	4,200 BC
6=	Faiyum	Egypt	4,000 BC
6=	Sidon	Lebanon	4,000 BC
6=	Plovdiv	Bulgaria	4,000 BC
9	Gaziantep	Turkey	3,650 BC
10	Beirut	Lebanon	3,000 BC
11	Jerusalem	Israel/Palestinian Territories	2,800 BC
12	Tyre	Lebanon	2,750 BC
13	Arbil	Iraq	2,300 BC
14	Kirkuk	Iraq	2,200 BC
15	Balkh	Afghanistan	1,500 BC
16=	Athens	Greece	1,400 BC
16=	Larnaca	Cyprus	1,400 BC
16=	Thebes	Greece	1,400 BC
19	Cádiz	Spain	1,100 BC
20	Varanasi	India	1,000 BC

Source: Compiled from several sources (2008)

The top 10 murder capitals

City	Country	Per 100,000 pop.
Belmopan*	Belize	46.67
Panama City	Panama	29.90
Distrito Nacional	Dominican Republic	29.26
Kathmandu	Nepal	24.71
San Salvador	El Salvador	16.30
Ulan Bator	Mongolia	15.29
Managua	Nicaragua	14.09
Quito	Ecuador	13.59
Almaty	Kazakhstan	12.96
Bishkek	Kyrgyzstan	12.56

*The UNODC's 9th report had Caracas, Venezuela, top with 130 homicides per 100,000 of the population, but the current report contains no data on the city.

Source: UNODC, 10th report on Intentional Homicide (2005-2006)

The 10 highest altitude

City	Country	Above sea level (m)
Wenchuan	China	5,099
Potosí	Bolivia	3,976
Oruro	Bolivia	3,702
Lhasa	Tibet (China)	3,684
La Paz	Bolivia	3,632
Cusco	Peru	3,399
Huancayo	Peru	3,249
Sucre	Bolivia	2,835
Tunja	Colombia	2,820
Quito	Ecuador	2,819

Source: UNESCO (2002)

The 50 oldest metro systems

Rank	City	Year opened
1	London	1863
2	Chicago	1892
3=	Budapest	1896
3=	Glasgow	1896
5	Boston	1897
6	Paris	1900
7	Wuppertal	1901
8	Berlin	1902
9	New York	1904
10	Philadelphia	1907
11	Hamburg	1912
12	Buenos Aires	1913
13	Madrid	1919
14	Barcelona	1924
15	Sydney	1926
16	Tokyo	1927
17	Osaka	1933
18=	Moscow	1935
18=	Newark	1935
20	Stockholm	1950
21=	Athens	1954
21=	Toronto	1954
23=	Cleveland	1955
23=	Rome	1955
25	St Petersburg	1955
26	Nagoya	1957
27=	Haifa	1959
27=	Lisbon	1959
29	Kiev	1960
30	Milan	1964
31	Tbilisi	1966
32=	Oslo	1966
32=	Stuttgart	1966
34	Montreal	1966
35=	Baku	1967
35=	Essen	1967
37=	Cologne	1968
37=	Frankfurt	1968
37=	Rotterdam	1968
40=	Beijing	1969
40=	Ludwigshafen	1969
40=	Mexico City	1969
43	Kamakura	1970
44=	Bielefeld	1971
44=	Munich	1971
44=	Sapporo	1971
47=	Nuremberg	1972
47=	San Francisco	1972
47=	Yokohama	1972
50	Pyongyang	1973

Source: www.metrobits.org and www.urbanrail.net (2004-2008)

The 50 longest metro systems

Rank	City	Length (km)
1	London	408
2	New York	368
3	Tokyo	304.5
4	Moscow	292.9
5	Seoul	286.9
6	Madrid	284
7	Shanghai	228.4
8	Paris	213
9	Mexico City	201.7
10	Beijing	198.95
11	Hong Kong	174
12	Washington	171.2
13	Mumbai	171
14	San Francisco	166.9
15	Chicago	166
16	Berlin	144.1
17	Osaka	137.8
18	Guangzhou	116
19	Singapore	109
20	Barcelona	106.6
21	Stockholm	105.7
22	St Petersburg	105.5
23	Hamburg	100.7
24	Busan	95
25	Munich	92.5
26	Nagoya	89
27	Santiago	83
28	Atlanta	79.2
29	Newcastle	76.5
30	Milan	74.6
31	Taipei	74.5
32	St Louis	73.4
33	Tianjin	71.98
34	Toronto	71.3
35	Vienna	69.8
36	Montreal	69.2
37	Delhi	68
38	Cairo	65.5
39	Kuala Lumpur	64
40	Bucharest	63
41=	Oslo	62
41=	Philadelphia	62
43	São Paulo	61.3
44=	Caracas	60.5
44=	Boston	60.5
46	Kiev	59.8
47	Prague	59.1
48	Yokohama	57.6
49	Daegu	53.9
50	Pittsburgh	53.56

Source: www.metrobits.org and www.urbanrail.net (2004-2008)

The 40 most expensive

Rank	City	Country
1	Moscow	Russia
2	Tokyo	Japan
3	London	UK
4	Oslo	Norway
5	Seoul	South Korea
6	Hong Kong	China
7	Copenhagen	Denmark
8	Geneva	Switzerland
9	Zurich	Switzerland
10	Milan	Italy
11	Osaka	Japan
12	Paris	France
13	Singapore	Singapore
14	Tel Aviv	Israel
15	Sydney	Australia
16=	Dublin	Ireland
16=	Rome	Italy
18	St Petersburg	Russia
19	Vienna	Austria
20	Beijing	China
21	Helsinki	Finland
22	New York City	USA
23	Istanbul	Turkey
24	Shanghai	China
25=	Amsterdam	Netherlands
25=	Athens	Greece
25=	São Paulo	Brazil
28	Madrid	Spain
29	Prague	Czech Republic
30	Lagos	Nigeria
31=	Barcelona	Spain
31=	Rio de Janeiro	Brazil
31=	Stockholm	Sweden
34	Douala	Cameroon
35	Warsaw	Poland
36	Melbourne	Australia
37	Munich	Germany
38	Berlin	Germany
39	Brussels	Belgium
40	Frankfurt	Germany

Source: Mercer, www.mercer.com (2008)

The 40 richest (GDP)

Rank	City/urban area	Country	GDP (US$bn)
1	Tokyo	Japan	1,191
2	New York	USA	1,133
3	Los Angeles	USA	639
4=	Chicago	USA	460
4=	Paris	France	460
6	London	UK	452
7	Osaka/Kobe	Japan	341
8	Mexico City	Mexico	315
9	Philadelphia	USA	312
10	Washington DC	USA	299
11	Boston	USA	290
12	Dallas/Fort Worth	USA	268
13	Buenos Aires	Argentina	245
14	Hong Kong	China	244
15	San Francisco/Oakland	USA	242
16	Atlanta	USA	236
17	Houston	USA	235
18	Miami	USA	231
19	São Paulo	Brazil	225
20	Seoul	South Korea	218
21	Toronto	Canada	209
22	Detroit	USA	203
23	Madrid	Spain	188
24	Seattle	USA	186
25	Moscow	Russia	181
26	Sydney	Australia	172
27	Phoenix	USA	156
28	Minneapolis	USA	155
29	San Diego	USA	153
30	Rio de Janeiro	Brazil	141
31	Barcelona	Spain	140
32	Shanghai	China	139
33	Melbourne	Australia	135
34	Istanbul	Turkey	133
35	Denver	USA	130
36	Singapore	Singapore	129
37	Mumbai	India	126
38	Rome	Italy	123
39	Montreal	Canada	120
40	Milan	Italy	115

Source: www.citymayors.com (2008)

40 best for quality of living

Rank	City	Country
1	Vienna	Austria
2	Zurich	Switzerland
3	Geneva	Switzerland
4=	Vancouver	Canada
4=	Auckland	New Zealand
6	Düsseldorf	Germany
7	Munich	Germany
8	Frankfurt	Germany
9	Bern	Switzerland
10	Sydney	Australia
11	Copenhagen	Denmark
12	Wellington	New Zealand
13	Amsterdam	The Netherlands
14	Brussels	Belgium
15	Toronto	Canada
16=	Berlin	Germany
16=	Ottawa	Canada
18	Melbourne	Australia
19	Luxembourg	Luxembourg
20	Stockholm	Sweden
21	Perth	Australia
22	Montreal	Canada
23	Nuremberg	Germany
24	Oslo	Norway
25	Dublin	Ireland
26=	Singapore	Singapore
26=	Calgary	Canada
28	Hamburg	Germany
29	Honolulu	USA
30=	Helsinki	Finland
30=	San Francisco	USA
30=	Adelaide	Australia
33	Paris	France
34	Brisbane	Australia
35=	Tokyo	Japan
35=	Boston	USA
37	Lyon	France
38=	Yokohama	Japan
38=	London	UK
40	Kobe	Japan

Source: Mercer, www.mercer.com (2009)

The 10 greenest

Barcelona, Spain
Built environment Hailed for its pedestrian-friendliness with 37% of all trips taken on foot.
Power All new buildings and major refurbishments are obligated to provide 60% of their hot water through solar energy.

Bogotá, Colombia
Transport Highly efficient bus transit system and more than 290 kilometres of cycle paths. An annual 'car-free day' and congestion initiatives aim to eliminate personal car use during rush hour by 2015.

Copenhagen, Denmark
Transport The city opened a new metro system in 2000 to make public transit more efficient and 36% of commuters cycle to work.
Built environment Recently won the European Environmental Management Award for cleaning up public waterways.
Power Middelgrunden offshore wind farm provides more than 10% of Denmark's energy.

Curitiba, Brazil
Transport A bus system hailed as one of the world's best with about three-quarters of residents relying on public transport.
Green space With municipal parks benefiting from the work of a flock of 30 lawn-trimming sheep, this midsized Brazilian city has become a model for other metropolises with over 580 square feet of green space per inhabitant.

London, UK
Transport Taxes on personal transportation to limit congestion in the centre of the city are waived for electric and hybrid vehicles. All London buses are to be hybrid vehicles by 2012.
Power Under London's Climate Change Action Plan the city will switch 25% of its power to locally generated, more efficient sources within the next 20 years.
Green space More than 40% of the city is parkland and green space.

Malmö, Sweden
Built environment With the goal of making Malmö an ekostaden (eco-city), several neighbourhoods have already been transformed using innovative design and are planning to become more socially, environmentally, and economically responsive.
Green space Known for its extensive parks and green space with 355 square feet per inhabitant.

Portland, Oregon, USA
Transport Portland runs a comprehensive system of light rail, buses, and bike lanes to help keep cars off the roads and is the first US city to enact a comprehensive plan to reduce CO2 emissions.
Built environment Has aggressively pushed green building initiatives.
Green space Boasts 92,000 acres of green space and more than 120 kilometres of hiking, running, and biking trails.

Reykjavik, Iceland
Transport The city runs hydrogen buses on its streets.
Power Heat and electricity come entirely from renewable geothermal and hydropower sources and the city is determined to become fossil-fuel free by 2050.

San Francisco, California, USA
Transport Nearly half the city's population take public transport, walk, or bike to work.
Built environment San Francisco has more than 70 projects registered under the US Green Building Council's LEED certification system. In 2001, San Francisco voters approved a $100 million bond initiative to finance solar panels, energy efficiency, and wind turbines for public facilities.
Green space Over 17% of the city is devoted to parks and green space.

Vancouver, Canada
Power Draws 90% of its power from renewable sources, is a leader in hydroelectric power and is now charting a course to use wind, solar, wave, and tidal energy to significantly reduce fossil-fuel use.
Green space The metro area boasts 200 parks and over 29 kilometres of waterfront.

Source: www.grist.org (2008)

The 40 tallest buildings (2009)

Rank	Building	City	Completed	Storeys	Height (m)
1	Taipei 101	Taipei	2004	101	509
2	Shanghai World Financial Center	Shanghai	2008	101	492
3 =	Petronas Tower 1	Kuala Lumpur	1998	88	452
3 =	Petronas Tower 2	Kuala Lumpur	1998	88	452
5	Nanjing Greenland Financial Center	Nanjing	2009	69	450
6	Sears Tower	Chicago	1974	110	442
7	West Tower	Guangzhou	2009	103	438
8	Jin Mao Building	Shanghai	1999	88	421
9=	Trump International Hotel & Tower	Chicago	2009	96	415
9=	Two International Finance Centre	Hong Kong	2003	88	415
11	CITIC Plaza	Guangzhou	1996	80	391
12	Shun Hing Square	Shenzhen	1996	69	384
13	Empire State Building	New York	1931	102	381
14	Central Plaza	Hong Kong	1992	78	374
15	Bank of China	Hong Kong	1989	70	367
16	Bank of America Tower	New York	2009	54	366
17	Almas Tower	Dubai	2008	68	363
18	Emirates Tower One	Dubai	1999	54	355
19	Tuntex Sky Tower	Kaohsiung	1997	85	348
20=	Aon Center	Chicago	1973	83	346
20=	The Center	Hong Kong	1998	73	346
22	John Hancock Center	Chicago	1969	100	344
23=	Rose Rotana Tower	Dubai	2007	72	333
23=	Shimao International Plaza	Shanghai	2006	60	333
25	Minsheng Bank Building	Wuhan	2008	68	331
26	China World Trade Center Tower III	Beijing	2009	74	330
27	The Index	Dubai	2009	80	328
28	Q1	Gold Coast	2005	78	323
29	Burj al Arab Hotel	Dubai	1999	60	321
30=	Chrysler Building	New York	1930	77	319
30=	New York Times Tower	New York	2007	52	319
30=	Nina Tower I	Hong Kong	2006	80	319
33	Bank of America Plaza	Atlanta	1993	55	317
34=	Menara Telekom Headquarters	Kuala Lumpur	1999	55	310
34=	U.S. Bank Tower	Los Angeles	1990	73	310
36	Emirates Tower Two	Dubai	2000	56	309
37	AT&T Corporate Center	Chicago	1989	60	307
38	The Address Downtown Burj Dubai	Dubai	2008	63	306
39	JP Morgan Chase Tower	Houston	1982	75	305
40	Baiyoke Tower II	Bangkok	1997	85	304

Source: Council on Tall Buildings and Urban Habitat, www.ctbuh.org (2009)

The 40 tallest buildings (2020)

Rank	Building	City	Completion	Storeys	Height (m)
1	Nakheel Tower	Dubai	2020	200+	1000+
2	Burj Dubai	Dubai	2009	160+	800+
3	Shanghai Tower	Shanghai	2014	128	632
4	Pentominium	Dubai	2012	122	618
5	Russia Tower	Moscow	2016*	118	612
6	Chicago Spire	Chicago	2013*	150	610
7	Goldin Finance 117	Tianjin	2014	117	600
8	Makkah Royal Clock Tower Hotel	Mecca	2010	76	577
9	Doha Convention Center Tower	Doha	2012	112	551
10	One World Trade Center	New York	2013	105	541
11	Burj Al Alam	Dubai	2012	108	510
12=	Federation Towers/Vostok Tower	Moscow	2010	95	509
12=	**Taipei 101**	Taipei	2004	101	509
14	**Shanghai World Financial Center**	Shanghai	2008	101	492
15	International Commerce Centre	Hong Kong	2010	107	483
16=	**Petronas Tower 1**	Kuala Lumpur	1998	88	452
16=	**Petronas Tower 2**	Kuala Lumpur	1998	88	452
18	Nanjing Greenland Financial Center	Nanjing	2009	69	450
19	**Sears Tower**	Chicago	1974	110	442
20	Kingkey Finance Tower	Shenzhen	2011	97	439
21	West Tower	Guangzhou	2009	103	438
22	Dubai Towers Doha	Doha	2010	84	437
23	**Jin Mao Building**	Shanghai	1999	88	421
24=	Trump International Hotel & Tower	Chicago	2009	96	415
24=	**Two International Finance Centre**	Hong Kong	2003	88	415
26	Princess Tower	Dubai	2010	101	414
27=	Al Hamra Tower	Kuwait City	2010	77	412
27=	Marina 101	Dubai	2010	101	412
29	Lighthouse Tower	Dubai	2011	64	402
30=	Emirates Park Towers Hotel & Spa 1	Dubai	2010	77	395
30=	Emirates Park Towers Hotel & Spa 2	Dubai	2010	77	395
32	**CITIC Plaza**	Guangzhou	1996	80	391
33	23 Marina	Dubai	2010	90	389
34	Eton Place Dalian Tower 1	Dalian	2012	81	388
35=	Hang Lung Plaza Tower 1	Shenyang	2013	76	384
35=	**Shun Hing Square**	Shenzhen	1996	69	384
37	The Domian	Abu Dhabi	2010	88	382
38	**Empire State Building**	New York	1931	102	381
39	Elite Residence	Dubai	2010	87	380
40	Mercury City Tower	Moscow	2011	70	380

*construction on hold Feb 2009

Bold indicates buildings that were completed before 2009

Source: Council on Tall Buildings and Urban Habitat, www.ctbuh.org (2009)

The 10 most polluted

City	Country	Pollutants/sources
Sumgayit	Azerbaijan	Organic chemicals and mercury from petrochemical and industrial complexes
Linfen	China	Particulates and gases from industry and traffic
Tianying	China	Heavy metals and particulates from industry. Average lead content in the air and soil are up to10 times higher than national standards
Sukinda	India	Hexavalent chromium from chromite mines. Waste rock and untreated water from the mines gets into local water supplies
Vapi	India	Over 50 industrial estates discharge heavy metals, pesticides and chemicals. Mercury in the groundwater is 96 times higher than WHO standards
La Oroya	Peru	Lead and other heavy metal mining and smelting over 80 years has caused significant lead contamination
Dzerzhinsk	Russia	Chemicals, toxic byproducts and lead from chemical weapons and industrial manufacturing
Norilsk	Russia	Heavy metals and particulates from mining and smelting
Chernobyl	Ukraine	Radioactive materials from the nuclear reactor explosion
Kabwe	Zambia	Unregulated lead mining and smelting operations resulted in lead dust covering large areas. Childrens' blood lead levels average up to ten times the recommended maximum

Source: The Blacksmith Institute (2008)

The 10 oldest functioning sewer systems

City	Country	Parts dating from
Rome	Italy	578 BC
Istanbul	Turkey	330 AD
Paris	France	1370
Tallinn	Estonia	1422
Vienna	Austria	1830
Hamburg	Germany	1843
London	UK	1844
Chicago	USA	1858
Brussels	Belgium	1867
Prague	Czech Republic	1907

Source: Compiled from several sources (2009)

HSBC Premier Centres

Country	City	HSBC Premier Centre	Address	Contact Number
Argentina	Buenos Aires	Casa Central	Florida 201, Ciudad Autonoma de Buenos Aires, Buenos Aires, C1005AAE	+54 1 143405010
Australia	Melbourne	Melbourne Branch	271 Collins St, Melbourne, VIC 3000	+61 2 9005 8114
Australia	Sydney	Sydney Branch	28 Bridge Street, Sydney, NSW 2000	+61 2 9005 8114
Brazil	Brasilia	Centro Brasilia	SHCS CR Quadra 502, Bloco A - Loja 13, Asa Sul Centro, Brasília - DF	+55 61 3208 2700
Brazil	Rio de Janeiro	HSBC Premier Centre Visconde de Pirajá	Rua Visconde de Pirajá, 608 - Loja A – Ipanema, Rio de Janeiro - RJ	+55 21 3206-5350
Brazil	Sao Paulo	Premier Centre MASP Paulista	Avenida Paulista, 1708 - Cerqueira César - 01.310-200, São Paulo	+55 11 3371 4600
Canada	Toronto	Toronto, Yorkville Branch	150 Bloor Street West, Suite M100, Toronto, Ontario	+1 604 216 8800
Canada	Vancouver	Vancouver Main Branch	885 West Georgia Street, Vancouver, British Columbia, V6C 3E9	+1 604 216 8800
Cayman Islands	Grand Cayman	HSBC House	68 West Bay Road, P O Box 1109, Grand Cayman KY1-1102	+1 345 914 7600
China	Beijing	China World Trade Centre	1 Jianguomenwai Dajie, Beijing	+86 10 5866 9866
China	Shanghai	Suite 106, G/F, and Suite 400, 4/F,	Shanghai Centre, 1376 Nanjing Road, Puxi Shanghai 200040	+86 21 6279 8582
China	Hong Kong	Hong Kong Office HSBC Premier Centre	Level 5, HSBC Main Building, 1 Queen's Road, Central, Hong Kong SAR	+852 2233 3322
Singapore	Singapore	Claymore Premier Centre	6 Claymore Hill, #02-01 Claymore Plaza, Singapore 229571	1800-227 8889 (in Singapore) +65 6216 9080 (from overseas)
Colombia	Bogota	Premier Center Cabrera	Calle 86, N10-88, Second Floor, Bogota	+57 1 257 0598
Czech Republic	Prague	Gestin Centre	V Celnici 1040/5 Praha 1, Prague	+420 225 024 121
Egypt	Cairo	Cairo Branch	Abou El Feda Building, 3 Abou El Feda Street, Zamalek, Cairo, 126D	+20 2 27381743
England	London	City of London Branch	60 Queen Victoria Street, London, EC3N 4TR	+44 1226 260 260
England	Manchester	Manchester Branch	PO Box 360, 100 King Street, Manchester, M60 2HD	+44 1226 260 260
France	Paris	Paris Elysées	103 Avenue Champs Elysées, 75419 Paris, Cedex 08	+33 1 55697575
Greece	Athens	Voukourestiou Branch	15 Voukourestiou Street, 10671, Athens	+30 210 3644313-7
India	Delhi	Brakhamba Road	25 Barakhamba Road, New Delhi, 110001	+91 11 41592055
India	Kolkata	Dalhousie	31 BBD Bagh, Dalhousie Square, Kolkata, 700 001	+91 33 225 42014
India	Mumbai	HSBC, 52/60	Mahatma Gandhi Road, Fort, Mumbai, 400 001	+91 22 6666 8815
Indonesia	Jakarta	World Trade Centre	HSBC Premier Lounge, 1st Floor, Jl. Jendral Sudirman, Kav 29 - 31, Jakarta 12920	+62 21 2551 4722
Japan	Tokyo	Ginza Branch	Ginza 888 Bldg. 8-8-8 Ginza, Chuo-ku, Tokyo, 104-0061	HSBC Premier customers: 0120 777 268 (Toll-free) +81 3 6254 6777 (Overseas Call Collect) Non-account holders: 0120 89 2028 (Toll-free)
South Korea	Seoul	Personal Banking Center (PBC)	HSBC Building #25 1-ga Bongrae-dong Chung-gu, Seoul, 100-161	+82 1577 3003
Lebanon	Beirut	St Georges Branch	HSBC Head Office Building, Mina El-Hos, St. Georges Bay, P.O.Box: 11-1380, Beirut	+961 1 760000
Malaysia	Kuala Lampur	HSBC Bank Malaysia Berhad	Level 2, HSBC Building, No. 2, Leboh Ampang, 50100 Kuala Lumpur	+60 3 22703702, 3797, 3728, 3798, 3731, 3789, 3509. Fax no: +60 3 20702076
Mexico	Mexico City	Palmas Branch	Av. Paseo de las Palmas No. 886, Col. Lomas de Chapultepec	+52 55 5202 1346
Philippines	Manila	Makati Branch	Mezzanine Floor, The Enterprise Center, Tower 1, 6766 Ayala Avenue cor Paseo de Roxas, Makati City 1200	+63 2 976 8080
Thailand	Bangkok	Bangkok Main Branch	HSBC Building, 968 Rama IV Road, Silom, Bangrak, 10500	+66 2614 4000
Turkey	Istanbul	Akatlar	Yildirim Oguz Goker Cad, Sumbul Sok, No 4 Akatlar	+90 212 4440112
UAE	Dubai	Bur Dubai Branch	312/45, Al Suq Road, P.O Box 66, Dubai	+971 42241000
USA	Los Angeles	Los Angeles Premier Center	660 South Figueroa Street, Los Angeles, 90017	+1 888 662 4722
USA	Miami	Miami Premier Center	55 Miracle Mile, Suite 330, Coral Gables, Miami, FL, 33134, US	+1 305 774 5400
USA	New York	Fifth Avenue Premier Center	452 Fifth Avenue, New York, NY 10018	+1 888 662 4722
USA	San Francisco	San Francisco Premier Center	601 Montgomery St., Suite 100, San Francisco, 94111	+1 888 662 4722

Contributors

All essays in this book have been written by current and recent residents of the featured city.

Lesley Abravanel [Miami] is a columnist for the *Miami Herald*, covering nightlife and celebrity nonsense emanating from the shores of South Beach. She is also the author of *Frommer's Florida*, *Frommer's South Florida*, *Frommer's Miami and the Keys Day by Day* and *Florida for Dummies*.

Nick Barley [Glasgow] is Director of The Lighthouse, Scotland's national centre for architecture, design and the city. He was formerly editor of Scotland's leading cultural magazine, *The List*.

Karl Baz [Beirut] is Editor-at-Large of *Time Out Beirut* magazine. He has written some 40 books in his head, and spends his time convincing foreigners to move to beautiful Beirut, the only woman he's ever loved.

Matt Bellotti [Kuala Lumpur] is the Editorial Director of *Time Out Kuala Lumpur*. When KL-ites aren't busy not laughing at his stand-up comedy nights, they're probably tied up not reading his work in *Expatriate Lifestyle*, *Golf Vacations* or *Newsweek* or www.spurscommunity.co.uk.

Amir Ben-David [Tel Aviv] is Deputy Publisher of *Time Out Tel Aviv* and the author of the novel *Top of the World*.

Rory Boland [Krakow] is a freelance journalist who splits his time between Poland and Hong Kong. He has contributed to *Time Out Flight Free Europe* and is editor of *National Geographic Traveler: Hong Kong*.

New Zealand-born **Adrienne Bourgeon** [Marseille] is a freelance writer who has lived in the south of France since the mid 1990s. She contributes to a variety of newspapers and magazines both in France and abroad.

Adam Bray [Hanoi] is a freelance writer, photographer and musician. He is a contributor to at least nine Vietnam and Cambodia guidebooks and owns the website www.muinebeach.net.

Toby Brocklehurst [Havana] runs tour company In Cloud 9 (www.incloud9.com), and also organises film and music production services in Cuba. He is currently building a hotel in Panama City.

Jessica Cargill Thompson [London] is a former Deputy Editor of *Time Out London*. She is the author of *40 Architects Under 40*, and the editor of *London Calling* as well as *The World's Greatest Cities*.

Rich Carriero [Istanbul] is a Staff Writer for *Time Out Istanbul* and has contributed to *Fodor's Turkey Travel Guide*. His work regularly appears on www.associatedcontent.com. Rich lives in Istanbul's Beyoglu district.

As Entertainment Editor of English-language monthly *That's Shanghai*, **Rebecca Catching** has covered everything from Chinese hip hop to propaganda in contemporary art. She also contributes to a range of publications including *Flash Art* and the *Far Eastern Economic Review*.

Carlos Celdran [Manila] is a performance artist who has been running historical tours of Manila's heritage districts for the last seven years. Carlos is known for his funny hats.

Tom Charity [Vancouver] is a film critic and programmer, and Co-Editor of the *Time Out Vancouver* city guide. His latest books are *The Rough Guide to Film* (2008) and *The Little Book of Film* (2009). He has lived in Vancouver for five years.

Nicholas Coldicott [Kyoto] is the Editor of the Time Out guides to Kyoto and Tokyo. He has lived in Japan since 1998 and works for national broadcaster NHK and the *Japan Times*.

Bryan Coll [Belfast] is a freelance print and radio journalist based in Northern Ireland. He previously worked as a television reporter in Paris and was awarded the *Irish Times* Douglas Gageby Fellowship in 2008.

Philip Cornwel-Smith [Bangkok] is the Editor of the *Time Out Bangkok* city guide and the author of *Very Thai: Everyday Popular Culture* and *Very Bangkok: A Subculture Guide*. Born in the UK, Philip has lived in Bangkok since becoming the founding Editor of *Bangkok Metro* in 1994.

Peterjon Cresswell [Budapest] is Editor-at-Large of the English-language monthly *Time Out Budapest* and has worked on all six editions of the *Time Out Budapest* city guide. He has lived in the city since 1992.

Keith Davidson [Edinburgh] is an Edinburgh-based freelance writer who has contributed to so many guidebook titles that he feels that he should have his own shelf in Waterstone's.

A Barcelona resident since 2001, **Sally Davies** [Barcelona] has written, edited and contributed to a number of books on Spain, including Time Out's guides to Barcelona, Madrid, Andalucia and Mallorca. She also writes on Spanish food and culture for publications including the *Guardian*, the *Sunday Times* and *Olive* magazine.

Shaun Davies [Tokyo] is Australian website ninemsn's 'Tokyo Insider' and makes a living writing about geeks, gadgets and good grub in Japan's neon-soaked capital.

John Dugan [Chicago] is the Nightlife Editor and Music Writer at *Time Out Chicago*. He plays drums in the Chicago Stone Lightning Band and has lived in Ukrainian Village and Bucktown for a decade.

Natasha Edwards [Paris] moved to the city over 15 years ago. Former editor of *Time Out Paris*, she is a specialist on food, art, design and observing the French. She writes regularly on travel and French culture for, among others, *Condé Nast Traveller*, *Contemporary*, the *Daily Telegraph*, *Elle Decoration* and the *Independent*.

Born and bred in the Little Red Dot, **Charlene Fang** [Singapore] spends almost all of her time dispensing personal concierge services to her friends. Luckily, she's Editor of the monthly *Time Out Singapore* magazine.

Jaqueline Fontenelle [Brasília] is a tourist guide in Chapada Dos Veadeiros, a national park near Brasília. She is the author of a collection of short stories about Chapada, *Luz Quartiada*.

Niels Footman [Seoul] is an Editor at *Morning Calm*, Korean Air's inflight magazine. A seven-year resident of South Korea, Niels is currently working on a book about the country's many and varied islands.

Paul French [Toronto] edits the *Time Out Toronto* city guide. When he's not unearthing the spoils of his native city, he's on the road writing travel stories for publications around the world.

Noam Friedlander [Los Angeles] is a former *Time Out London* writer and has written scripts for the TV show *Dream Team* (Sky1) and questions for the quiz show *Are You Smarter Than a 10-Year-Old?*. She moved to Los Angeles in 2008 to work on the film *Warrior*.

Nick Funnell [Madrid] edits the monthly magazine *InMadrid* and has contributed to the *Time Out Madrid* city guide, *Time Out London* magazine, specialist film journal *Sight & Sound* and British Airways' *High Life* magazine.

Joshua Goodman [Bogotá] is a reporter for Bloomberg News in Rio de Janeiro. Previously he lived in Colombia and Argentina, where he was a writer for the *Time Out Buenos Aires* and *Patagonia* guidebooks.

Anne Hanley [Rome] has lived in Italy for 25 years. When not editing Time Out guides she designs and restores gardens.

Chad Henderson [Stockholm] is the Consultant Editor of the *Time Out Stockholm* city guide. He has lived in the city for ten years and is completing his PhD in English literature.

Gary Hills [Brussels] is Editor of the *Time Out Brussels* city guide and has been writing reams for various Time Out publications over the years.

Anca Ionita [Bucharest] is Editor-in-Chief of *Time Out Bucuresti*. She is a theatre critic and a professor of Theories of Drama and History of Theatre at Bucharest's Film and Theatre Academy. Bucharest is her native town.

Anna Katsnelson [São Paolo] is the editor of *Time Out São Paulo*. She is a former Fulbright scholar to Brazil, and is writing her PhD on Brazilian literature.

Cork-born **Fergal Kavanagh** [Naples] is an expert in the Neapolitan art of *arrangiarsi* (getting by), having dabbled in teacher training, DJ-ing in clubs and on radio, writing for guidebooks, translating and organising cultural exchanges.

Roberta Kedzierski [Milan], who is based between Milan and Lake Lugano, combines travel guidebook writing and editing with business reporting for British and US clients. She has also contributed to a number of publications on cultural issues.

After years of travel subsidised by carpentry and B-movie acting, writer **Steve Korver** [Amsterdam] came to the city in 1992 to reverse the journey his parents made as emigrants to Canada. He got his first real job in 2005 as Editor-in-Chief of the cultural paper *Amsterdam Weekly* but has now returned to freewheeling and freelancing.

Alexey Kovalev [Moscow] is a translator, author and editor currently working for *Time Out Moscow* magazine. With his photographer wife Maja he has produced a number of stories for Russian editions of international publications such as *Rolling Stone* and *National Geographic Traveler*.

Rachel Lopez [Mumbai] edits the Around Town section of *Time Out Mumbai*. She has a keen interest in Mumbai's civic issues and history and has lived in the city for over 25 years.

Becky Lucas [Dubai] is Deputy Editor of *Time Out Dubai*. Previously she worked on *New York Times* Bestseller *Pick Me Up*. She has lived in Dubai for three years.

Paul McGann [Dublin] is an Irish landscape architect from Dublin, currently living and working in London.

Bradford McKee [Washington, DC], a writer specialising in architecture, landscape and design, is a former arts editor of *Washington City Paper* who has lived in Washington, DC for 20 years. His latest book is *The Civilized Jungle*.

Sergey Medvetsky [Almaty] runs a design studio in Almaty and does freelance translation and interpreting for a number of local and international NGOs and businesses.

Anna Mzwena [Marrakech] runs Dar Masoud, a small guest house in Mouassine, Marrakech, and is renovating a 10-bedroom guest house in Bab Hmar.

Slobodan Obradovi [Belgrade] was born and lives in Belgrade. He specialises in theatre criticism, drama, and film and TV screenplay, and is an expert on the history and theory of drama, film and performing arts.

Deepanjana Pal [Kokata] writes for the art and books sections of *Time Out Mumbai*. Having lived in six major cities in three continents, she hopes to cover every continent eventually (with the possible exception of Antarctica).

British born **Tom Pattinson** [Beijing] is Editor-in-Chief of *Time Out Beijing* magazine and a commentator on Chinese society and culture. Formerly a journalist at the *Sunday Times*, he contributes to *Esquire*, *Travel and Leisure*, the *Guardian*, National Geographic channel and the BBC. He moved to Beijing in the 1990s and has a passion for lamb kebabs.

Tom Phillips [Rio de Janeiro] is a journalist and documentary maker who has spent the past five years reporting on Brazil for the *Guardian*. Tom's blog can be found at www.brazilnuts.com.br.

Claire Rigby [Buenos Aires] was the Editor of Time Out's first Mexico City guide, and is currently editor of Time Out's *Buenos Aires for Visitors*.

Travel writer, rock journalist, author and filmmaker, **Dave Rimmer** [Berlin] has had a suitcase in Berlin for over 20 years. His *Once Upon a Time in the East* documented the last days of the divided city. He is currently working on a book about Bowie and Iggy in Berlin.

Jeff Risom [Copenhagen] is an urban designer and architectural engineer. He works for the urban quality consulting firm Gehl Architects and teaches Urban Studies at the Danish Institute for Study Abroad (DIS) in Copenhagen.

Native New Yorker **Lisa Ritchie** [New York] recently returned to the city after two decades in London. She is Editor of the *Time Out New York* city guide, *NYC for Visitors*, ongoing Shortlist guides, and special projects for *Time Out New York* magazine.

Alison Roberts [Lisbon] is a freelance radio and print journalist who has been based in Lisbon for a decade. She has edited the *Time Out Lisbon* city guides and worked on the launch of Time Out's *Lisbon for Visitors* magazine. She is the author of a history of the British Council's 70 years in Portugal, *A Small but Crucial Push*.

Jane Rocca [Melbourne] is a freelance music journalist whose work appears in *The Age*, *Sydney Sun Herald*, *West Australian* and *Rolling Stone*. She is the author of *The Cocktail* and *Cocktails and Rock Tales*.

Dan Rookwood [Sydney] is the Editor of *Time Out Sydney* magazine, and a contributing editor for *Madison*, *GQ* and the *Sydney Morning Herald*'s Sport & Style magazine.

Nicholas Royle [Manchester] teaches creative writing at Manchester Metropolitan University. His most recent books are novellas *The Appetite* and *The Enigma of Departure* and short-story collection *Mortality*.

Architect **Salma Samar Damluji** [Sana'a] is an authority on mud brick building in Yemen and the Middle East. Her publications include *A Yemen Reality*; *The Valley of Mud Brick Architecture – Shibam, Tarim & Wadi Hadramut*; *The Architecture of Oman* and *The Architecture of the United Arab Emirates*. She is currently based in London.

Abdoulie Sey [Cairo], a former newspaper editor and Associate Editor for tourism magazine *Concern*, now works as a private media consultant for the Gambia Tourism Authority.

Dmitry Shestakov [St Petersburg] contributes to several magazines, including *Time Out Saint Petersburg*.

Diane Shugart [Athens] is the Editor of *Odyssey*, a magazine about Greece, and author of *Athens By Neighborhood*. She was also Consultant Editor for the *Time Out Athens* guide.

Ebrima Sillah [Dakar] has worked for the BBC and many news agencies, reporting from West Africa.

Avtar Singh [Delhi] is the Editor of *Time Out Delhi* magazine. His novel, *The Beauty of These Present Things*, was published by Penguin India.

A musician by training, **Nicky Swallow** [Florence] moved to the city in the early 1980s. For the past decade, she has been writing about Florence for various guidebooks and international magazines and served as Consultant Editor of the *Time Out Florence & Tuscany* guide.

Author, columnist and writer **Josef Talotta** [Johannesburg] is the editor of *Sandton* magazine, dedicated to 'the good life' in Johannesburg's northern suburbs. He has contributed to most of South Africa's glossies (*Condé Nast House & Garden*, *GQ*, *InStyle*, *Style*) as well as UK-based Time Out online, *Condé Nast Traveller*, *Wallpaper** and *Spruce*.

Having escaped his soul-destroying former life as a lawyer in Perth, Australia, **Mark Tjhung** [Hong Kong] is now a writer for *Time Out Hong Kong* magazine, finding time to indulge in jamming with his yet-to-be-named band and nurture an unhealthy addiction to Facebook poker.

Jo-Ann Titmarsh [Venice] has been living and working in Venice since 1992. She is the author of *Venice Walks* and a contributor to the *Time Out Venice* city guide and Shortlist.

Former California crime reporter **Will Tizard** [Prague] is the Editor of the *Time Out Prague* city guide and a correspondent for *Variety*, and has documentary and video production credits in Prague.

Lisa van Aswegen [Cape Town] is a born and bred Capetonian whose love of travel and eating out marry marvellously in her roles as Editor of *Time Out Cape Town* and Assistant Editor of local restaurant guide *Eat Out*. She's at her happiest gazing at Table Mountain from her front garden, while carrying out research on local wine.

Born and raised in San Francisco, **Bonnie Wach** [San Francisco] is the author of *San Francisco As You Like It: 23 Tailor-Made Tours for Culture Vultures, Shopaholics, Neo-Bohemians, Famished Foodies, Savvy Natives & Everyone Else*. She currently writes about food, travel, and all things San Francisco for the *San Francisco Chronicle* and USAToday.com.

Dionne C Walker [Kingston] is a cultural critic and fellow at the National Art Gallery in Kingston. She has published a book, *The Informer for Filmmakers*, and is now developing an environmental Caribbean project on sustainable cities.

Klive Walker [Kingston] is a reggae historian, expert on Caribbean cinema, cultural critic and author of the book *Dubwise: Reasoning from the Reggae Underground*.

Penny Watson [Seville] is a freelance travel writer and co-author of *Cool Camping Europe* and Lonely Planet guides to Australia and Sydney and New South Wales. She now lives in Seville.

Photographers

Héloise Bergman has worked as a photographer for 10 years, taking on a variety of projects to feed her fascination with people and the worlds they inhabit. Her work has featured in exhibitions, magazines and books. www.heloisebergman.com

Karl Blackwell is a travel photographer freelancing for Time Out, Michelin, the AA and Lonely Planet, among others. He has also worked for the BBC and exhibited worldwide and has been interviewed for *Professional Photographer* and *DPI*, Taiwan's leading design magazine. www.karlblackwell.com

After completing a Professional Photography postgraduate course at Central St Martins, **Lydia Evans** was commissioned to shoot the *Time Out Havana* city guide. She has since been published by Thames & Hudson, *Condé Nast Traveller*, Rough Guides, Insight and *Time Out Lisbon*. www.lydiaevans.com

Born in New York, **Elan Fleisher** has been photographing destinations around the world for 15 years. Based in Berlin, he has worked for Time Out, Condé Nast, Rough Guides and numerous travel publications in Europe, Asia and the USA. www.elantravelpix.com

Years of travelling and living in different countries inspired **Michelle Grant**'s love of travel photography, but it wasn't until finally settling in London that she pursued it as a career. A summer of travel shoots resulted in an exhibition in 2007 and several private commissions. www.michellegrant.com

Jitka Hynkova is a Czech-born photographer whose images reflect her passion for food and travel. She works on commission and on personal projects in the Czech Republic and the UK. Her photographs have been published in Time Out guides and magazine. www.jitkahynkova.com

Britta Jaschinski's first book, *Zoo*, was a critical and commercial success and led to a well-received exhibition that toured internationally. Her second book, *Wild Things*, was published in 2003 in English and German editions. Her award-winning images feature in publications and exhibitions worldwide. www.brittaphotography.com

Texan **Michael Kirby** is a freelance photographer based in New York. He specialises in editorial and documentary photography, and is particularly passionate about travelling, outdoor expeditions and covering under-reported social issues. He also carries out multimedia assignments. www.mikirby.com

Oliver Knight is a freelance documentary photographer specialising in contemporary subjects and themes. Aside from his longstanding relationship with *Time Out London* magazine and Time Out's city guides, he regularly shoots for other publications in both the UK and France. Oliver divides his time between London and Paris. www.oliver-knight.com

Vancouver-based **Shannon Mendes** is interested in the quiet moments in peoples' lives that lie in the inbetween. Her editorial, lifestyle and portrait work attempts to capture the natural gestures and expressions that exist in a non self-conscious state. www.shannonmendes.com

A native of Florence, **Gianluca Moggi** has travelled all over Italy and beyond for his photojournalistic work. Time Out commissions include Florence & Tuscany, Rome, Turin and Milan guides, and he has also shot Cape Town for Insideout and Naples for Frommer's. He is co-owner of the Florence-based New Press Photo photographic agency. www.newpressphoto.it

Mark Parren Taylor is a travel and culture editorial photographer. His work appears in inflight magazines, consumer titles and travel guides published throughout Asia, Europe and the US. www.mptphoto.com

Based in London, **Jonathan Perugia** has more than 15 years' experience in travel, news and commercial photography, and has helped define Time Out Guides' photographic style. He has worked on over 40 books, and been published worldwide. The results of the photography workshops he conducted with marginalised young people in Indonesia were published in the acclaimed book *A Child's Eye*. www.jpfoto.com

Olivia Rutherford, nominated as Travel Photographer of the Year 2008, has travelled extensively in Europe, America, Africa and Asia for her work. Her vibrant style uses strong colour and movement. She has shot for publications including *Time Out*, *Condé Nast Traveller*, *The Face*, *ID Saturday Telegraph Magazine*, *Scotland on Sunday* and the Sunday Times' *Travel* magazine. www.oliviarutherford.co.uk

Fumie Suzuki specialises in travel photography, focusing on Hungary, Romania, Bulgaria, Serbia, Croatia, Ukraine, Moldova, Turkey and Austria. She has documented Eastern European traditions and cultures in Hungary and Romania, especially among groups such as Roma musicians. She has also worked extensively as a newspaper and magazine photographer in Japan. www.suzukifumie.com

Alys Tomlinson has shot for several Time Out city guides including New York, Toronto, Miami, Venice and Barcelona. She is currently working on a personal project documenting alternative communities in the UK. In 2009 she was named one of 30 photographers to watch by *Photo District News*. www.alystomlinson.co.uk

Martha Williams is a native Chicagoan who has been shooting in the city for over 10 years. She specialises in vibrant photographs of spaces, food, and people. She is currently an Associate Photo Editor at *Time Out Chicago* magazine. www.marthawilliamsphotography.com.

Photography credits

Photography pages 5,100, 101, 102, 103 Martha Williams; pages 8 (left), 11 (right), 34, 35 (bottom right), 104, 105, 106, 107, 187 (bottom middle), 302/303, 304, 305 Heloise Bergman; pages 8 (middle left), 299, 300 Tove K Breitstein; pages 8 (middle right), 144, 145, 146, 147 Andrew Moore; pages 8 (right), 35 (top and middle left), 36, 37, 290/291, 292 (top middle, bottom middle and right) Mark Parren Taylor; pages 9 (left, middle left), 10 (left), 24, 25, 27 (top and bottom left), 40 (top), 41, 42 (top left and right, middle right, bottom left), 43, 124, 125, 126, 127, 133, 135 (middle left and right, bottom right), 187 (middle), 207 (bottom), 208, 209 (top), 226/227, 229 (top right, bottom middle and left), 250/251, 252, 324/325, 326, 327 Olivia Rutherford; pages 9 (middle right), 254, 255, 256 (left, top middle, bottom right) Jitka Hynkova; pages 9 (right), 11 (middle left), 60, 61, 62, 63, 65, 120/121, 122 (top left and right, middle row), 187 (top and bottom left), 328, 329, 330, 331 Britta Jaschinski; page 10 (middle left), 42 (middle left) Greg Gladman; pages 10 (middle right), 242/243, 244 (mid and bottom row middle), 244 Michael Kirby; pages 10 (right), 128/129, 130 (bottom right), 228, 229 (top left and middle, bottom right), 262, 263, 264, 265 Gianluca Moggi; pages 11 (left), 40, 42 (top middle, bottom right), 64, 206, 208 (top second from left), 209 (bottom), 222/223, 224 (bottom right), 256 (top right, bottom middle), 257, 274, 275 (bottom), 276 (top), 277, 294/295, 296, 297, 332/333, 334, 335 Elan Fleisher; pages 11 (middle right), 130, 131, 152/153, 154, 155, 185, 187 (top middle), 241 (bottom), 244 (top right, middle left, bottom row left & right), 247 Jonathan Perugia; pages 20/21, 22 Aziz Mamirow; page 23 Arman Berdalin; pages 26, 27 (middle and bottom right), 29, 304 (top right, bottom right) Michelle Grant; page 27 (middle left) Anne Binckebank; pages 31, 32, 33, 122 (top middle, bottom left), 123, 185 (bottom), 187 (top right), 224, 225, 244 (top row left and middle), 316, 318, 319 (bottom) Alys Tomlinson; pages 44/45, 47 Ben McMillan; page 47 (top middle) Chen Chao; pages 48, 49, 50, 51 Rania Chalfoun and Vincent El Khoury; pages 52, 53, 54, 55 Northern Ireland Tourist Board; pages 56, 57, 58 Touristic Organization of Belgrade; page 59 Nenad Petrovic; pages 66/67, 68 (top), 69, 160/161, 163, 217 (top right) Alamy; pages 68 (bottom), 138 (top), 202/203, 204, 205 www.photolibrary.com; page 70/71 South American Pictures/Tony Morrison; pages 86, 87, 89 Gonzalo Gil; page 88 Marc van der Aa; page 89 (bottom left) Diego Ortega; pages 72, 73 Christian Knepper; pages 74, 75, 76, 77 Oliver Knight; pages 78/79, 80 TO Bucharest; page 81 Andrei Spirache; pages 82, 83, 84, 85, 148, 149, 150, 151, 168/169, 170, 171, 312 (right), 313 (top right, middle row, middle and right, bottom row middle and right) Fumie Suzuki; pages 92/93, 110 (bottom), 111 www.photolibrary.com; pages 94, 95 (right) Gardel Bertrand/www.Hemis.fr; pages 95 (top left), 139 (bottom), 164/165 Panos; pages 108/109 Morandi Bruno/SIME; pages 95 (bottom left), 138, 139 (top), 166, 214/215, 273 Getty Images; page 110 Prisma/Superstock; pages 112/113, 114 (bottom left, top and bottom right), 115 Cherian Thomas; page 114 (top and middle left) Dhruba Dutta; pages 114, 115, 116, 117 ITP Images; page 126 (top middle) Muir Vidler; pages 132, 135 (top, bottom left) www.seeglasgow.com; page 134 Sandy Young; page 136/137 Masterfile; pages 140/141, 142, 143, 180, 181, 182, 183 Lydia Evans; pages 156/157, 158, 159 South African Tourism PR; page 162 (top, bottom left) Dionne Walker; page 162 (bottom right) SIME-4 Corners Images; page 167 Steve Raymer/NGS Image Collection; pages 172/173, 174, 175 Lim Chee Wah; page 174 (bottom right) Ministry of Sound/Euphoria; pages 176, 177, 178, 179 Chris McCooey; page 184 Time Motion; page 189 Piers Allardyce; page 187 (bottom right) Rogan Macdonald; pages 190, 191 (top & middle), 193 (middle right, bottom left) Max Malandrino; pages 191, 192, 193 (top, middle left) Sarah Hadley; page 193 (bottom right) Amanda C Edwards; pages 194, 195 (middle), 197 Jon Santa Cruz; pages 195, 196 Venetia Dearden; pages 198/199, 200 John Oakey; page 201 (top left, middle row middle and right, bottom left) Nathan Cox; page 201 (top right) David Oakey; page 201 (middle row left, bottom right) Simon Buckley; pages 210 (top), 212, 213 Charlie Pinder; pages 210, 211, 212 (left), 238/239, 240, 241 (top), 286, 287, 288, 289, 310/311, 312 (left), 313 (top row left & middle, middle left, bottom left) Karl Blackwell; page 216 Mark Chew PR; page 217 (left) Peter Dunphy PR; page 217 (bottom right) Axiom; pages 218/219 (top), 220, 221 (middle left and bottom) Hector Barrera; pages 218, 219, 221 (top right) Bruce Herman/Visit Mexico; page 221 (top left, middle right) Carlos Sanchez/Visit Mexico; pages 230/231, 231 (top and bottom), 232 (top left) Max Avdev; page 231 (middle) Maja Kucova; pages 232 (bottom left), 233 Andrey Kunitsky; page 232 (bottom middle) Dmitry Iskahov; page 232 (top and bottom right) Grigory Polyakovsky; page 234 (top) Time Out Mumbai; pages 234 (bottom), 237 Pouloni Basu; pages 234/235, 236 (right) Chirodeep Chaudhuri; page 236 (top left) Apoorva Guptay; page 236 (bottom left) Vikas Munipalle; page 244 (middle row left) Ben Rosenzweig; page 246 Jael Marschner; pages 258/259, 260, 261 Ana Schlimovich; pages 266/267, 268, 269 Kirill Efimov; pages 270/271 Axiom; page 272 (top) Michele Falzone/Jon Arnold Images; page 271 (bottom) Peter Adams/Jon Arnold Images; pages 275, 276 Hans Kwiotek; pages 278, 279, 280, 281 Anna Katsnelson; pages 282/283, 284, 285 Korea Tourism Organization; pages 292 (top left and right, middle left and right, bottom left), 293 Jackson Lowen; pages 298, 300 (middle), 301 Mathew Lea; pages 306/307, 308, 309 Natat Dvir, Ilya Melnikov and Anatoli Michaelo; pages 314, 315 Kazunari Ogawa; pages 316 (top), 316/317, 318 (bottom left), 319 (top) Matei Glass; pages 320, 321, 322, 323 Shannon Mendes.

The following pictures were provided by the featured establishments: pages 30, 31 (middle), 32 (middle row middle).